THE
AUTHORITY
OF THE OLD
TESTAMENT

THE
AUTHORITY
OF THE OLD
TESTAMENT

JOHN BRIGHT

BAKER BOOK HOUSE
Grand Rapids, Michigan

© 1967 by Abingdon Press
Reprinted 1975 by
Baker Book House Company
with the permission of the
copyright owner

Fourth printing, August 1978

Library of Congress Catalog
Card Number: 67-14989

ISBN: 0-8010-0637-6

PHOTOLITHOPRINTED BY CUSHING - MALLOY, INC.
ANN ARBOR, MICHIGAN, UNITED STATES OF AMERICA
1977

TO
C. L. B.

FOREWORD

What is the nature of the authority of Scripture, and in what sense does the Old Testament share that authority? What place does the Old Testament legitimately occupy in the Christian's Bible and in the church's proclamation? What principles ought to guide one in interpreting it to the congregation? These are the questions with which this book will attempt to deal, with what success the reader must judge.

The book has had a rather long history. As its title page indicates, the substance of it was delivered as the James A. Gray Lectures at the Divinity School of Duke University. That was in November of 1959. But the book actually had its genesis much earlier, for the problem which it treats is one that had plagued me for many years prior to that time. I suppose that it is inevitable that it should have: it is a problem that no teacher of Old Testament studies can forever evade. Certainly I was unable to do so. I had long found myself troubled by the fact that so few preachers—myself included, I fear—really seemed to know how to proceed with the Old Testament, or were guided in their preaching from it, if they preached from it at all, by any conscious hermeneutical principles. I had had it brought home to me by the questions—not to say the complaints—of my students that many of them took a rather patronizing view of the Old Testament and, because uncertain of the usefulness of great parts of it in their preaching, were less than convinced that a thorough mastery of it was essential to their training; now and then some of them (and some of their elders too) would go so far as to ask if much of the time devoted to its study might not better be spent elsewhere. It early became clear to me that the place of Old Testament studies in the theological curriculum was not something that could be taken for granted. I was driven to the realization that if I could not present my students with some positive position with regard to the place of the Old Testament in the Bible, and provide them with some guidance in their use of it in the pulpit, they might justifiably regard all that I was trying to teach them, however interesting it

7

might be historically, as of questionable theological and practical importance.

So it was that for a number of years I had been wrestling with the problem of the Old Testament and groping for satisfying solutions. More than once I had attempted to formulate my thoughts on the subject and to present them through lectures or informal discussion to my students, and also, as occasion offered, to students in other theological institutions, as well as before groups of pastors and laymen. I had never been satisfied with what I had said and, needless to say, did not always gain the agreement of my hearers. But on almost every occasion I found that the subject was one that excited intense interest, among pastors, theological students, and laymen alike. It seemed that Christians of all degrees of theological sophistication were aware of the problem, sensed its importance, and were eagerly searching for answers. When, therefore, the invitation to deliver the Gray Lectures came, I accepted it gladly, grateful for the opportunity to formulate my thoughts more precisely and to present them before so discriminating an audience.

When I agreed to deliver the Gray Lectures I knew that, because of other commitments, there would be a considerable delay before the material could be placed in publishable form. But I had not dreamed that the delay would be so long. Although it was occasioned by circumstances beyond my control, I am nevertheless embarrassed by it, and apologize for it. Still, I believe that it has worked out for the best. The time that has elapsed has afforded opportunity for further reflection on the subject and for wider reading in the relevant literature; and this has both brought new insights and at more than one place helped to clarify my thinking. Moreover, I have been able to test some of the positions here developed in the preparation of sermons, chapel talks, and the like. And this, too, has proved most beneficial, for, as the proof of the pudding is in the eating, so the proof of hermeneutical principles must be in the preaching. In addition to this, there have been further opportunities to present the subject matter of the lectures in various forms before audiences of theological students, college undergraduates, pastors, and laymen. Again and again questions raised by my hearers have indicated to me ambiguities or questionable points in my presentation, and have forced rephrasing or rethinking. I deeply regret the delay, but I believe that the book is the better for it.

Through its first four chapters the book follows the outline of the lectures as delivered orally. Though the material has been completely rewritten and considerably expanded by the inclusion of points not touched upon in the oral presentation, the argument remains in all essentials the same. (I suspect, too, that in spite of revision the style of oral delivery at many places still shines through.) The final chapter, on the other hand, was not a part of the lectures at all. This consists of a few selected examples designed to give concrete illustration to the hermeneutical principles developed in the preceding chapters by applying them to specific texts. These are in no sense offered as sermons, or even as outlines of sermons, but have the aim solely of lifting the discussion above the abstract and, I hope, making its relevance to the practical task of preaching clearer.

The lectures as originally delivered had a very practical aim. They were addressed primarily to the theological student and to the pastor whose task it is week by week to interpret the Scriptures to the congregation. Every effort has been made to hold the book to that aim. No attempt has been made to provide a comprehensive review of the history of the interpretation of the Old Testament (which, after all, the reader may find elsewhere), or to present the views of all the contemporary scholars who have expressed themselves on the subject in a significant way. That would have made for a very large book indeed, would have involved still further delay, and would have resulted in something that would have corresponded but little to what was actually delivered as the Gray Lectures. Rather I have sought, as in the lectures, merely to present in a positive way, for what they are worth, my own views with regard to the matter. Scholars whose positions are described, and perhaps debated with, are selected as representative examples; most of them were mentioned, if more briefly, in the lectures. I trust that the footnotes (which, however, I have tried to use as sparingly as possible consistent with fairness) and the bibliography at the end of the book will be of assistance to any who may wish guidance toward further reading.

I am, of course, keenly aware of the magnitude and the difficulty of the subject that I have undertaken. It is a most controversial subject, which has always evoked the sharpest disagreement among Christians. I have no illusions that I have disposed of it in these pages. On the contrary, I am acutely conscious that at a number of points I am still groping for positions that may elude me, and that yet further thinking remains to be done. I suspect that this will always be the case. Aside from this, there is

9

the fact that any discussion of such a subject must of necessity be some-what subjective. That is to say that each of us will find his approach to it, and the conclusions that he reaches with regard to it, to be deeply conditioned by his background and training and by his personal theological convictions. I am sure that my own grounding in the Reformed tradition will more than once be evident in the pages that follow. The reader who is of different background and convictions will doubtless see many things differently. He will understand that I am here voicing my own convictions, at times tentatively and subject to reversal, with full awareness that other points of view are both possible and defensible. Since this is so, I cannot hope that what is said here will command the reader's assent at every point. But if he should be stimulated, perhaps by his very disagreement, to ponder the matter and to search for positive answers of his own, this book will have achieved its purpose. My overriding concern throughout has been that the Scriptures both of the Old and the New Testaments be accorded their rightful place in the church as the ground and norm of her preaching, and her supreme rule of faith and practice.

I must here express my thanks to those who in one way or another have had a part in bringing this book into being. First of all, I am grateful to the members of the faculty of the Duke University Divinity School, especially to Dean Robert E. Cushman and to Professor James T. Cleland —through whom the invitation was extended to me—for the honor they accorded me, and the challenge they laid before me, in inviting me to deliver the Gray Lectures. I trust that what is so tardily written here will not prove a disappointment to them. I also owe particular thanks to my colleague, Professor Mathias Rissi, who has read the entire manuscript in its semifinal form and has discussed with me various points at which my presentation was questionable or less than clear. I appreciate his counsel and encouragement more than I can say. The typing of the manuscript in all its various drafts was done by Mrs. F. S. Clark and, as usual, done to near perfection. Again, as on many previous occasions, I must express my thanks to her. Finally, I owe thanks to my wife, not only for her help in checking and correcting the copy, but also for keeping after me and encouraging me till the job was done. The book, as it ought to be, is dedicated to her.

CONTENTS

ABBREVIATIONS

BWANT	*Beiträge zur Wissenschaft vom Alten und Neuen Testament*
BZAW	*Beihefte zur Zeitschrift für die alttestamentliche Wissenschaft*
CBQ	*The Catholic Biblical Quarterly*
EOTH	*Essays on Old Testament Hermeneutics* ed. by C. Westermann
ET	*The Expository Times*
EvTh	*Evangelische Theologie*
IDB	*The Interpreter's Dictionary of the Bible* ed. by G. A. Buttrick
JBL	*Journal of Biblical Literature*
JNES	*Journal of Near Eastern Studies*
JSS	*Journal of Semitic Studies*
OTCF	*The Old Testament and Christian Faith* ed. by B. W. Anderson
RB	*Revue biblique*
RThPh	*Revue de théologie et de philosophie*
SBT	Studies in Biblical Theology
SJT	*Scottish Journal of Theology*
ThZ	*Theologische Zeitschrift*
USQR	*Union Seminary Quarterly Review*
VT	*Vetus Testamentum*
ZAW	*Zeitschrift für die alttestamentliche Wissenschaft*
ZThK	*Zeitschrift für Theologie und Kirche*

I

THE AUTHORITY OF THE OLD TESTAMENT:

THE NATURE OF THE PROBLEM

As its title indicates, we shall be concerned in this book with the authority of the Old Testament. Or, to put it more accurately, we shall be concerned with the authority of the Bible, and the problem presented by the Old Testament once we attempt to take it seriously as a part of canonical Scripture. That is a large subject, and one that has many ramifications. It opens up before us a veritable Pandora's box of issues far broader in scope than the simple statement of the title might suggest, none of which will it be possible for us to avoid. We shall be obliged to inquire into the nature of biblical authority, and the sense in which the Old Testament shares that authority; and this, in turn, will require us to examine the theological relationship of Old Testament to New within the canon of Scripture. Moreover, because our concern is an intensely practical one, we cannot avoid the problems of biblical hermeneutics and the question of the proper use of the Old Testament in the pulpit and in the teaching of the church. All these issues, and others besides, will claim our attention in the pages that follow. Yet the title is, I think, not amiss, for it lays the finger on the crux of the matter that is before us. To ask about the authority of the Old Testament is—stated in the simplest and bluntest terms—to ask what place the Old Testament legitimately occupies in the canon of Scripture, and whether it ought to be included in the Christian's Bible at all.

That is, granted, a blunt way of stating the question. But the question is certainly no new one frivolously concocted in these pages for purposes of discussion, nor yet one that has arisen only in recent times with some "modern" understanding of Scripture. On the contrary, it is a very old question, one of the oldest and most persistent that has vexed the church. It was raised as far back as the second century when Marcion (of whom more later) declared the Old Testament to be no part of the Christian revelation and, accordingly, removed it from his canon. Indeed, we may see the problem adumbrated in the pages of the New Testament itself, for there we read that while one group in the primitive church maintained that all Gentile converts must shoulder the yoke of the Jewish law in order to be Christians, others (notably Paul) declared that Christians had been freed from the way of the law, which had no authority over them.

This controversy regarding the Old Testament, begun in the church's infancy, has never been resolved, but has continued with greater or less intensity throughout the church's history from that day to this. No agreed solution to it has ever been arrived at among Christians. As the reader is aware, one may find among the various communions, and not infrequently within the same communion, the most widely divergent viewpoints with regard to the Old Testament. Among theologians the same is true. In theological circles today few subjects are being more warmly and voluminously debated—and with a greater measure of disagreement—than those that relate to the Old Testament, its place in the canon, its theological relationship to the New, and the principles that ought to govern its interpretation in the church.

Nor are questions of this kind of such a nature that they might occur only to trained theologians. Many a private Christian has asked them too, albeit perhaps unable to formulate them with precision and quite unaware of the magnitude of the theological issues involved. It is simply that he is troubled by the Old Testament. To be sure, he finds in it much that is noble, profound, and moving, much that speaks to his condition and nurtures his spirit: that he gladly concedes. But he also finds much that is strange to his way of thinking, much that is tedious and seemingly irrelevant, and not a little that offends his moral sensibilities. He comes to these endless genealogical lists, these interminable chapters giving detailed instructions for offering the various kinds of sacrifice, the specifications for the tabernacle drawn out to utter tedium, and he cannot imagine how such things concern him. So he reads, and is bored—and ceases to read. He encounters a narrative of matchless lucidity that captures

16

his interest, but he has to admit that much of it is not especially edifying. Again and again it presents him with instances of immorality and violence, and with customs, attitudes, and conceptions of God that seem to him much less than Christian. Many a reader has been troubled by these things. He is puzzled to know how he can receive the Old Testament as the Word of his God. He wonders what advantage there is in reading it, and whether it is wise to teach it to his children. And many a pastor, too, betrays by his preaching—perhaps openly confesses—that he does not know how to begin with the Old Testament.

The Old Testament, then, presents a problem to many Christians, and always has. And the problem, fundamentally, is one that lies between the Old Testament itself and the affirmations the church is accustomed to make about it. Or, to put it in another way, the Old Testament is a problem because it is in the Bible, and because of what the church declares the Bible to be. If the Old Testament were not in the Bible, it would be just another body of ancient religious literature (albeit infinitely superior to any other), and it would occasion the Christian no problem whatever. Or if the church regarded the Bible as a book like any other book, there would again be no problem. But the church has *not* regarded the Bible as a book like any other book, and the Old Testament *is* in the Bible. It has been there since the church's canon was first formed, indeed was regarded in the church as Holy Scripture before the New Testament was written; and till this day it is bound in our printed Bibles alongside the New Testament. Nor has the mainstream of Christianity ever drawn any formal distinction in value between the Testaments, but has in one way or another always declared the scriptures of both Testaments to be the Word of God and the church's supreme authority in all matters of doctrine and practice.[1] And that sets the problem. What do we mean by statements of this kind when applied to the Old Testament? In what way is this ancient book, with its ancient laws, customs, and institutions— its record of ancient events, by no means all of them edifying—to be received by the Christian as a part of his supreme rule of faith and practice and applied as such in his daily life?

The place of the Old Testament in the Bible and in the life of the

---

[1] I suspect that no tradition has stated this more strongly than my own, whose standards declare: "Under the name of Holy Scripture, or the word of God written, are now contained all the books of the Old and New Testaments [they are then listed] all of which are given by inspiration of God, to be the rule of faith and life" (Westminster Confession of Faith, Ch. I, Sec. II).

church hangs ultimately on the question of its authority. It is, in the final analysis, profitless to attack the problem at any other level. Little would be gained by arguing that the Old Testament contains many things of abiding value, or that some knowledge of it is essential for the proper understanding of the Christian faith. That would be to stress the obvious. Neither point, one would think, is in dispute. And, in any event, the canonical status of the Old Testament cannot be defended on these grounds alone. Nor can the place of the Old Testament be secured merely by insistence upon its divine inspiration or by appeal to the doctrine of revelation, for, however important and relevant both these doctrines are, the problem of the Old Testament is not necessarily linked with a denial or "low" view of either of them. True, the Old Testament *has* been rejected on the grounds that it was not inspired by, and is in no sense a revelation of, the Christian's God (Marcion). Any who take such a view will of course dismiss the Old Testament from the canon. But even those who hold the "highest" view of the Old Testament as an integral part of Holy Scripture have not escaped the problem of its authority. Indeed, the more strongly the doctrine of Scripture is stated, and the more seriously the Old Testament is taken as a part of Scripture, the more acute the problem becomes, or should become. Even he who affirms that the old Testament is in each of its texts inspired of God and affords in all its parts a revelation of his character, purpose, and will (let the reader state it in the strongest terms he cares to employ), must still face the question: How are these ancient laws, institutions, and concepts, these ancient narratives, sayings, and expressions of an ancient piety, actually to be taken as authoritative over the faith and life of the Christian, and how proclaimed as such in the church?

That, then, is the problem. Our first task—and it is the sole task of this chapter—must be to state the problem, and to do so as clearly and as sharply as possible, so that we may understand what sort of problem it is and not be tempted to evade it. Nothing whatever is to be gained by minimizing it or, as so many of us seem to prefer to do, closing our eyes to it and pretending it does not exist. It *does* exist, and it *is* a real problem. It must be met and, for the health of the church, met squarely. If we fail to do so, all our statements regarding Scripture are in danger of becoming empty statements, with the inevitable result that the very place of the Bible in the life and preaching of the church will be thrown into question.

18

I

But we must begin at the beginning. The authority of the Old Testament is not a subject that can be discussed in isolation, for it is, after all, but an aspect of the larger problem of the authority of the Bible as a whole. It is quite idle to discuss it in any other context. Indeed, as we have already hinted, it is only in this context that the problem even arises. If we made no insistence upon the authority of the Bible, or if we did not attempt to take the Old Testament seriously as a part of the Bible, there would be no problem. We cannot, therefore, proceed until we have asked what we mean when we speak of the supreme authority of the Bible. But that, in turn, presses us to a still broader question. There are many today to whom the very notion of authority in religion is unwelcome, and who would be reluctant to concede that a supreme authority over belief and practice (unless it be that of God himself) is either necessary or desirable. Since this is so, we have to begin by asking what place authority legitimately occupies in religion generally and by distinguishing the sense in which we wish, and the sense in which we do not wish, an authority to direct us.

1. Let us, then, leap straightaway into midstream and sum up the issue in the form of a question: Is there such a thing as a supreme authority that governs Christian belief and Christian action and, if so, what is it? Or, to put it differently: Is there a final authority to which Christians may appeal in deciding all matters of faith and conduct and, if so, what is it?

So stated, the question has a certain formal, old-fashioned sound about it that will doubtless jar upon the sensibilities of some, and perhaps may even serve to prejudice in their minds the relevance of our entire discussion. As it is popularly understood, the notion of authority in religion is not one that this day and age—to speak in general—feels that it can take seriously. People today tend to feel that they have gotten beyond such a notion, and they believe that they have done well to do so. In the minds of many, authority in religion connotes a spiritual authoritarianism of some sort, which may dictate what one is to believe and what one is to do, and which is to be obeyed meekly and without question. And this, in turn, connotes an intrusion upon the freedom of reason and conscience of which our contemporaries wish to hear nothing. So understood, the question just asked can only seem a futile one, not worth discussing, to be answered peremptorily in the negative. Is there an authority that can tell a man what he has to believe and what he must do? No, there is not! That is an old-fashioned notion best gotten rid of. It is in a class with the unicorn, the centaur, the hippogriff, and other such mythical creatures. "There ain't no such animal," and people ought not to be so gullible as to suppose that there is.

People today have, in general, little patience with the notion of authority in religion as they understand it. It suggests to them the acceptance of beliefs as true, and the adoption of patterns of conduct, entirely in submission to some external directive or influence: perhaps the dominant personality of a parent, or the prestige of a pastor or a teacher, or the mores of the religious community, or the claims of church dogma. And that is not something that most of us are willing to do, or think it healthy to do: we reserve the right to question. Of course, children must be guided (and are almost certain to be influenced) by the beliefs of their parents, and ought to do as their parents say. But that's for children. The grown man who parrots beliefs the meaning of which he has never examined, or who follows patterns of conduct for no other reason than that he was taught to do so as a child, would be regarded by most thinking people, one suspects, as intellectually and emotionally immature.

By the same token, to speak of the authority of the Bible is to speak of something foreign to the thinking of many people—even of many Christians—today. They will take the term to mean simply that one is supposed to believe what the Bible says—totally, without question, and to the letter. And modern man wants to ask questions of the Bible. He claims the right to approach the Bible with his reason, and he is likely to resent the notion of biblical authority, as he understands it, as an infringement upon his intellectual integrity. Are you seriously going to argue, he will say, that the Christian is supposed to accept patterns of belief passively, on external authority? Are you saying that whatever is in the Bible is by that very fact validated as true, and that the Christian is simply required to believe it and ask no questions? Is it suggested that the deepest questions that trouble one's spirit have meekly to be suppressed whenever the preacher slams the desk and quotes a verse of Scripture? How can a thinking person acquiesce in such a notion? Surely if one's belief—even one's belief in the Bible—is to mean anything at all, it must be submitted to the test of reason and experience. Now of course, the Christian faith requires of us no docile surrender of the intellectual faculties, but rather commands us to use them to the fullest. It does not ask of us a *sacrificium intellectus* before the biblical text. Yet it is to be feared that this is just

20

what acceptance of the authority of the Bible has come to connote to many people today. And because this is so, we find ourselves at times hesitant to use the term.

2. But we have not, for all that, outrun the problem of authority. There is another sense in which authority is desperately needed in the church, and desired by all who think seriously on the matter. It is most urgently necessary that the church become clear in her mind as to what that authority is.

There is not a parish pastor who does not collide head on with the problem of authority each Sunday when he rises to exhort and instruct his congregation. It is wrapped up with the very nature of his function as a minister of the Word. In what capacity does he speak? Certainly he does not speak merely as an educated man who propounds his personal opinions, although he has, of course, both a right to his opinions and the right to express them. Nor does he invite the congregation to join him in the search for truth, though it is a tragedy if both he and they are not open to all truth. He does not claim a hearing as one who *is* an authority, whether in philosophy, ethics, history, political science, economics—or even theology. In all likelihood he is *not* an authority in any of these things. He speaks as a teacher and advocate of the Christian gospel—nothing else. Indeed, there is fundamentally no other reason that he should speak at all, and certainly none that the faithful should trouble to listen to him fifty-two times *per annum*, give or take a few.

His task, then, is to expound the Christian gospel, to summon his hearers to accept that gospel and to live in a manner consonant with it. But just that places him squarely before the problem: How can he be sure, as he attempts to do this, that the beliefs he enunciates and the patterns of behavior he advocates are indeed Christian beliefs and Christian practices? What *authority* has he for asserting that they are, and urging them upon his people as such? He must know, if he has any historical sense, that the wildest beliefs and the most ungodly deeds have been advocated in the name of Christ. How does he know that what he preaches is any better, is in fact Christian doctrine? How shall he be sure that the content of his homily faithfully represents the Christian faith to his people? Is there any authority by which he may test his preaching on this score?

The church, too, faces the problem of authority, and it behooves her to be clear as regards her understanding of it. If she is not, all her debates on matters of faith and practice are at cross-purposes. For example, a queer and exotic belief intrudes in her midst, accompanied perhaps by certain unaccustomed practices. How does she evaluate it? Let the right of each free individual to believe what he will without let or hindrance, or threat of coercion, by all means be granted. But must the church then agree that one belief is as Christian as another, provided only that it be held sincerely? Certainly not. But, in that event, how is the matter to be settled? With our fists? By the counting of noses (the voice of the majority is the voice of God)? By appeal to tradition alone (the thing is without precedent, therefore wrong)? By forensic skill (a euphemism, perhaps, for the ability to shout the loudest)? Or is there some authority, recognized by all parties as competent to determine what is, and what is not, in accord with the Christian faith, to which the church may appeal in attempting to referee the matter?

Likewise, the church is called upon to face the social and moral issues of the day and to guide her people toward Christian courses of action. On no account can she shirk this responsibility. But upon what will she base her pronouncements? Upon some vague Christian sentiment or humanitarian feeling, or (God save the mark!) political or ecclesiastical expediency? It is the duty of the church to call upon her people to seek the divine will and to act in accordance with their Christian commitment in all areas of life; but when men disagree, as they almost always do, as to what the divine will is in the specific situation, is there any authority upon which the church may base herself in formulating her directives? Or is she to be so helpless in the face of such questions that she can only say that anything done in good conscience is Christian?

Examples of this problem as it confronts the church could be multiplied at will. It may concern matters of ecclesiastical law or polity (such as the question of the remarriage of divorced persons or the question of the ordination of women, to mention two issues that have been before courts of my own church in recent years); or matters of personal demeanor (say, as regards sex, the use of alcohol, or the proper observance of the sabbath); or the great social and moral issues of the day (race or nuclear warfare). We shall not take sides on any of these issues here. The point to be made is that all such questions will inevitably evoke differences of opinion. Moreover, representatives of every viewpoint, with those rare exceptions whom God alone can ferret out, will be sincere in their conviction that the course they advocate is the Christian one. Is it, after all, really conceivable that any should rise in church court or assembly and say: We freely admit that the solution we propose is not a Christian one and, furthermore, we do not care what the Christian solution is? No, in such debates all participants, even those whom we in our arrogance may be quick to brand as perverse, are normally convinced that their way is the Christian way. And this one thing is certain: All cannot be equally right. How, then, is the church to proceed? That all can be brought round to the same opinion is, in most instances, too much to hope for. Failing that, the matter can be settled by vote, or a compromise acceptable to the majority can be arrived at. But is the Christian course of action necessarily what a majority of those present and in session thinks it is? Is there no authority that can tell us what the applicable Christian teachings are, so that we may at least begin our debating and voting from that point? We are helpless indeed if we have none.

3. But enough has been said to make it clear that the problem of authority is as alive as it ever was, and of desperate importance to the church. The church has need of an authority to which she may appeal in order to determine what is in accord with Christian teaching and what is not.

But where is she to find such an authority? One might object that to ask such a question is wholly superfluous, for Protestantism has historically always had its clear answer ready: The final authority in all matters of faith and conduct is the Bible. The great confessional documents of the major Protestant traditions affirm that point explicitly. In the standards of my own church it is clearly stated that the Scriptures of the Old and New Testaments were inspired by God and have been preserved by his providence, and that "in all controversies of religion the Church is finally to appeal unto them." [2] And all ordained persons are obliged to avow their belief that the Scriptures are "the Word of God, the only infallible rule of faith and practice." Other Protestant communions of course employ other phraseology and lay various shadings of interpretation upon it. Yet it is only correct to say that Protestantism in general has historically been in agreement with the sense of the statements just quoted: the final authority to be appealed to in all matters of belief and practice is the Bible.

But how seriously can we take such a statement today? What do we mean by the authority of the Bible? It is to be feared that many of us

[2] *Ibid.*, Ch. I, Sec. VIII.

have no clear answer to that question. Do we mean that the Bible's doctrines and moral and religious directives must command our belief and practice to the last detail? Do we regard the Bible as authoritative only in the sense that, as the primary witness to our faith, we may expect it to provide us with the broad, general principles that must guide us in our doctrinal and ethical decisions? Or do we look upon the Bible as *an* authority, not to be ignored to be sure, but to be consulted along with other authorities in determining matters of faith and practice? We are far from clear on the point; certainly there is little agreement on it in present-day Protestantism, where all the above views of the matter, and others besides, can be found represented. [3]

In view of this confusion, it would be well if we were to pause to clarify the sense in which the word "authority" is intended. In current English parlance "authority" is used in a variety of senses, two of which are germane to the discussion here. The reader will no doubt have detected that both of these have been employed in the paragraphs immediately preceding. On the one hand, there is authority in the sense of that which secures assent, compels or constrains belief; or, in another context, that which can compel conformity of conduct, enforce obedience. Thus, we speak of the authority of the government to make laws and enforce them, or of a school to set its rules and compel its students to abide by them. Or we speak of parental authority, meaning the right and duty of parents to guide and discipline the conduct of their children. Again, should an eminent professor of physics make a statement of fact within the area of his competence, I am compelled to take his word for it; he is an authority in his field—about which I know next to nothing—and his authority guarantees to me, short of further information, the truth of what he says. Thus the primary meanings of the word given in my dictionary: "1. The right to command and to enforce obedience; the right to act officially. 2. Personal power that commands influence, respect, or confidence." [4]

[3] Some even go so far as to question if "authority" is a useful term. See, for example, C. T. Craig in A. Richardson and W. Schweitzer, eds., *Biblical Authority for Today* (London: SCM Press, 1951), pp. 30-44, who would prefer to substitute "source of guidance" for "authority." The Bible is a "source of guidance" (which itself must be sifted of chaff by the Christian consciousness, p. 35) to be consulted alongside other sources of guidance: the ethical experience of the race, the traditions of the church, the witness of the Holy Spirit.

[4] I have no opinion as to which is the best English dictionary at the moment. The one currently in use on my desk happens to be Funk and Wagnalls, *Standard Dictionary of the English Language, International Edition* (New York: Funk and Wagnalls, 1958).

But the word is also used in another sense—namely, of a recognized source or standard to which one may appeal in order to justify the accuracy of a statement made or the correctness of a position taken, or in order to test the propriety of an action performed or contemplated. Thus, one who lectures or writes upon the thought of a given scholar will appeal to the published works of that scholar as his primary authority for the statements he makes about it. (Whether he agrees with that scholar's position or not is another matter.) Or the umpire on the baseball field will conduct the game in accordance with the rules and, in case of a disputed decision, will appeal to the rulebook as his authority. (Whether or not he believes the rules could be improved is another matter.) Thus my dictionary also gives this definition of authority: "4. That which is or may be appealed to in support of action or belief, as an author, volume, etc."

The authority of the Bible may, of course, be discussed in either of the above senses. The confessional statements of the church in fact embrace both of them. In the first sense, authority is viewed in its more subjective aspect, frequently with a strong apologetic concern. That is to say, the Bible's authority refers to its right to be believed and obeyed; it refers to that in the Bible which impels one—or should impel one—to give assent to its teachings, which constrains one to believe, and which may be expected, *deo volente,* to constrain others to believe. This is the authority that the church has in mind when it speaks of the Bible as the inspired Word of God: because it is God's Word, its witness is trustworthy and ought to be believed. Many a Christian accepts the teachings of the faith unquestioningly on no other authority than this, which he finds all-sufficient; in support of his beliefs he appeals to the Bible. Others, however, aware that such convictions are not shared by all, seek to defend the authority of the Bible by pointing to those of its teachings which commend themselves to the reason and conscience as worthy and true, and which, they believe, might serve to awaken in the minds of all open-minded people a belief in the truth of the biblical revelation. But, whether stated strongly or less strongly, authority in this sense refers to the power that resides in the Bible to compel conviction and create belief. Concern is primarily with asserting the validity of the biblical teaching, perhaps before those of contrary opinion.

In the second sense of the word, however, authority is viewed in its more objective aspect. Here authority has less to do with establishing the truth of the biblical revelation, or with its compelling power, than with

25

its definition. Authority in this sense is primarily of concern to those who stand within the Christian faith and are committed to it, and who desire to know the content of that faith in order that they may test their own beliefs and actions in the light of it. To these the Bible is authoritative because, as the primary document of the Christian faith, it is the source that must finally be appealed to in any attempt to decide what the Christian faith actually teaches; because they desire to conform to those teachings, the Bible is their authoritative rule of faith and practice.

4. It is probable that most people are accustomed to think of biblical authority almost exclusively in the first sense—namely, of the power that resides in the Bible to certify the truth of its teachings and to constrain belief. If I am not mistaken, most treatments of the subject that have appeared in recent years tend to approach it from this angle.[5] Nor would anyone wish to deny that this is a legitimate approach. If God in any way speaks his Word in the Bible, then the Bible carries with it something of the authority of God. And the Bible does indeed have an authority that commands assent and awakens faith in the minds of those who read it humbly and openly. It is, therefore, quite proper to inquire into the nature of that authority, its role in creating belief, and its relationship to other factors that operate to the same end, especially the human reason. Certainly no one factor has exclusive authority in this area. If by authority is meant those forces that have constrained us to give assent to the truth of the Christian revelation, and have shaped our apprehension of it, it is clear that the Bible has not been our only authority, and it may not have been —and in the case of many Christians in fact has not been—even the supreme and final one. And that obligates us to ask what we mean when we hail it as such.

What actually does constrain a man to give assent to the Christian faith, or to adopt whatever beliefs he may hold and whatever patterns of conduct he may follow? What caused any of us to believe as we do?

---

[5] See, for example, C. H. Dodd, *The Authority of the Bible* (London: Nisbet & Co., Ltd, 2nd ed., 1938 [New York: Harper Torchbooks]). p. ix: "I assume that the function of authority is to secure assent to truth; that for us the measure of any authority which the Bible may possess must lie in its direct religious value, open to discovery in experience." See also H. H. Rowley, "The Authority of the Bible" (*Joseph Smith Memorial Lecture*, Overdale, Selly Oak, Birmingham, England, 1949) who asks (p.5) "whether a belief in the authority of the Bible can approve itself to reason, when reason is free and unfettered" (he takes an affirmative position). For a similar understanding of the matter see Leonard Hodgson in the symposium, *On the Authority of the Bible* (London: SPCK, 1960), pp. 1-24, and D. E. Nineham, pp. 81-96. Other examples could be added.

Factors too numerous to mention. The teachings of the Bible, of course; but also our early training in the home (which may or may not have included much instruction in the Bible), the example of parents, the influence of persons whom we admired in formative years and after, the doctrines of the church we happen to belong to as learned in Sunday school and communicants' class, the preaching we have heard (which may have been biblical preaching and, again, may not have been), the experiences we have undergone, the thinking we have done, and more besides.[6] We have, in fact, been constrained to accept the Christian faith, and our apprehension of it has been shaped, by many authorities. The degree to which the authority of the Bible has been effective varies with each individual. All of us have known upright and loyal churchgoers who seldom look inside the Bible, and who are all but ignorant of its contents. Such people have scarcely formed their patterns of belief and conduct primarily on biblical authority. Whatever their creedal profession may be, the Bible has exercised authority over them only in a most indirect and attenuated sense; other authorities have played a major role in making them what they are.

Whatever we mean by the supreme authority of the Bible, we do not mean that the Bible can, alone and of itself, override reason and compel belief. The Bible has no such dead authority over belief. Unless one has been persuaded, through the witness of the Holy Spirit, of the trustworthiness of the biblical revelation, one will grant the Bible no authority at all.[7] And even those who have been so persuaded are not required for that reason to surrender their intellectual faculties: we may and must respond to the biblical teaching as thinking individuals. Indeed, it is only as the biblical word attests itself to the reason, conscience, and experience of the individual that real belief in the Bible takes shape. Belief that has not been tested by experience and reason is scarcely yet real belief. Perhaps the

---

[6] See, e.g., Nineham, *On the Authority of the Bible*, pp. 95-96, who clearly recognizes this and finds the authority of the Bible "inextricably connected with other authorities"; he lists the authority of the church, of the saints, of the liturgy, and of reason and conscience. If one approaches the subject from this point of view, one must agree that Nineham is right, save perhaps that his list of "authorities" could be greatly expanded.

[7] As Calvin said long ago: "Wherefore the Scripture will then only be effectual to produce the saving knowledge of God when the certainty of it shall be founded on the internal persuasion of the Holy Spirit. . . . But those persons betray great folly, who wish it to be demonstrated to infidels that the Scripture is the Word of God, which cannot be known without faith" (*Institutes of the Christian Religion*, I, viii, 13; cf. also I, vii, 5).

reader learned, as I did, in the kindergarten of the church school the song that goes:

> Jesus loves me, this I know,
> For the Bible tells me so.

Now the Bible does so tell us, and it is very well for children to be taught as much. I confess that I cannot hear the song, banal though some may think it, without many haunting recollections. But if I believe at all in the love of Christ, it is not *just* because "the Bible tells me so"; it is because the Bible's assurance to that effect has been tested in experience and found in one way or another to be trustworthy. Had it not stood the test of experience, I should scarcely be prepared to believe it, in the Bible or not.

In any event, we know that in practice it usually does little good to attempt to "prove" things on the authority of the Bible alone. Unless the person to whom we speak already accepts the Bible unquestioningly, it is no convincing argument to call upon it for support. All who have had occasion to discuss matters of faith with some intelligent but skeptical person who doubts the goodness—or even the existence—of God, or who cannot bring himself to believe in some cardinal doctrine of the Christian religion, will understand the point perfectly. In such cases it helps little to say: "But, man, you must believe it! It says so in the Bible!" No doubt he knows that it says so in the Bible—and still doesn't believe it. The authority of the Bible, whatever we may think of it, will convince no one who does not grant it such authority. And it is because biblical authority has come to suggest to so many people the power of the Bible to compel conviction, its right to be believed unquestioningly—and perhaps also our own right to prove things by appeal to the Bible—that we find ourselves embarrassed by the term. We are puzzled to know in what sense the Bible may be spoken of as supremely and finally authoritative in matters of faith and practice, as the creedal statements have it.

5. But when we view the authority of the Bible in that other sense mentioned above, we are on much firmer ground. We speak now of the Bible's authority, not in the sense of that which guarantees its truth or constrains men to believe in its teachings and obey them; rather, we speak of the Bible as the authoritative source to which Christians must appeal in attempting to determine the nature and content of the Christian faith as originally held, in order that they may evaluate their own beliefs and

actions in the light of it.[8] The question is not now primarily one of demonstrating the correctness of the biblical teaching, or of determining what it is that constrains men to believe in the Christian faith; rather, it is a question of what the Christian faith *was*, and, by extension, properly *is*. Viewed in this light, one may say that the Bible is not only the supreme authority in matters of faith and practice; it is the only sure and primary one.

Perhaps one or two illustrations might serve to clarify what is meant by authority in this sense. They are not perfect illustrations, but they will have to do. We might mention *Robert's Rules of Order*. As is well known, these are accepted rules for regulating parliamentary procedure. They have, of course, no authority to compel anyone to believe in their wisdom, or to abide by them, who does not wish to do so. One may regard them as capable of improvement, or may think some of them to be needlessly complicated, if not downright ridiculous; one may even reject the ideal of orderly parliamentary debate altogether. But for those who have accepted parliamentary procedure as a desirable way of conducting public assembly, these rules have become the authority to be appealed to in deciding whether a given action is or is not "in order."

Better still, perhaps, let us take the Constitution of the United States. The Constitution is the final authority over legislation and over judicial and governmental procedure, in that it is the norm by which laws, decisions of lower courts, official regulations, and the like are tested in order to determine whether or not they are in accord with those basic principles upon which our nation was founded and which that Constitution expresses. Laws or decisions that are held to be out of harmony with the Constitution are declared "unconstitutional," and are "struck down" or reversed. Now the Constitution is not an authority in the sense that it can guarantee the truth of its own presuppositions or compel any to believe in them who do not wish to do so. Citizens of other lands are in no way governed by it; one does not have to accord its ideas any objective validity at all, and millions in the world do not. But if one is or becomes a United States citizen, and swears allegiance to our government, then one accepts the normative authority of the Constitution. This does not mean that one must regard the Constitution as sacrosanct and beyond improvement (it

---

[8] For a somewhat similar understanding of biblical authority, see Hubert Cunliffe-Jones, *The Authority of the Biblical Revelation* (London: James Clarke and Company, 1945), esp. pp. 13-25; see also *Biblical Authority for Today*, pp. 45-58.

has been amended many times); still less does it mean that one must necessarily agree with every decision of every court in interpretation of it. Yet it remains for all who accept its authority the norm that is to be appealed to in deciding what is and what is not in harmony with a given tradition, in this case American constitutional democracy.

Now it is somewhat in this latter sense that we speak here of the supreme authority of the Bible. Whatever else we may affirm that it is, the Bible provides us with the primary, and thus the normative, documents of the Christian faith; it has, therefore, normative authority—constitutional authority, if you will—over all who claim to be Christians. To ask, as we continually do, Is this teaching truly Christian? Is this course of action in accord with the Christian gospel? is to be driven inevitably back to the Bible, for these are questions that can ultimately be answered only in the light of the Bible. On what basis can we say what is truly in accord with the Christian faith if we fail to consult the only documents that tell us what the Christian faith originally was? And since those documents are found in the Bible, the Bible remains the final authority to be appealed to in discussing such questions. Men may, of course, disagree in their understanding of what the Bible teaches at any given point. Many biblical texts are ambiguous and capable of more than one interpretation; and no interpreter is infallible. But the authoritative position of the Bible is in no sense impaired by this. If all parties to the debate are honestly seeking to discover what the biblical teaching is, there may be disagreement; but it is no longer a clash of free opinion regarding what is Christian and what is not, but rather a disagreement regarding the correct interpretation of an agreed norm. And that norm remains the Bible.[9]

This is not to say, of course, that to establish the biblical teaching is *per se* to establish its validity, still less to compel men to believe it. Men can refuse to believe it. To ask: What does the Bible teach? and to ask: Is that teaching something that I as a thinking individual can believe? is to ask two questions, not one. Both ought to be taken with the utmost seriousness, but they ought not to be confused. Yet I would submit that before one has a right to declare that a given teaching or course of action is the Christian one, one must first have tested it by the normative authority of

---

[9] I regret that "norm" and "normative" have acquired pejorative connotations in the minds of some when used in this connection. The first definition of "norm" given in my dictionary is: "a rule or authoritative standard." The word is used in that sense here: the Bible is our supreme rule (norm) of faith and practice.

the Bible to see if it accords with the biblical teaching or not. Let us, at least, raise it as a question to be pondered: Can a belief or practice that is demonstrably out of accord with the biblical teaching, whatever its intrinsic merits, with propriety be labeled a *Christian* belief or a *Christian* practice?

II

For my own part, in the sense just defined, I should be prepared to affirm without hesitation, in line with the mainstream of Protestantism, that the Bible is the final authority to be appealed to in all matters of faith and practice. The Bible *must* be the final authority; nothing else can safely be accorded that position.

1. Now, of course one does not mean by such a statement—nor did the Reformers mean—that the final authority over the Christian is a *book*. We do not worship a book. On the contrary, the sole legitimate object of worship, and the supreme authority to whom the Christian submits himself, is God—the God who, according to the Scripture, worked his redemptive purpose in Israel and, in the fullness of time, revealed himself in Jesus Christ. The Christian's God is the Creator and Lord of all things, and is the Lord also of Scripture. He existed before there was a Bible, and quite independently of it. He performed his work of creation when no man was there to record it. He gave his covenant law at Sinai, and that law had authority in Israel before the Pentateuch was written. He did his saving work in Jesus Christ, who came, did mighty works, died, and rose again, and this would be just as true had the Gospels never been penned. The Bible, therefore, derives its authority from God; it does not have authority of itself, but rather by virtue of the God to whom it witnesses and who speaks in its pages. The God of the Bible is the Christian's supreme authority in all senses of the word.

True. Yet there is a practical sense in which this comes to much the same thing. What, after all, would the Christian know of his God, of Christ, and of the nature of the Christian faith apart from the Bible? Suppose for a moment the Bible had never been written or had been lost to us. What would we know of the history and faith of Israel? What would we know of Jesus, his life, his teachings, and the significance of his saving work as the early church understood it? The answer is: precious little. Perhaps there would have come down to us a vague and fluid oral tradition, tenacious indeed, but so refracted in the telling that we could scarcely be sure of a single detail. Jesus would be to us as shadowy a figure as is Zoroaster, the very century of whose activity has long been a subject of dispute. Virtually all that we know of the God whom we worship, of Christ, and of the nature of the primitive Christian faith has come to us directly or indirectly from the Bible. The Bible, therefore, speaks to us with the authority of God, of Christ, and the gospel. And since it is, in the final analysis, only through the Bible that we can know anything tangible of the gospel, the Bible remains the supreme and final authority to be appealed to in any discussion of it.

To say this is in no sense to deny that God can be known to us in other ways than through the Bible. The mainstream of Christian theology has always maintained that he can be, and is. One thinks of the inward witness of the Holy Spirit without which—so the classical confessions have always declared [10]—not even the words of Scripture can rightly be heard and received. One thinks also of God's witness to himself in the life of his church and in the lives of individual believers. One might further feel, as many do, that some knowledge of God may be gained through contemplation of nature and through reflection upon history and experience. That is a point which we cannot debate here. But one would, in any event, have to concede that such knowledge is, to borrow the language of my own church's Confession of Faith, "not sufficient." [11] Certainly nothing that we know of God or of the Christian faith apart from the Bible is adequate to provide the church with a norm by which her doctrine and practice may be tested. Had we no Bible, we should have no basis for discussing the will of Christ at all; we should scarcely know who he was.

Perhaps the point would be made clearer if we were to turn it around. If the Bible is not to be regarded as the final authority to be appealed to in determining what the Christian faith teaches and requires, to what authority, then, can we appeal? I can think of but two possibilities. If we do not look to the Bible as the final authority in such matters, then either the church or the conscience and reason of the individual (illumined, let us hope, by the Holy Spirit) must be accorded that position. Now I should, for one, readily agree (it has already been expressly affirmed) that God witnesses to himself and manifests his will through both these means; I should further agree that both have a decided authority in shaping belief

---

[10] It is not necessary to document the point at length. It has certainly been strongly insisted upon in my own tradition: cf. Westminster Confession of Faith, Ch. I, Sec. V; see also the quotation from Calvin in note 7.

[11] Westminster Confession of Faith, Ch. I, Sec. I.

and guiding conduct. Yet it is to me unthinkable that either should be elevated above Scripture when it comes to saying what the Christian faith actually teaches and actually requires.

2. As regards the church, this is no more than the historic Protestant position. Protestantism has never been willing to accord the church the degree of authority in matters of doctrine that the Roman Catholic Church has. This is probably, indeed, the point which more than any other separates the Protestant from his Roman Catholic brother. Now it is of course most wrong to suppose, as I fear many Protestants do, that the Catholic does not acknowledge the final authority of Scripture in matters of doctrine, for he does so explicitly. Yet from the Protestant's point of view, he so states the point as, in effect, to deny it.[12] Alongside authoritative Scripture the Catholic lays the church's ongoing tradition, which is likewise authoritative and of which the church is the sole repository. The authority of Scripture is thus linked with the authority of the church. Not only can the church alone define what inspiration is and determine which writings are inspired; the church has the sole authority to declare, in the light of her tradition, how these writings are to be interpreted.[13] Indeed, the church may promulgate dogma that has no support in Scripture at all, solely on the basis of tradition (the bodily assumption of the Virgin Mary is a recent example); and such dogma has binding authority over the faithful. But if Scripture is to be accepted on the authority of the church, if the church alone can determine the interpretation of Scripture and can even promulgate dogma without basis in Scripture, then it would seem that the church has assumed a certain authority *over* Scripture.[14] And

[12] One may find a convenient presentation of the Roman Catholic position regarding Scripture, from a Protestant point of view, with documentation, that is both fair and critical in J. K. S. Reid, *The Authority of Scripture* (London: Methuen and Co., 1957), Ch. IV.

[13] Clearly stated in the decree *Insuper* of the Council of Trent in 1546: "No one . . . shall presume to interpret Sacred Scripture contrary to the sense which Holy Mother Church —to whom it belongs to judge the true sense and interpretation of Holy Scripture—both held and continues to hold; nor (shall any one dare to interpret) Sacred Scripture contrary to the unanimous consent of the Fathers, even if interpretations of this kind are never published." The quotation is taken from J. E. Steinmueller, *A Companion to Scripture Studies* (2nd ed.; New York: Joseph F. Wagner, 1941), I, 394. For other quotations from Catholic sources in similar vein, see Rowley, "The Authority of the Bible," pp. 2-5.

[14] The relationship of Scripture and tradition is, of course, debated among Catholics. See, for example, the recent discussion of P. J. Cahill, "Scripture, Tradition and Unity," *CBQ*, XXVII (1965), 315-35. Cahill argues that Trent affirmed only one *source* of revelation (the gospel), of which tradition is the official interpreter. A tradition may be subject to corruption, but the total church can never be in error.

it was just at this point that the Reformers uttered their emphatic protest. This was, indeed, the pivotal issue of the Reformation; and even with the climate of openness that prevails today (for which we ought to thank God) the issue remains.

The Catholic, to be sure, is able to accord the church this authority through a virtual identification of the church with her Lord. She is his visible body on earth, and her voice is his voice; she can, no more than can he, promulgate error. When, therefore, the pope speaks *ex cathedra,* as the head of the church, he is infallible.[15] Protestants, however, both reject this claim and have resisted the temptation to transfer it to any one of their own denominations. This does not at all mean that Protestants are necessarily involved thereby in a "low" view of the church, or in a denial of the actual and rightful authority that the church exercises in shaping the beliefs and guiding the conduct of her people. The church in fact has tremendous authority in this regard, as we have said. After all, it is in the church that the gospel is preached and taught; many a believer knows his Bible and the tenets of the faith only as he has heard them expounded there and, indeed, may even have taken well-nigh his entire pattern of beliefs and attitudes on the authority of his church's teachings. No thinking Protestant would wish to deny this. But he is not driven thereby to accord to his church an authority alongside that of Scripture in matters of faith and practice. Rather, he maintains that his church is subordinate to Scripture in such matters. He would agree with Luther, who said: "The Church cannot create articles of faith; she can only recognize and confess them as a slave does the seal of his lord." [16]

The church is a community of believers called into being through faith in its Lord, organized about that faith, and commissioned to transmit it and proclaim it in the world. As such, she has both the right and the duty to define and interpret that faith to her people. She has also the right to set such standards of belief and conduct as she means to require of her members. But that right is not unlimited: it is subject to correction. The church can never of herself determine the content of the Christian faith, nor can any church court or council on its own authority say infallibly what

---

[15] On the somewhat similar position of the Greek Orthodox Church regarding the authority of tradition and the infallibility of the decisions of its ecumenical councils, see P. I. Bratsiotis in *Biblical Authority for Today,* pp. 17-29.

[16] I owe this quotation to F. W. Farrar, *History of Interpretation* (New York: E. P. Dutton & Co., 1886; reprinted Grand Rapids: Baker Book House, 1961), p. 326. I have been unable to check it, since Farrar does not give its exact source.

the Christian teaching is. The church may be, and on occasion has been, in error regarding matters of faith and practice. And when in error, she must be corrected by a norm outside and above herself—lest she correct herself by herself. And this norm can be nothing else than the very faith she is commissioned to transmit, the records of which are in the Bible. We hold, therefore, that the church does not have authority over Scripture, but quite the other way around. The church teaches with authority only so long as her teachings accord with Scripture; should they fail to do so, and to the degree that they so fail, they have no authority over the Christian at all.

3. So the historic Protestant position. But there seems to be a growing number of Protestants today who are either not altogether clear on the point or not wholly convinced of its correctness. No doubt some will say: But has not the above position been stated a bit too strongly and perhaps somewhat naïvely? Did not the church produce the New Testament Scriptures? Did not the church establish the canon of Scripture which we still today accept as normative? Have not most of the churches claimed in one way or another that their practice is patterned upon that of the New Testament church? Must we not, then, to some degree find our source of authority in the church?

Not a few would give an affirmative answer to that last question. As an excellent example of this view of the matter one might point to the book of John Knox, *The Early Church and the Coming Great Church.*[17] The author is here concerned to find some norm, some model for the great universal church of the Christian ideal. He asks if this can be discovered in the pages of the New Testament and comes to the conclusion that it cannot, for the church as we see it there was not itself united. The New Testament church, to be sure, had unity in its common life and its common faith in Christ; but it had no single, formal creedal expression, no one order of government and worship, and it was, moreover, no stranger to strife and schism. It cannot, therefore, serve as a model for a united Christendom, for the church—so the author argues—must be united not only in spirit but in outward form. The New Testament, since it embodies and expresses the primitive church's memory of its Lord and its experience

---

[17] (Nashville: Abingdon Press, 1955). If I mention only this one work, it is not because I wish to single it out for especial criticism, but because it is the clearest and most persuasive presentation that I have seen of what seems to be a widely held opinion, and because Professor Knox is himself a scholar whose stature requires that his views be taken seriously. For a more recent expression of Professor Knox's views, see his book, *The Church and the Reality of Christ* (New York: Harper & Row, 1962).

of the Spirit, is indeed authoritative over our faith; but as regards the outward aspects of unity—creedal expressions, forms of government and worship—the very matters that divide us most sharply, it provides us with no sure guidance. We must, therefore, look elsewhere. The author then goes on to reason that since the church gradually gained formal unity and was given a common order with the development of the early Catholic Church in the second century, we must to some degree look to that church as our model and must extend the locus of authority to include it.

For my part, I find myself unable to agree with this line of reasoning. It is, to be sure, most lucidly and persuasively presented and in a thoroughly irenic spirit; but it leads, I think, to highly dangerous conclusions. Now of course the New Testament church cannot serve directly as a model for the churches today, or for the ecumenical church of the Christian ideal. Not only did it lack the formal marks of unity and exhibit great variety in its practice; it had its share of sinful men, who behaved as sinful men will, and was on occasion plunged into overt controversy over matters of doctrine and even personality. What is far more serious, it belonged to an age that we cannot repeat; we could not in any event slavishly copy first-century forms of organization and corporate life and expect them to be adequate in the twentieth century. I know of no church that seriously attempts to do this. However loyal to the New Testament the churches may be, all have actually developed their particular forms of worship, government, and organization on the basis of later reflection and experience. But are we for this reason to extend the locus of authority beyond the New Testament to include the early Catholic Church? Leaving aside the question of whether the New Testament church was actually disunited or merely not formally united; leaving aside the question of whether one hopes for the time when diversity of practice and differences in creedal expression will no longer be permitted in the church; are we to seek the norm of the church in the church of the first century, or of the second century, or of any other century? To do so leads to dangerous consequences. It is, in the final analysis, to say that the model upon which the church is to pattern itself is the *church*. We have then only to decide which phase in the church's development we shall take as our model, and we will never agree on that. If one is to sanctify the second century with special authority, why stop there? Why not the third century, or the fourth, or the fifth? Why, after all, not the papacy? As will be argued later, the church's norm can never safely be the New Testament church, or the church of any age, but must be the

New Testament *doctrine,* the New Testament *theology* of the church. In our outward forms we may differ vastly from the New Testament church and from one another; but all of us must strive to express through those forms that are ours the New Testament doctrine of the church—what it may mean to be the body of Christ, the branches of the vine which is Christ.

But did not the church produce the New Testament Scriptures? Does not the New Testament provide us precisely with the witness of the primitive *church* to its Lord? Did not the church, moreover, in establishing the canon define the limits of Scripture? Does it not therefore follow that the authority of Scripture is in some way inextricably linked with that of the church? Many people today seem to believe so. But I, for one, find myself unable to follow this line of reasoning without considerable qualification.

As for the statement that the church produced the New Testament Scriptures and therefore has, as it were, a certain parity with them—that is, in my opinion, a rather loose way of speaking. Of course there is a truth in it, for the New Testament was produced in the church, by men of the church. But one fears that there has been a tendency in certain circles to exaggerate the creative power of the amorphous community, specifically the worshiping community. It is true that the material of the Gospels in particular was handed down for a time through oral transmission (though it ought to be added that the period of purely oral transmission was relatively brief), and we may assume that in the course of this transmission it was shaped by the uses to which it was put and by the needs of the community. Nor is it to be denied that the New Testament as a whole presents us with Christ as the earliest church understood him and believed in him; we can know of Christ only through this primitive Christian witness. Yet to say that the church, anonymously as it were, produced the New Testament is not to speak very precisely.[18] Leaving any doctrine of inspiration aside, the New Testament was not produced by the church corporately and anonymously, but by leading spirits in the church who sought to inform the church of Christ and the significance of his work, and to instruct and correct it in the light of his will. This is emphatically true of its epistolary literature. Would anyone, for example, say that the

---

[18] As C. H. Dodd remarks, "Creative thinking is rarely done by committees. . . . It is individual minds that originate." See *According to the Scriptures* (London: James Nisbet and Company, 1952), pp. 109-10. See also the excellent article of Otto Piper, "The Origin of the Gospel Pattern," *JBL,* LXXVIII (1959), 115-24, esp. p. 123.

church at Corinth produced the Corinthian letters? As well say that the royal cult of Bethel produced the book of Amos! These letters were anything but products of the church, expressive of its corporate thinking. Rather, they are expressive of the mind of Paul, as he strove to instruct the church and correct it by a norm outside it and above it—namely Christ. Even in the case of the Gospels, though the material had doubtless been shaped through transmission in the church, each evangelist in his own way laid the distinctive stamp of his mind upon the material, and each had the aim of proclaiming *to* the church the truth about the One who is the church's Sovereign Lord.

As regards the question of the canon, we cannot delay upon it here. We shall return to it briefly in a later chapter. It is true that the church did establish the canon which we accept as normative. It is also true that the line between canonical and noncanonical is at many places a fine one, and not infrequently a fluid one. The various branches of the church have never been in complete agreement as to which books belong in the Bible. The problem of the canon, therefore, is a real one. Very well to say that the canonical Scriptures are authoritative—but which church's canon do you mean? We cannot undertake to discuss that problem here, although I trust that the position taken in these pages will have the effect to some degree of drawing its sting. The point, however, to be made here is this: that in establishing the canon the church did not create a new authority, but rather acknowledged and ratified an existing one.[19] Books were selected because they were already recognized as authoritative. By the same token, the fact that we accept the canon which the early church established does not in any sense mean, at least in my judgment, that we accept the authority of the church, but rather that we ratify its judgment regarding *authoritative Scripture.* Indeed, I should say that we no more accept the authority of the church in this than I would accept the reader's authority were I to agree with him in his selection of the hundred greatest books or of an all-star baseball team. This would not be to accept his authority, but only by my free judgment to concur with his judgment. To accord to the church an authority above or equal to Scripture as the arbiter of faith and practice is to step outside the historic Protestant tradition, and dangerous in the extreme.

4. But if we cannot allow that the church can be the final authority in

---

[19] See, for example, F. V. Filson, *Which Books Belong in the Bible?* (Philadelphia: The Westminster Press, 1957), p. 40; B. Nagy in *Biblical Authority for Today,* p. 82.

matters of faith and practice, what about that other possibility mentioned above? Can we accord final authority to the conscience and reason of the individual and grant to each individual the right to decide, as the Spirit gives him guidance, what is Christian and what is not? Many Protestants seem to think so—or at least behave as if they thought so. But again the answer must be an emphatic *no*.

To be sure, no thinking person would wish to minimize the role that conscience and reason play in determining for each individual what he can believe and how he ought to act. Conscience and reason have a decided authority over belief and action in the first sense of the word as defined above (i.e., in compelling belief and constraining obedience), perhaps an authority which in actual practice may in many cases be more determinative than that of Scripture. After all, one can really believe in the Bible only as (through the work of the Holy Spirit) its truth attests itself to one's mind and conscience and in one's experience. Moreover, conscience gives the believer insights and speaks to him imperatives not specifically set forth in Scripture; and when conscience speaks its categorical imperative, it has an authority that does not wait for proof texts. Reason, conscience, and experience all have compelling authority in shaping belief and guiding conduct—that is, authority in the first sense of the word. But it is unthinkable that they should ever be accorded final authority in the second sense of the word—that is, as the norm to be appealed to in deciding what is and what is not in accord with Christian doctrine and ethics. And for two reasons.

First, the fallibility of conscience. I do not trust the reader's conscience, nor does he trust mine. It is notorious that men have often in good conscience done horrible things. Nor does the desire to do the will of God, or the conviction that God's will is indeed being done under the guidance of the Holy Spirit, ensure that such is in fact the case. How does one know that it is the Holy Spirit that speaks? What passes for the Holy Spirit impels some to roll frothing on the floor or to handle snakes. What passes for the Holy Spirit leads others to read from the Scriptures bizarre beliefs that have little or no relationship to the authentic Christian faith. The conscience is a very subjective authority that speaks to each man with a different voice; and there are no tests for determining the presence or absence of the Holy Spirit, save the test of the biblical teaching itself.[20]

[20] Probably no one ever put this more strongly than Calvin; see the *Institutes of the Christian Religion*, I, ix.

If the conscience and reason of the individual, however enlightened, be the final authority in matters of faith and practice, then let us face it: Each individual is his own authority, and the Christian faith is what each individual thinks it is.

But there is a second reason. It is very well to speak of the authority of conscience in matters of belief and conduct; but we ought also to ask about the roots of conscience. Let the reader ask himself where he got this Christian conscience of his. How did his conscience and mine, and the conscience of society generally, come to be conditioned by Christian attitudes? Answer: Because directly or indirectly we have been subjected to Christian teaching, we and our fathers before us. Of course, if we go on to inquire as to the manner in which that teaching was mediated to us, no simple answer is possible. Some of us, indeed, may have absorbed Christian attitudes, by osmosis as it were, from the general cultural environment, which has to such a large degree been permeated by them. Others of us have received intensive religious instruction. But it is certain that Christian attitudes have been shaped within us as, directly or most indirectly, the biblical teachings about God and Christ, about right and wrong, have made impress upon our thinking. The Bible is the great, ultimate shaper of conscience and as such has normative authority over conscience. Had the Bible never been written, had its teachings made no impact upon society, had our generation no awareness of those teachings, however vestigial, there would be no Christian conscience worth mentioning. And it may as well be added that if through our carelessness we allow knowledge of the Bible to lapse, this Christian conscience of which we like to speak will not long survive.

III

We have argued, then, that the Bible is the Christian's supreme authority in matters of doctrine and practice in that it is the one primary and reliable source to which he may appeal in determining what the Christian faith actually affirms and teaches. But does this assertion dispose of the problem of authority? Most emphatically not! On the contrary, it only introduces us to it. The real question before us is not simply whether or not we shall recognize the canonical authority of Scripture, but rather:

How is Scripture to be appealed to, how understood, and how used, so that it may actually serve as our rule of faith and life? [21]

1. First, let us make a preliminary point which need not be belabored at length, since it is probable that most readers of these pages would find themselves in agreement upon it. If the Bible is to be normative in matters of faith and conduct, it must be the Bible rightly interpreted. The Bible can seem to mean, and can be made to mean, many things; to acknowledge it as authoritative settles nothing so long as the principles by which it is to be interpreted are not agreed upon. What, then, are these principles? How shall we be sure what a given text means? Who has the right to say what it means?

Answers given to such questions of course range from one extreme to the other. The Roman Catholic Church stands at one extreme. Catholics, appalled as they are by the multiplicity of interpretation characteristic of Protestantism, which must seem to them a veritable Babel of confusion, have always declared that final authority to interpret belongs to the church. To be sure, Roman Catholic scholars are permitted far more latitude in their research than many Protestants realize, and this latitude has markedly broadened in recent years. Moreover, the exegetical principles employed by competent Catholic scholars in interpreting the Bible differ in no essential from those followed by their Protestant colleagues. Yet latitude has its limits, for in all matters of dogma the church has the final word: no meaning may be gotten from Scripture that contravenes the church's teachings in any way.[22] At the opposite extreme there stands a certain Protestant individualism. Protestants—rightly, we hold—shrink from church-dictated interpretations and rejoice in the freedom of each individual to study the Bible for himself, relying upon the guidance of the Holy Spirit as he does so. But many Protestants, though their piety may be admirable and their sincerity beyond question, are so innocent of *any* principle of interpretation that the biblical text means, quite simply, what it means *to them*. That, and nothing else. After all, cannot each man find in the Bible what the Spirit leads him to see there? Is not one man's interpretation, therefore, as valid as another's?

---

[21] For a clear recognition and statement of this point specifically as it relates to the Old Testament, see A. A. van Ruler, *Die christliche Kirche und das Alte Testament* (Munich: Chr. Kaiser Verlag, 1955), p. 7.

[22] See note 13 above. It must be said, however, that the texts the interpretation of which has been dogmatically fixed are relatively few.

But surely the correct answer lies between these extremes. To be sure, only a fool would scoff at the accumulated wisdom of the church as this is embodied in her traditional positions. Only a fool would come to his Bible as if he were the first to do so, or as if all the labors of the best minds of the church in the past had nothing to teach him.[23] But we cannot allow that the results of interpretation may be dictated in advance. This would be to throttle honest scholarship and, to a significant degree, to render its labors pointless. After all, if the meaning of a text must in the end always be what dogma has already said it is, what profit is there—other than apologetic—in an exhaustive examination of it? The church can never be granted final authority to interpret, for this is to give the church authority over Scripture—and even she is not great enough for that.[24] On the other hand, though we certainly do affirm that each man both can and should study the Bible for himself (nor is a degree in theology neces- sary in order to begin), to insist that one man's interpretation is as good as another's is downright irresponsible. The right of the individual to study the Bible for himself, relying on the guidance of the Holy Spirit, is not the right to make ignorance equal to knowledge. An erroneous interpretation arrived at in ignorance is not authoritative in the church at all.

But how is the Bible to be interpreted? As scholars today would unani- mously agree, there is but one admissible method for arriving at the meaning of the biblical text: the grammatico-historical method. That is to say, the text is to be taken as meaning what its words most plainly mean in the light of the situation (historical situation or life situation) to which they were originally addressed: the "grammar" is to be interpreted against the background of "history." It becomes, therefore, the task of the student to determine as accurately as he can, with the aid of all the tools that lie at his disposal, what Isaiah or Jeremiah or the Psalmist, Paul or Matthew or John, *actually intended to say*. In this way alone can the true meaning of the biblical word be arrived at; and it is the biblical word in its true meaning, and that alone, that can claim to be normative in the church. We have, in a word, the task of exegesis—of reading from the biblical

---

[23] Not even Calvin rejected the authority of tradition to this extent; cf. H. J. Forstman, *Word and Spirit: Calvin's Doctrine of Biblical Authority* (Stanford: Stanford University Press, 1962), pp. 23-26.

[24] The point applies to the authority of the confessional documents of the Protestant churches just as much as to the authority of the Roman Church. We hold that neither can dictate interpretation; cf. W. Schweitzer in *Biblical Authority for Today*, pp. 138-41.

text the meaning its author intended to convey. We are not permitted the luxury of eisegesis—of reading our own ideas into the text or finding there meanings which its author did not have in mind.

To insist upon this is no more than to take one's stand in the Reformation tradition. Whatever their mistakes in detail, and whatever their inconsistencies in practice, the Reformers held steadfastly to the principle that it is the business of the interpreter to expound the text in its plain, literal meaning. Both Luther and Calvin were emphatic on the point, and could be quoted almost endlessly. As for Luther, no one insisted more strongly on the necessity of arriving at the *sensum grammaticum-historicum* than did he; and one could scarcely wish for a more lucid description of what is involved in this task than is found in the preface to his exposition of Isaiah.[25] Again and again he expressed himself on the subject. For example: "There are strong reasons for my feeling, and especially that violence should not be done to the form of the words of God, by man or angel. But wherever possible their simplest meanings are to be preserved; and, unless it is otherwise manifest from the context, they are to be understood in their proper, written sense." (He goes on to censure Origen for his fanciful allegories and for being "contemptuous of the grammatical meaning.")[26] Or again: "Only the single, proper, original sense, the sense in which it is written, makes good theologians. The Holy Spirit is the simplest writer and speaker in heaven and earth. Therefore his words can have no more than a singular and simple sense, which we call the written or literally spoken sense."[27]

Calvin was no less emphatic than Luther. Said he, in commenting upon Gal. 4:21-26: "For many centuries no man was considered to be ingenious who had not the skill and daring necessary for changing into a variety of curious shapes the sacred word of God. This was undoubtedly a contrivance of Satan to undermine the authority of Scripture and to take away from the reading of it the true advantage . . . the true meaning of Scripture is the natural and obvious meaning; let us embrace and abide by

---

[25] For the quotation, see conveniently A. Jepsen, "The Scientific Study of the Old Testament," in *Essays on Old Testament Hermeneutics*, ed. C. Westermann (Richmond: John Knox Press, 1963), pp. 246-84; see pp. 254-55.

[26] *Martin Luthers Werke* (Weimar: Hermann Böhlau), VI (1888), 509. I am indebted to R. C. Johnson, *Authority in Protestant Theology* (Philadelphia: The Westminster Press, 1959), p. 29, for bringing this and the ensuing quotation to my attention. The translations are his.

[27] *Ibid.*, VII (1897), 650.

it resolutely." [28] Or again (in a dedicatory letter to his commentary on Romans written to his friend Simon Grynaeus): "We were both of this mind that the principle point of an interpreter did consist in a lucid brevity. And truly, seeing that this is in a manner his whole charge, namely, to show forth the mind of the writer whom he hath taken upon himself to expound, look by how much he leadeth the readers away from the same, by so much he is wide of the mark. . . . Verily the word of God ought to be so revered by us that through a diversity of interpretation it might not be drawn asunder by us, no not so much as a hair's breadth. . . . It is an audacity akin to sacrilege to use the Scriptures at our pleasure and to play with them as with a tennis ball, which many before this have done." [29] Or again, with unmistakable clarity: "It is the first business of an interpreter to let his author say what he does say, instead of attributing to him what we think he ought to say." [30]

From citations such as these it is evident that the Reformers were committed no less than are present-day scholars to the proposition that right interpretation consists in discovering the plain sense of the biblical word. No preacher may claim to stand in their tradition who plays irresponsibly with his text, or who advertises by ignoring it that he does not think its meaning very important. It is true that the Reformers were primarily concerned to combat allegory and did not define the plain, or literal, sense precisely as a modern exegete might; we shall return to that subject in the next chapter. But this does not alter the fact that they vehemently insisted that the text has but one meaning, the plain meaning intended by its author, and that it is the business of the interpreter to arrive at it. We hold, therefore, that right interpretation must begin with a grammatico-historical study of the text aimed at doing just that. The interpreter must seek to set forth with all possible objectivity what the writer intended to convey; he must resolutely refuse to allow his own predilections to influence his interpretation, and he may on no account feel free to find in the text

---

[28] See *Commentaries on the Epistles of Paul to the Galatians and Ephesians,* trans. William Pringle (Edinburgh: The Calvin Translation Society, 1854), pp. 135-36.

[29] The citation follows generally the wording found in Henry Beveridge, ed., *Commentary upon the Epistle of Saint Paul to the Romans* (Edinburgh: the Calvin Translation Society, 1844), pp. xvii, xxi. But the reader will find a more up-to-date and pleasing translation by Ross Mackenzie in D. W. and T. F. Torrence, eds., *The Epistles of Paul the Apostle to the Romans and to the Thessalonians* (Edinburgh: Oliver and Boyd, 1961).

[30] Quoted in Farrar, *History of Interpretation,* p. 347, from the Preface to Romans. I have myself been unable to find this precise wording; but the sense is certainly Calvin's.

meanings, however edifying, which the author clearly did not have in mind. Only when it is thus interpreted objectively, in its plain intention, can the Bible be appealed to as authoritative in the church.

But perhaps some reader will exclaim: This is all very fine, but is it not a bit naïve? Is a completely objective, unbiased exegesis of the text really possible? Will not the interpreter inevitably bring his presuppositions with him to the text, and will this not just as inevitably influence his understanding of it? And does this not mean, in turn, that in the final analysis the objective and authoritative biblical word is delivered over to the subjectivity of the individual interpreter?

The question of the possibility of "presuppositionless exegesis" has been much discussed in theological circles in recent years, no doubt owing particularly to the stimulus of various writings of Rudolf Bultmann.[31] The question is a legitimate one, and it is quite proper to raise it; but it can give rise to considerable misunderstanding if one is not clear as to what is meant by the word "presuppositionless."[32] If by presuppositionless exegesis one means that the exegete must divest himself of his predilections, his inherited beliefs, and personal convictions—all those factors in his background and training that have made him what he is—and come to the text as a newborn babe, then no such thing is possible. The exegete cannot be expected to be neutral toward the text, or to approach it with complete unconcern. On the contrary, his Christian commitment (or want of it), his professional training and interests, his personal needs and concerns, will inevitably condition his approach to the text and, to a large degree, determine the questions he will ask of it and the use he will make of it. In this sense of the word presuppositionless exegesis is not possible—nor is it really desirable. But this must not be taken as meaning, as some seem to have done, that the possibility of *objective* exegesis has been impeached. If by presuppositionless exegesis one means an unbiased exegesis, an exegesis the first presupposition of which is that one's presuppositions shall not be read into the text, an exegesis that is controlled by a grammatico-historical examination of the text and not by one's presuppositions, an exegesis that is aware of presuppositions but allows them to be corrected

---

[31] See, for example, Rudolf Bultmann, "Das Problem der Hermeneutik," *ZThK* XLVII (1950), 47-69; reprinted in *Glauben und Verstehen* (Tübingen: J. C. B. Mohr, 1952), II, 211-35; idem, "Ist voraussetzungslose Exegese möglich?" *ThZ* XIII (1957), 409-17. It is not my intention to enter into a specific discussion of Bultmann's views here.

[32] Bultmann himself seems to have used the word in more than one sense; cf. K. Frör, *Biblische Hermeneutik* (Munich: Chr. Kaiser Verlag, 1961), pp. 34-44, esp. p. 40.

by the text—then that not only is possible, but is practiced by thousands of honest scholars every day of the year, all over the world. [33]

But is perfect objectivity, in the sense just defined, really attainable? Probably not. At least, not completely. Probably no scholar has ever succeeded in being completely objective at all times—any more, I should say, than anyone has ever achieved complete sinlessness. But we do not for that reason give up the struggle in either area. Objectivity in exegesis, like righteousness, remains an ideal to be striven after and, within the limitations of our humanity, to a significant degree possible of attainment. An exegesis that subordinates presuppositions to the text is indeed possible. This is of course not to say that exegetes, however objective, will ever reach agreement on all points of interpretation, for it is certain that they will not. Many texts are ambiguous and difficult of understanding; exegetes vary in their competence, and none is infallible. But differences between exegetes who are equally unbiased in their approach will not arise primarily from their differing presuppositions, but—as in the case of two equally competent physicians who differ in their diagnosis of identical symptoms —from differing interpretations of the evidence. Exegetes with identical presuppositions (say, of the same communion and with the same theological convictions) may often disagree regarding the meaning of a text, while exegetes with widely different presuppositions may just as often agree. Objective, grammatico-historical exegesis is, we repeat, possible; and through it alone is a right interpretation of the biblical word to be arrived at. And it is the biblical word, thus rightly interpreted, that is normative in the church.

2. But merely to say that the Bible must be rightly interpreted does not get us past the question with which we started. Few would disagree with the proposition that if the Bible is to be appealed to as the church's rule of faith and practice, it must be interpreted in accordance with sound exegetical principles. The Bible cannot be allowed to mean what each individual wants it to mean. If the meaning of the biblical text were thus delivered over to whim, it would in practice be fruitless to appeal to the Bible on any question. Agreed! But that does not relieve us of the problem. Even granting that the Bible's texts have been correctly inter-

---

[33] It should be noted that Bultmann, in denying the possibility of "presuppositionless exegesis," does not deny the possibility of an objective, unprejudiced understanding of the biblical text as a historical phenomenon; cf. *Glauben und Verstehen*, II, 228-29; also Frör, *Biblische Hermeneutik*, p. 53; H. Wildberger, *EvTh* XIX (1959), 74-75.

preted in the plain sense intended by their authors, the question still remains of the right *use* of the Bible's authority. It is, unfortunately, quite possible to believe in the supreme authority of the Bible and yet, in attempting to apply its teachings to the specific issues that confront us, to appeal to it in an illegitimate way. How ought we to proceed?

The question is a crucial one, and it will continually be before us in succeeding chapters. We must be satisfied here with making a point negatively. We are not to appeal to the Bible's authority in a mechanical way, as if the Bible were a rule book or a dictionary, the authority of which resides equally and independently in each of its parts. The Bible is not a rule book or a dictionary. It cannot, therefore, be used as if it were no more than a vast collection of proof texts which one may call upon at discretion in order to support one's own arguments or confute those of one's opponents. That is a misuse of the Bible's authority. This is in no sense to say that one ought never to cite a proof text. To quote a text is no sin. Indeed, it is only by citing its texts that one can appeal directly to the Bible at all. Yet adducing proof texts can be a dangerous thing and can lead to the breakdown of biblical authority. The danger exists that the Bible will be appealed to in an arbitrarily selective way—that texts will be adduced in evidence as convenient, while other texts, equally but inconveniently germane, will be passed over, played down, or artificially harmonized. The danger further exists that texts, lifted from their context, will become little more than mottoes, or will be improperly thrown together with other texts in support of an argument as if authority attached to them regardless of the use to which they are put. And this opens the way to the ultimate danger that the Bible's authority will become, not something to be submitted to, but something to be *used*.

A former generation in orthodox Protestantism was all too prone to appeal to the Bible in this way. Examples could be cited almost at will from sermons and theological treatises of the day.[34] The preacher would defend his position (whether Calvinist or Arminian or some other) with liberal quotations from Scripture, and would demolish his opponents (whether Arminian or Calvinist or some other) in the same way. In like manner the theologian would develop his system of doctrine step by step in logical propositions, backing up the argument at each step with verses

---

[34] I have no wish to single out or criticize the work of any particular individual here. Readers who were raised on such works—as, theologically speaking, I was—will understand the point.

of Scripture. This procedure undoubtedly rested upon a profound conviction that the Bible is fully inspired and authoritative in all its parts, and it took that conviction seriously. No position was held to be tenable if it could not be supported from Scripture, or by reasonable inference from same. And the systems of theology thus developed were certainly biblical in that they were based on Scripture, scrupulously endeavored to be true to Scripture, and had as their aim merely to set forth in a systematic way the truths contained in Scripture. Yet the method employed was too often not really Bible-centered. The argument was essentially logical and rational in its structure, at times (dare one say it?) well-nigh rationalistic in tone. (One thinks, for example, of the classic "proofs" of the existence of God, or of the resurrection.) [35] The Bible tended to be assigned somewhat of a supporting role. Too seldom was it allowed to speak for itself in the full range and variety of its teaching. Rather, propositions were propounded —based, to be sure, on biblical teaching—and the authority of the Bible was then called upon to back up the propositions. The Bible, though recognized in the system itself as the ultimate authority, in practice served to give authority to the system. The end of it was that, in the minds of many, the system itself became the supreme authority, or, what comes to the same thing, the authoritative interpretation of Scripture.

I do not wish to belabor the point and certainly do not mean to imply that Protestant orthodoxy fell uniformly into the pitfall just described. The point to be made here is that the Bible, appealed to on the basis of isolated texts or random collections of texts, can be made the authority for almost anything; and an authority that can be made to support almost anything ceases, in effect, to be usable as an authority at all. So appealed to, the Bible becomes an arsenal of ammunition—and the battle of proof texts is on. Luther long ago saw this clearly. Speaking of those who misused the principle of *analogia scripturae* (i.e., the interpretation of Scripture by Scripture) by heaping together proof texts in an arbitrary way, he sarcastically declared, "If this is to be the way, I can prove from the Scriptures that bad beer is better than good wine." [36]

[35] My colleague, James P. Martin, has clearly called attention to the rationalistic strain in older Protestant orthodoxy in his book, *The Last Judgment in Protestant Theology from Orthodoxy to Ritschl* (Edinburgh: Oliver and Boyd; Grand Rapids: Wm. B. Eerdmans Publishing Co., 1963), esp. Ch. II.

[36] See *Werke*, VI, 301. I am again indebted to R. C. Johnson in *Authority in Protestant Theology* (pp. 28-29) for bringing this quotation to my attention.

We have illustrations enough from an earlier time in our country's history, when quarrels between denominations were more frequent and bitter than they are today, of the way in which proof texts could be massed in support of conflicting theological positions. Presbyterian, Episcopal, and Congregational forms of church government were defended on biblical grounds, each to the exclusion of the others. The various modes of baptism were each heatedly advocated and combated, with all parties supporting themselves upon biblical texts. The doctrine of predestination and the principle of the freedom of the will were argued from the Bible, not infrequently each to the virtual exclusion of the other. And so on and on. Now it is certainly not suggested that it was wrong to have appealed to the Bible. Still less is it suggested that one ought to be neutral with regard to such things. (I am not; I cheerfully admit to my presuppositions which were shaped by my rearing in the Reformed tradition and lie within it.) The point is that the most diverse opinions have been defended on biblical authority. But if the Bible can be made to support a given position and, to its exclusion, its exact opposite, then this must indicate some misuse of the Bible's authority. It is, indeed, effectually the breakdown of biblical authority. The Bible remains, perhaps, the court of final appeal; but it is a court which seems unable to settle anything, which in fact initiates litigation.

Let us press the point one step further. The Bible, so appealed to, can even be made the authority for things that are patently wrong. Examples could be adduced almost at will: the justification of massacres and holy wars on the basis of the narratives of Joshua and Judges, or of the execution of "witches" on the basis of Pentateuchal law ("You shall not permit a sorceress to live," Exod. 22:18).[37] But perhaps an example from our own nation's past would best serve to point up the insidious danger of a misuse of the Bible's authority. The grandfathers of many of us who live in the southern United States used to defend slavery on biblical grounds as a divinely ordained—or at least permissible—institution. (Robert Lewis Dabney, professor of systematic theology in Union Theological Seminary in Virginia, and for a time adjutant to General Stonewall Jackson, was eloquent on the point.) Now nothing would be more pointless at this late date than to scoff at our grandparents, or to look down upon them in condescending pity. The point is that, using the Bible as was customary in

[37] For selected examples, with documentation, see Farrar, *History of Interpretation*, pp. 38-43.

their day (and not in the South only), they made an excellent case for their position and sincerely believed themselves to be (for who shall say to the contrary?) in accord with Christian teaching. Let me paraphrase the argument as Grandfather might have made it.

Appeal was made first of all to the Old Testament law which legislates in the name of God regarding slavery (cf. Exod. 21:1-11, 20-27; Lev. 25; Deut. 15:1-18). The details of that legislation need not concern us, nor the fact that of all the ancient law codes the Pentateuchal law was far the most humane as regards the treatment of slaves. Those of our grandparents who justified slavery from the Bible were Christian men, and would have been unanimous in their insistence that the Christian must treat his slave humanely. The point is not that the Old Testament law is humane, but that it regulated slavery; for what is regulated by law is by that very fact not forbidden, but sanctioned. To illustrate: the state of Virginia, like other states, regulates the sale of liquor by means of its ABC laws. This means that in the eyes of Virginia law liquor, though liable to obvious abuses which that law seeks to guard against, is not prohibited but legal. Virginia law does not, on the other hand, similarly regulate—let us say—prostitution. Prostitution is not regulated but forbidden. Just so, the fact that Old Testament law regulates slavery implies that, although the institution must be guarded from abuse (as must virtually every other institution), the institution itself is sanctioned. Old Testament law does not similarly regulate, say, the practice of the fertility cult. It simply forbids it and requires the punishment of those who engage in it. But if the Old Testament law sanctions slavery, and if the Old Testament law is the law of God, then—so Grandfather reasoned—slavery is sanctioned of God.

Shall we then appeal to the New Testament to refute this? We shall not get very far. Jesus uttered no recorded word about slavery. The institution was certainly well known to him: it was common enough in his day. And Jesus was no coward when it came to attacking religious and social abuses. Why, then, did he not somewhere say plainly that slavery is wrong? Surely it could not have been a moral blind spot on his part! And as for the various New Testament writers, though they now and then admonish the slave to be diligent in service as under God (e.g., Col. 3:22-23), and the master to treat the slave in the recollection that he too has a Master in heaven (e.g., Col. 4:1), never once did they say: In the name of Christ, have done with it! On the contrary, the Bible from end

50

to end assumes the existence of the institution. And so it was that Grandfather reasoned from his Bible that slavery was ordained of God.

Now our grandparents did not begin with the Bible and, after exhaustive study of it, come to the conclusion that slavery was in accord with God's will, and so adopt the institution. On the contrary, they appealed to the Bible in support of the then-existing system, of which they were a part. But the fact that no one today that I know of would wish to defend slavery on biblical grounds must not blind us to the fact that, appealing to scriptural authority as was customary in their day, our grandparents were on very sound ground indeed. In fact, their justification of slavery from the Bible is as good an example as could be wished for of what may happen when the Bible is "flattened out," as it were, accorded equal authority in all its parts, and appealed to via the proof text method.

The authority of the Bible is a problem not so much in the theory as in the practice. One who stands in the Protestant tradition may find it easy—indeed necessary—to affirm, as we have done, that the Bible is the church's supreme authority in matters of faith and practice; it is when one attempts to appeal to the Bible in this capacity, and to apply its teachings to specific questions, that one may run into difficulty. The Bible cannot be appealed to mechanically as if it had the flat authority of law in each of its texts. Not everything in the Bible—its institutions, customs, sentiments, directives—is equally binding on the Christian. And this obliges us to ask what it is in the Bible that commands us, and how its authority is rightly to be appealed to, and how brought to bear on the doctrinal, moral, and ethical problems that confront us. That is a fundamental problem of biblical hermeneutics, and one that will claim our attention further in the chapters that follow.

3. But, finally, there is the special problem posed by the Old Testament in this connection. Our purpose in this chapter, as was said at the outset, is to state that problem and to do so as bluntly as possible, so that we may see that it is indeed a problem and not be tempted to evade it. In what sense is the Old Testament authoritative over the Christian at all? That the problem is most acute where the Old Testament is concerned is beyond question: the illustration just given indicates as much. Our grandparents were able to justify slavery on biblical grounds because the institution is permitted and regulated in the Old Testament, and not explicitly forbidden in the New. In other words, an institution which most of us would feel to be contrary to the spirit of Christ was defended primarily on the authority of the Old Testament. And that points us to the heart of the

51

problem. We have affirmed that the Bible is the church's supreme authority in matters of doctrine and practice, because it is the source that must finally be consulted in any attempt to determine what the Christian faith actually teaches. Yet we have at the same time to admit that there is a great deal in the Old Testament—however divinely inspired we may believe it to be, and however binding it may have been upon those to whom it was first addressed—that cannot serve directly as a model for Christian faith and piety, and that is not—and never has been—proper to normative Christian practice. Since this is so, what do we mean by the authority of the Old Testament?

To say that the problem of authority is at its sharpest in the Old Testament is not to say that the New Testament is exempt, for it is not. There is not a little in the New Testament that reflects the ancient situation and ancient patterns of thinking, and that cannot be slavishly carried over into the belief and practice of today. The New Testament writers expressed themselves in categories that were at home in Jewish or Hellenistic thought, many of which are scarcely understandable to modern man, who does not think in these categories, without considerable interpretation. Their world view was a pre-Copernican one (though why that should seriously trouble anyone I do not know); but no one supposes that modern man must for that reason adopt a similar world view. The moral and social standards that the New Testament urges upon the churches were appropriate for the first-century situation, but in many cases it is debatable how they are to be applied to the situation today. For example, is Paul's pronouncement to the effect that women should be silent in church and accept their subordinate status as ordained of God (I Cor. 14:34-35) to be regarded as binding on the present-day church, or does it apply only to the circumstances then existing? (My own church has recently voted to permit the ordination of women. This is not the place to discuss the correctness of that action; but I am confident that protagonists of both sides of the debate acknowledged the authority of the New Testament and intended to be obedient to it.) The question of how to interpret the New Testament teaching and apply it to the modern situation can give rise to all sorts of debate. Nevertheless, there can be no question that the New Testament is in a peculiar sense authoritative in the church in all matters of faith and practice. As the primary document of the Christian faith, it must be the starting point and final arbiter of any discussion of that faith. If we wish to know what the Christian faith first was, and properly is, we have to consult the New Testament, for it is the primary authority on the subject.

The Old Testament, however, is different. It was not in the first instance a document of the Christian faith at all, but of the faith of Israel. It contains much that is strange to Christian belief and that has never been practiced by Christians, together with not a little that may even be offensive to Christian sentiment. How is this ancient book, which presents a religion by no means identical with the Christian religion, to be appealed to by the church as normative over Christian belief and Christian conduct? How is the Christian to learn from it, with its ancient thought patterns and alien institutions, of the nature of his God, the tenets of his faith, and the duty that his God requires of him? How is the Old Testament to be preached as authoritative and binding in the church, when so many features of its religious practice and so many of its concepts have never been taken into normative Christianity?

Let us sharpen the issue by a few examples. To begin with a relatively obvious one, the Old Testament offers us large blocks of material having to do with ceremonial matters: laws and directives regarding the various kinds of sacrifice, regarding ritual cleanness and uncleanness, the duties and the support of the clergy, feasts and other sacred occasions, and the like. Now it is clearly stated that these regulations were commanded of God; it is equally clear that they had binding authority over the life of old Israel. Yet we take our stand with Paul and the mainstream of the New Testament church: however binding these laws may have been in the life of Israel, they have no authority over the Christian. The Christian is not obliged to offer animal sacrifice at all; he need not observe the Jewish feasts (and he can have a ham sandwich whenever he wishes), for he is free from the ceremonial law. To be sure, the reader may object that this is not really a problem. The church has always had its answer ready, the answer of the New Testament itself—namely, that the ceremonial law has been set aside through the perfect sacrifice of Christ and is no longer binding on the Christian. Quite so. Agreed! But let us face the consequences of what we have just said. We have said, in effect, that the Scriptures of the Old and New Testaments are the supreme authority in all matters of doctrine and practice, but that parts of the Old Testament, having been set aside, are no longer authoritative at all.

But in that case, which parts, and how does one distinguish them? Most of us, I fear, are not altogether clear on the point. The ceremonial law, we say, is set aside for the Christian; but the moral law is not. The Ten Commandments, one supposes, retain their validity! But how does one tell which laws are "moral" and therefore valid, and which "ceremonial" and therefore superseded? The Old Testament itself draws no such distinction, but presents all laws as equally commanded of God. For example, in Lev. 19:18 we read the well-known commandment, "You shall love your neighbor as yourself," and in the very next verse—and in identical form—the strange injunction, "You shall not sow your field with two kinds of seed." [38] The one we instinctively accept as valid and normative (and we frequently preach upon it); the other we leave aside (for I have never heard anyone attempt to preach upon it) as of no concern to us. But what canon have we, other than our common sense, for making such a judgment? Who picks and chooses in this regard?

But even as regards laws that are obviously ceremonial in character we are not always clear. No Christian, to be sure, would suggest that we return to animal sacrifice or to the dietary laws of Judaism. But what about tithing? Church boards recommend it. And many Christians have adopted the tithe as an ideal by which to measure their giving. Indeed, there are those who look upon the tithe not as a goal or an ideal, but as a binding obligation, and confidently expect—for so their pastor may have assured them (basing himself, no doubt, on Mal. 3:6-12)—that if only they are faithful in this regard their financial affairs will prosper. (I once knew such a man well and shall never forget his agonized perplexity when he lost everything that he had.) This is to say that there are Christians who regard the law of the tithe, probably in the form in which it is recorded in Lev. 27:30-33 (it is hard to imagine a church board urging the law as stated in Deut. 14:22-27 as an ideal), as in some way normative —a thing they would never dream of doing in the case, say, of the laws regarding clean and unclean, ritual purification, and the like, also found in Leviticus. No criticism of tithers is intended, but rather praise of their good stewardship. But why is one ritual regulation to be regarded as having normative authority, and not others?

But the problem is broader and involves much more than ceremonial regulations set aside in Christ. For example, the Old Testament contains many laws of a civil rather than a ritual nature which are abrogated for us simply by the fact that we are not ancient Israelites. Although ancient

[38] I thank L. E. Toombs, *The Old Testament in Christian Preaching* (Philadelphia: The Westminster Press, 1961), p. 23, for reminding me of this odd juxtaposition of commands.

Israelite society was simple in comparison with our own, it was anything but primitive; all aspects of everyday life were regulated by a highly developed system of customary law, much of which we find preserved in the legal portions of the Pentateuch. There were laws regarding the ownership and transfer of real property, moneylending and indebtedness, marriage and divorce, cases of rape and adultery, of murder and manslaughter, theft, damage to person or property, and much more. Now these laws are clearly presented as given by God, and they undoubtedly were regarded as authoritative in ancient Israelite society. But what possible authority can they have over us today? How could we possibly obey them? In cases of suspected adultery, should we require the woman to demonstrate her innocence by drinking some noxious potion, as prescribed in Num. 5:11-31? Should we establish cities of refuge so that those who have taken life unintentionally might flee to them for sanctuary, as commanded in Num. 35, Deut. 19:1-13, etc.? To ask the question is to answer it. Manifestly not! These are laws of an ancient society quite unlike our own; to take them over and try to apply them in our complex society would be nothing short of ridiculous. But then the question: Since we frankly make no attempt to obey these laws, in what sense are they normative for our faith and practice? What do we mean when we say that the Old Testament (which contains them) is authoritative Scripture? Do we mean that it has authority once suitable exceptions have been made? But, in that event, who shall have the authority to say what these exceptions should be?

But that is still not all. There is much in the Old Testament—and it ought frankly to be admitted—that offends the Christian's conscience. Its heroes are not always heroes, and are almost never saints. They lust, they brawl, and commit the grossest immorality; they plot, they kill, or seek to kill. And often enough their conduct receives no whisper of rebuke: it is just recorded. How are the stories of such things in any way a guide for the faith and conduct of the Christian? How shall he learn from them of the nature of his God and of the duty that his God requires of him? Many a sincere Christian has, explicitly or tacitly, asked that question. Scarcely a part of the Old Testament is exempt from it. Not even the prophets! Noble they were and stirring their words, but did they not hate right well, and on occasion curse their enemies most heartily? And the psalms? Here is piety indeed, the most exalted and touching the world has ever known. But here is also that vengeful and wholly unforgiving spirit whose voice we hear in Ps. 109; here is also that embittered exile who, in Ps. 137, spat out his hatred of his oppressors and wished that he might take their babies and dash their brains out against a rock. And many a troubled reader has asked how he can hear in such things the authoritative Word of God, how he can possibly receive them as a legitimate part of his supreme rule of faith and practice.

But what has probably troubled Christians the most about the Old Testament is that it now and then records deeds of violence and bloodshed that were performed—so it is clearly stated—at God's express command. For example, one reads in the book of Joshua of the holy war of conquest and of the *ḥerem*, the butchery of the Canaanite population to the last thing that breathed; and more than once it is said that God expressly ordered this. Or one reads of the prophet Samuel, that hero of the faith, who (I Sam. 15) gave to Saul God's command to exterminate the Amalekites (vs. 3) and who, when Saul failed to carry this out completely, publicly rebuked him and himself hewed the Amalekite king in pieces "before the Lord" (vs. 33). Or one reads of the man caught gathering sticks on the sabbath (Num. 15:32-36) who was summarily stoned at the behest of a direct command of God to Moses.

We could go on. Things of this kind have always troubled sensitive spirits and have caused many to question the place of the Old Testament in the Bible. What pastor has not heard the questions: But is God really like that? How do you reconcile such things with the teachings of Jesus? They are fair questions. And whoever asks them has—whether he is aware of that fact or not—raised the problem of the authority of the Old Testament. He wants to know in what way such narratives can contribute to the Christian's understanding of his God, and how they can furnish guidance for Christian conduct. Nor will it do to turn the question aside with an easy answer, for it is clear that whatever authority such passages may possess, they do not provide the Christian with examples which his God wishes him to imitate. Are we, after all, to advocate the death penalty for those who absent themselves from church in order to pick up sticks— well, golf sticks at any rate—on Sunday? Is the church to deal with its foes by butchering them in the name of Christ? Christ forbids it! Are we, then, to regard such things as but examples of human fanaticism and ignorance or, alternatively, as actions which may have been necessary at the time but which are in no way to be imitated by us? But, in that event, wherein is their authority?

That, then, is the problem: In what sense is the Old Testament authoritative for the Christian in matters of faith and practice? We have tried so far only to state the problem, and to do so in the sharpest way possible. We have stated it against the background of the affirmations the church is accustomed to make with regard to the Bible, for it is only against that background that the problem emerges. We have affirmed with the mainstream of Protestantism—for we could do no other—that the Bible is the church's supreme authority in matters of doctrine and practice, for it is the primary and authoritative document to which all discussions of the Christian faith, its nature and demands, must finally be referred. But what is meant by such a statement when we make it of the Old Testament? We have admitted—for it is not to be denied—that the faith of the Old Testament is not identical with the Christian faith and that many features in its practice cannot be, and never have been, followed by Christians. In what sense, then, is the Old Testament legitimately to be spoken of as a part of the Christian's supreme rule of faith and practice? Ought we to modify our statements regarding the Bible where the Old Testament is concerned? Or must we, by some canon yet to be developed, undertake to separate what is valid in it from what is ancient, time-conditioned, and irrelevant? Or has the very admission of the problem invalidated the whole thesis of biblical authority and reduced it to empty rhetoric?

The problem is a serious one, and it behooves us to face up to it squarely, for it is certain that, if we will not, we shall never find an adequate solution; we shall remain forever crippled in the ministry of the Word because of ambiguity regarding the authority of the Word. For myself, I believe that a positive solution is possible. If I did not, these pages would never have been written. But we cannot rush to solutions prematurely, as though we were the first to come at the problem. Many have wrestled with it before us, and they have much to teach us. We would do well, therefore, first of all to examine some of the solutions that have been proposed in the past and attempt some evaluation of them. And that now becomes our task.

II

THE PROBLEM OF THE OLD TESTAMENT:

THE "CLASSICAL" SOLUTIONS

In the preceding chapter we tried to make clear the nature of the problem that arises when one attempts to take the Old Testament seriously as authoritative Scripture. It will be recalled that we stressed the crucial importance to the church of a supreme and recognized authority to which she may appeal in all matters of doctrine and practice. It will also be recalled that we spoke of authority not in the sense of a spiritual authoritarianism of some sort, but in the sense of a standard, a source from which the church may ascertain the nature and content of the Christian faith as originally proclaimed and in the light of which she may test her preaching, her ecclesiastical pronouncements, her doctrinal positions, and her actions, in order to see if what she says and does is a true reflection of that faith or not. Such an authority, we argued, is imperatively necessary. We also argued that this authority can in the final analysis be found only in the Bible, for the Bible provides us with our one firsthand record of what the Christian faith originally was. Without reference to the Bible it is impossible to say what is in accord with the Christian faith and what is not. We were obliged, therefore, to affirm the correctness of the church's historic assertion that the Bible is her supreme authority in all matters of doctrine and practice.

But what do we mean by such an assertion when we extend it to the Old Testament and thereby place the Old Testament on a level of formal equality with the New? That is the problem. That the New Testament is supremely authoritative in the sense just defined can hardly be questioned. Whatever intellectual difficulties men may have with it, and however hard it may be to interpret its teachings to the modern mind and apply them to present-day situations, the New Testament, as the primary document of the Christian faith, remains the final authority to be appealed to in any discussion of that faith and its demands. But in what sense is this true of the Old Testament? How can we hail it as normative for our belief and conduct when so many of its concepts seem alien to us and when there are so many features of its practice that we do not even pretend to follow? When we speak of the authority of the Bible, what are we to make of the Old Testament?

As was hinted at the outset, the problem is by no means a new one. It was keenly felt at the very beginning of the church's history, and has continued to be a sore subject ever since. Wherever men have taken the authority of the Bible seriously, it has followed inevitably that the Old Testament has become a problem. The very things that we have pointed out about it—and others besides—have always been noticed, with the result that the place of the Old Testament in the Christian's Bible has always been a debated one. And still today the debate continues, producing books and articles by the dozen, yet bringing us no nearer to a consensus than ever. Manifestly we cannot attempt to review the history of that debate in a book of this kind.[1] We shall, rather, single out certain typical solutions to the problem that have been proposed over the years and attempt some evaluation of them. These can, I believe, be discussed without oversimplification under three headings since, in spite of infinite variation in detail, certain family likenesses may be observed. The vast majority of the solutions that have been proposed tend to fall into three major types or categories. Two of these first made their appearance in the earliest days of the church and, though it is probable that few today

---

[1] The standard treatment of F. W. Farrar, *History of Interpretation* has now been reprinted, but it is woefully out-of-date, and not without bias. The reader may supplement it with E. G. Kraeling, *The Old Testament Since the Reformation* (London: Lutterworth, 1955), or, if he reads German, with H. J. Kraus, *Geschichte der historisch-kritischen Erforschung des Alten Testaments* (Neukirchen: Verlag der Buchandlung des Erziehungsvereins, 1956). Shorter and more popular treatments include: D. E. Nineham, ed., *The 'Church's Use of the Bible, Past and Present* (London: S.P.C.K., 1963); J. D. Wood, *The Interpretation of the Bible* (London: Gerald Duckworth & Co., 1958); R. M. Grant, *The Bible in the Church* (rev. ed.; New York: The Macmillan Company, 1948). For orientation to the current debate regarding the Old Testament the following two titles are especially recommended: C. Westermann, ed., *Essays on Old Testament Hermeneutics* (hereafter *EOTH*), and B. W. Anderson, ed., *The Old Testament and Christian Faith* (hereafter *OTCF*; New York: Harper & Row, 1963).

would care to defend either of them as they were originally proposed, they still have their advocates in more or less modified forms. The third is of more recent vintage and, though one would think that its inadequacy has been made abundantly clear, it continues to command an enormous following, at least in this country. Because of their tenacity and popularity and because they might seem logically to exhaust the possibilities, I have ventured to call them the "classical" solutions. In spite of their differences one from another, they have it in common that all take the New Testament as their point of orientation and evaluate the Old Testament from that perspective. Although this might seem a reasonable procedure for a Christian to follow—in a sense an inevitable one—it can, if pursued in the wrong way, lead to unfortunate results.

I

One who makes himself at home in the New Testament and then from that vantage point turns his gaze backward toward the Old is likely to be struck first of all by the differences. And indeed there are differences, as we have said. It may be that the Christian will be so impressed by these differences that he will feel the Old Testament religion to be a strange religion, quite other than his own. He may then go on to draw the conclusion that, since its religion is not the same as Christianity, the Old Testament is of no concern, or at best only of subsidiary concern, to him. Through the centuries men have for various reasons drawn just this conclusion. There have always been those who would solve the problem raised by the Old Testament by declaring that it has no rightful place in the Christian's Bible and ought therefore to be deposed from canonical status. Others, unwilling to go so far and perhaps finding great positive value in the Old Testament, would nevertheless place it on a lower level of value than the New and would regard it, so to speak, as Scripture of the second rank.

1. The attempt to get rid of the Old Testament was encountered by the church as far back as the second century in the first great heresy with which it had to deal, that of Marcion.[2] It is impossible to understand

---

[2] The definitive treatment is that of A. von Harnack, *Marcion, Das Evangelium vom fremden Gott* (2nd ed.; Leipzig: J. C. Hinrichs Verlag, 1924; reprinted, Darmstadt: Wissenschaftliche Buchgesellschaft, 1960). For briefer discussions in English, see John Knox, *Marcion and the New Testament* (Chicago: University of Chicago Press, 1942); E. C. Blackman, *Marcion and His Influence* (London: S.P.C.K., 1948).

Marcion and the impact of his teachings apart from Gnosticism, a strange mishmash of philosophical and religious speculation which in various forms swept over the ancient world in the early centuries of our era and attracted so many adherents that Gnostic sects became a serious rival to orthodox Christianity. Now one cannot generalize regarding Gnostic beliefs, for the various Gnostic systems differed from one another chaotically.[3] But one feature was common to them all: a dualistic notion of the universe, together with the belief that the material world is originally and incurably evil. This, of course, made the creation of the world a theological problem for them: If the world is thus evil, how could the good God have made it? Their answer was that he did not do so. They were able to give this answer and so escape the dilemma by recourse to a doctrine of emanations, or aeons: by a process of generation a series of descending emanations was produced (in some systems many, in others only a few) through which the divine essence was manifested in forms ever more and more attenuated, till eventually there emerged a being so imperfectly divine that he could come into contact with matter without shock to himself. This final emanation was sometimes known as the Demiurge, sometimes by other names (Pro-archon, Cosmocrator, etc.). He was so far removed from God, and the divine essence in him was so weak, that he worked without awareness of the divine will, if not in active hostility to it. And this Demiurge being was the creator of the universe and is its present ruler. Christ, on the contrary, was concieved of by Christian Gnostics as the highest emanation, firstborn of the true God, who came to reveal to men the hidden knowledge (*gnosis*) of God and to save them from the power of the evil world which the Demiurge had made.

This strange doctrine logically led, and in fact did lead, to a drastic devaluation of the Old Testament. The dualism of the universe was transferred to Scripture, and the Testaments rent asunder thereby. Since the Demiurge (by whatever name) is the creator, he is the god revealed in the Old Testament; the Old Testament is his book and like the

[3] The best introduction to Gnosticism is Hans Jonas, *The Gnostic Religion* (Boston: Beacon Press, 1958); see also R. M. Grant, ed., *Gnosticism: an Anthology* (London: William Collins, 1961). Texts recently discovered at Nag Hammadi in Egypt have enormously enlarged our firsthand knowledge of Gnostic belief. For an introduction to these, see Jean Doresse, *The Secret Books of the Egyptian Gnostics*, trans. Philip Mairet (London: Hollis and Carter, 1960); W. C. van Unnik, *Newly Discovered Gnostic Writings* (SBT, 30), trans. H. H. Hoskins (London: SCM Press, 1960); R. M. Grant, *The Secret Sayings of Jesus* (New York: Doubleday & Company, 1960).

Demiurge himself is full of imperfections. The New Testament, on the contrary, is the book of Christ, son and perfect revealer of the true God. The Old Testament, since it is not a revelation of the true God at all but of a different and vastly inferior being, has no theological continuity with the New Testament whatever. It goes without saying that such a view would inevitably lead to the demand that the Old Testament be removed from the canon; and this was the demand that Marcion made.

The degree to which Marcion was influenced by Gnostic teaching is a disputed subject which cannot detain us. But some dependence must be assumed.[4] Marcion separated the two Testaments completely. The redemption in Christ was to him in no way to be understood in terms of Judaism or the Scriptures of Judaism, in which he found much to offend him. The God of the Old Testament is another and inferior being, the Demiurge-creator, the vindictive God of the law, wholly opposed to the gracious God revealed in the gospel. The Old Testament therefore has nothing to say to the Christian of his God or of Christ. Its messianic prophecies could not possibly refer to Christ, for Christ was as totally unlike the Old Testament Messiah as could be. The Messiah of the Old Testament is the Messiah of the Old Testament's god who, unable to give his people world supremacy, promised them a deliverer who would achieve it for them in the future. Christ, on the contrary, was sent by the true God to redeem men from this cruel Old Testament god and the evil world of which he was the creator. As the book of another and hostile god, the Old Testament—said Marcion—is no part of the Christian revelation and has no place in the Christian canon.

2. All this was roundly rejected by the church as heresy, and we may be thankful that it was. Though Marcionist and Gnostic teachings survived for some centuries outside the church in various forms, and though teachings of similar character cropped up among certain heretical sects of the Middle Ages (the Cathari), Marcionism was effectively excluded from the mainstream of Catholic Christianity. The church officially committed itself to the Old Testament as a part of its canon, and has continued to do so ever since. Nor did the Reformation bring any change in this regard,

---

[4] This was vigorously denied by Harnack in *Marcion, Das Evangelium vom fremden Gott,* p. 4 and Excursus II. But although certain characteristic features of Gnostic speculation are lacking in Marcion, others (e.g., dualism, creation by an inferior and hostile god, salvation as liberation from his power) are strikingly present; cf. Jonas, *The Gnostic Religion,* pp. 137-46. Marcion's teachings as developed in succeeding generations were emphatically Gnostic; cf. Doresse, *The Secret Books of the Egyptian Gnostics,* pp. 24-26.

for the great Reformers never questioned the place of the Old Testament as an integral part of Scripture.[5]

Nevertheless, there is a sense in which the Reformers prepared the way for the reopening of the Marcionist question in that they demanded that Scripture be interpreted in its plain meaning and, while retaining the Old Testament, repudiated the then-current practice of finding mystical meanings in its text by means of allegory—which, as we shall see, had been precisely the means by which the church had saved the Old Testament against Marcion. This does not mean that the question was reopened at once. The hermeneutical principles of both the great Reformers were such that they could, each in his own way, understand the plain meaning as a Christian meaning; and so could the first generations of their followers in the days of Protestant orthodoxy, few of whom were exegetes of half the stature of the Reformers. But in the eighteenth and nineteenth centuries, with the Age of Enlightenment and the rise of the critical study of the Bible, a change took place. Scholars, finding themselves increasingly uneasy with the christological or typological interpretation of the Old Testament then so popular in the churches, were driven to the conviction that the plain meaning is the literal, philological-historical meaning expressed in the text, and they felt obliged to insist that the Old Testament is to be read in that literal meaning. But to read the Old Testament in its literal meaning is to see it in its strangeness; and to see it in its strangeness is to raise again the question of Marcion.

In any event it is scarcely a coincidence that just at this time voices were raised with a distinctly Marcionist tone. There were many of these, and we cannot listen to them all. Again and again one hears it asserted that the Old Testament does not stand on a level with the New or share its authority, that the religion of Israel is a different religion from Christianity, which stands on a level with the heathen religions of the world— and more in the same tenor. One hears such sentiments from the poet Goethe, from the great theologian Schleiermacher, from Schelling, from Feuerbach, and from a host of others right on down through the nineteenth

[5] Harnack sees a latent Marcionist tendency in Luther, and even more so in Agricola (pp. 218-19 in *Marcion*). But, although Luther had harsh words to say about "Judaizing," and although his use of the antithesis of law and gospel, if pushed to extremes (as it has been by some in recent years, as we shall see), could lead to a downgrading of the Old Testament, it apparently never entered this great Reformer's mind to question the place of the Old Testament in the canon. On the whole subject, see especially H. Bornkamm, *Luther und das Alte Testament* (Tübingen: J. C. B. Mohr, 1948).

century to the anti-Semitism of Paul de Lagarde.[6] Of all these, perhaps no one was more explicit on the point or more influential than was Schleiermacher (he is cited again and again by those of like opinion). Though Schleiermacher did not deny that Christianity had a special historical relationship to Judaism, he snapped the theological link between the Testaments by placing the religion of the Old on a par with heathenism. Said he: "The relations of Christianity to Judaism and Heathenism are the same, inasmuch as the transition from either of these to Christianity is a transition to another religion."[7] Schleiermacher saw no objection to printing the Old Testament in the Bible, but he thought it would be better if it followed the New as a sort of appendix. "The Old Testament Scriptures do not . . . share the normative dignity or the inspiration of the New."[8] It is clear from this that Marcion, excommunicated and long dead, was once again seeking reinstatement in the church.

3. This Marcionist strain, so clearly evident in the centuries that preceded us, has never died out but has continued on down to the present day. And always it has voiced the complaint that there is so much in the Old Testament that is alien and unedifying to the Christian, and that cannot be normative for him, that he would probably be better off without it. To mention all those who in recent generations have expressed themselves in this way would be tedious and pointless. Rather, we shall single out a few outstanding examples with the aim simply of making it clear that the way of Marcion, though long rejected by the church, has by no means been abandoned.

One such example is Adolf von Harnack, the great historian of dogma, whose work on Marcion is the definitive one.[9] Although Harnack criticizes Marcion at certain points, his evaluation of that worthy is extremely sympathetic. Of course, scholar and child of the modern world that he was, Harnack had no place in his thinking for Gnostic speculative nonsense (he denied—wrongly, I think—that Marcion had), nor did he share Marcion's pessimistic view of the universe. Moreover, he was well aware that the roots of Christianity lay in the faith of the Old Testament, and

[6] The reader who is interested may check these and other examples from the works of Kraeling or of Kraus cited in note 1.

[7] *The Christian Faith,* 2nd ed., trans. H. R. Mackintosh and J. S. Stewart (Edinburgh: T. and T. Clark, 1928), Par. 12 (pp. 60-62).

[8] *Ibid.,* Par. 132 (pp. 608-11).

[9] See *Marcion,* esp. pp. 215-35; cf. also W. Pauck, "The Significance of Adolf von Harnack's Interpretation of Church History," *USQR,* XIII (1958), 31-43.

he conceded that for the church to have followed Marcion in the second century would have been disastrous, for it would have resulted in the uprooting of the Christian faith from history. Nevertheless, he held that Marcion was correct in his major contention: the Old Testament ought to be deposed from canonical rank and placed at the head of the Apocrypha.[10] The very fact that it is in the canon makes it a source of offense to many people and provides them with occasion for ridiculing the gospel. These words of Harnack's are worth quoting, for they state his major theme: "To have cast aside the Old Testament in the second century was an error which the church rightly rejected; to have retained it in the sixteenth century was a fate which the Reformation was not yet able to avoid; but still to keep it after the nineteenth century as a canonical document within Protestantism results from a religious and ecclesiastical paralysis." [11] In other words, now that the historical background of Christianity is clearly seen by everyone to lie in the Old Testament, the dangers inherent in discarding it, so real in the second century, no longer exist; the church, since it has outgrown its need of the Old Testament, ought now to go on to take the step implicit—says Harnack—in Luther, but not taken by him, and eject it from the canon. So the voice of Marcion in modern speech.

But if Harnack unequivocally called for the dismissal of the Old Testament from the canon, he at least expressed himself through reasoned argument and in temperate language. That is more than can be said for Friedrich Delitzsch who, just as the first edition of Harnack's work appeared (in 1920), let fly with a broadside entitled *Die grosse Täuschung* (The Great Deception).[12] Seldom has the Old Testament been subjected to more vicious abuse than in this book. It is really a very bad book (I should say a "sick" book),[13] and we should pay it no attention were it not for the fact that its author was a scholar of outstanding ability who was one of the founders of the science of Assyriology and who was moreover of a family that was partly of Jewish origin. His father was none other than Franz Delitzsch, eminent Old Testament scholar and man of conservative

---

[10] *Marcion*, pp. 221-22. Incidentally, Harnack calls upon Schleiermacher at this point.
[11] *Ibid.*, p. 217.
[12] (Stuttgart: Deutsche Verlags-Anstalt, Vol. I, 1920; Vol. II, 1921).
[13] It should be noted that Harnack in the 2nd ed. of his book (in 1924) vigorously dissociated himself from Delitzsch's views which, he declared, "are as deficient from a scholarly point of view as they are religiously objectionable" (cf. Harnack, *Marcion*, p. 223, n. 1).

evangelical piety, many of whose commentaries retain their usefulness until this day. The younger Delitzsch had been well trained in the Old Testament and was himself a Hebraist of stature. But he tells us that the Old Testament had caused him difficulty from a moral and intellectual point of view ever since his student days and that he had been driven to the conclusion that it was from end to end a book full of literary fraud, immorality, and bad history. As he said:

I might summarize . . . by saying that the Old Testament is full of all kinds of deceptions: a veritable hodge-podge of erroneous, incredible, undependable figures, including those of Biblical chronology; a veritable maze of false portrayals, misleading reworkings, revisions and transpositions, together with anachronisms; a never-ending jumble of contradictory details and entire narratives, unhistorical inventions, legends and folktales, in short a book full of intentional and unintentional deceptions, in part self-deceptions, a very dangerous book, in the use of which the greatest care is necessary.[14]

This sort of thing goes on and on and is fully typical; but we need not put up with any more.

Delitzsch, in a word, found the Old Testament unsuitable for use in the church. Even in its noblest portions, he said, it has no proper significance for the Christian.[15] He uprooted Christianity from its Jewish background, declaring it to be a new and independent religion which did not develop out of Judaism at all.[16] Delitzsch was Marcionist in the fullest sense, even to the point of denying that Yahweh, God of Israel, is to be identified with the Christian's God: the making of such an identification is itself "the great deception." [17] The fact that the New Testament writers on occasion refer to the church as the spiritual Israel, or speak of a spiritual circumcision and the like, is regrettable and simply shows that they had not yet escaped their own Jewish background. Delitzsch, incidentally, was one of those who went so far as to advance the shocking and ultimately silly suggestion that Jesus himself was a Gentile.[18] Since in his view the Old Testament is a thoroughly unchristian book, he urged that the study of

[14] *Die grosse Täuschung*, II, 52-53.
[15] *Ibid.*, I, 71, 93, 95.
[16] *Ibid.*, II, 69.
[17] *Ibid.*, I, 70, *et passim*.
[18] *Ibid.*, I, 94; II, 59, 61, 68-69. I was surprised to learn from I, 114, n. 33, that Delitzsch could call upon the support of Paul Haupt, predecessor of my own teacher at Johns Hopkins University, in this connection.

it be dropped from the theological curriculum and handed over to the professor of comparative religions or to the department of Oriental studies. A general introduction to Hebrew history and religion is all that the average theological student needs; to compel him to learn Hebrew is to ask of him an unjustifiable waste of his time.[19] As for the average Christian, he would do better to contemplate the works of German thinkers and the heroes of German saga and history than to trouble with the Old Testament.[20] In a word: The Old Testament is not needed in the church, is an encumbrance to the church, and should be gotten rid of.

As a work of scholarship Delitzsch's book is not worthy of mention. It is so intemperate and its arguments often so petty and biased that it would convince no fair-minded person. One wonders indeed to what degree its author may have been motivated by the desire, whether conscious or unconscious, to dissociate himself from his own Jewish background in the face of the tide of anti-Semitism then rising in Germany. It is not ours to judge. But for the venom of its attack upon the Old Testament, Delitzsch's book remains without parallel in scholarly literature; and its anti-Semitic tone undoubtedly did its part in preparing the climate for the Nazi abomination.[21]

In the course of the Nazi years in Germany attacks on the Old Testament were frequent and vicious. But these were for the most part pure propaganda, devoid of theological significance and beneath contempt. Nevertheless, there were exceptions. That is to say, there were also works by competent scholars, which stood in the Marcionist tradition, but which cannot be dismissed simply as propaganda. Among these one thinks especially of a book by Emanuel Hirsch, a leading New Testament scholar, on the Old Testament and the preaching of the gospel.[22] Though Hirsch was a Nazi (and on occasion betrays his sympathies)[23] his

---

[19] *Ibid.*, I, 94-95; II, 70-71. Incidentally, Delitzsch quotes Harnack as also expressing the feeling that Hebrew might well be dropped as a compulsory subject (See II, 86, n. 15).

[20] *Ibid.*, I, 95-96.

[21] Delitzsch was hotly accused of anti-Semitism, and as hotly denied it (see II, 3-4). But in view of certain of his remarks (e.g., I, 102-4, where he calls the Jews "a fearful danger" of which the German people must be warned) the accusation seems justified. Kraus, *Geschichte der historisch-kritischen Erforschung des Alten Testaments*, p. 279, says that Delitzsch had been influenced by Paul de Lagarde and Houston Stewart Chamberlain—both noted anti-Semitists.

[22] *Das Alte Testament und die Predigt des Evangeliums* (Tübingen: J. C. B. Mohr, 1936).

[23] See, for example, *ibid.*, p. 62.

arguments are based not on political but on theological grounds. Hirsch takes his stand on the classical Lutheran doctrine of the two kingdoms and the antithesis of law and gospel; and this last he pushes to the extreme of identifying the Old Testament with law. He does not, therefore, explicitly advocate the exclusion of the Old Testament from the canon, but he believes it to be of value chiefly because of the contrast that it provides to the New. The Old Testament religion is in fact the great antithesis of Christianity in the light of which alone the meaning of the gospel can properly be appreciated. It is a special case among non-Christian religions in that it is the soil from which Christianity sprang, but its relationship to the latter is one of "antithetical tension." [24]

It is evident from this that Hirsch, while he does not actually dismiss the Old Testament from the Bible, clearly does not regard it as a ranking partner with the New: stress falls entirely upon the discontinuity between the two. Hirsch asserts that the Old Testament was included in the church's canon in the first instance for reasons that would not carry weight today (not least the fact that the early church was able to impart a Christian meaning to the Old Testament rather than understanding it in its plain historical sense).[25] Read in its plain meaning, said he, the Old Testament is an alien book to the Christian. It presents a religion bound by cultic regulations, indissolubly linked with Jewish nationalism, without hope of eternal life, a religion of law in which even grace is legally conditioned. [26] We cannot, to be sure, do without it, for it not only has many valuable things to say but provides the indispensable background for the understanding of the gospel. But it is not to be placed on a level with the New. The Old Testament has been superseded for the Christian; Christians of non-Jewish blood have no direct relationship to it.[27] Indeed, the Christian, if he would be true to his Lord, should adopt a polemical attitude toward it.[28] Hirsch, it may be added, built upon none other than the great Danish theologian, Kierkegaard, whom he quotes with approval on the flyleaf of his book (it is a sort of motto). Here is the quotation in part:

[24] *Ibid.*, pp. 27, 59, 83.
[25] *Ibid.*, pp. 67-71.
[26] *Ibid.*, pp. 72-78. The last statement strikes one who is familiar with the Old Testament as decidedly inaccurate. It is partially explained, perhaps, by the fact that Hirsch believes (p. 22) that the only legitimate understanding of the Old Testament is that of postexilic Judaism.
[27] *Ibid.*, pp. 16, 31, 44.
[28] *Ibid.*, pp. 48, 61.

It cannot be made clear enough, or repeated often enough, that Christianity does indeed have a relationship to Judaism but, be it noted, of this sort, namely, that Judaism is for Christianity that with the help of which the latter makes itself negatively recognizable, that is, its dialectical opposite.[29] . . . For one will find that almost all, so to speak, of the more pious aberrations in Christianity have a common relationship to the fact that the Old Testament has been elevated to the same level as the New.[30]

This may not be Marcionism as outright as that of Delitzsch. But it is Marcionism nonetheless, and it leads to the same result: the effective removal of the Old Testament from its position of authority as a part of the Christian's rule of faith and practice.

4. We have, then, observed a definite Marcionist strain in Christian theology that has persisted down into modern times. It is scarcely surprising that some of its clearest expressions should have issued from Germany in the years between the two world wars, for Marcionism and anti-Semitism undoubtedly have affinities. But the two are not synonymous. Marcion's answer to the problem of the Old Testament is not necessarily motivated by anti-Semitism, nor did it have its origin in German nationalism. It is therefore not to be supposed that the passing of the Third Reich automatically disposed of it. Still today, answers akin to that of Marcion continue to be given. That is to say, there are scholars who, without trace of anti-Semitism and on purely theological grounds, would solve the problem of the Old Testament not by eliminating it from the Bible but by frankly placing it on a level of value secondary to the New.

Notable among such scholars is Rudolf Bultmann. We are not here concerned with Bultmann's views in general, specifically not with regard to the "demythologizing" controversy, but only as they relate to the Old Testament. These he has expressed in various articles, the two most important of which are now available in English.[31] Whether or not it is fair to classify Bultmann with Marcion has provoked a considerable

---

[29] Literally, "the counter-thrust of offence" (*Gegenstoss des Ärgernisses*); the paraphrase is for the sake of clarity.

[30] I am not competent to say whether Hirsch has quoted Kierkegaard in context or not; but a Marcionist tendency has been observed in Kierkegaard. See, for example, R. C. Johnson, *Authority in Protestant Theology*, pp. 93-94.

[31] See Rudolf Bultmann, "The Significance of the Old Testament for the Christian Faith," trans. B. W. Anderson in *OTCF*, pp. 8-35; and "Prophecy and Fulfillment," trans. J. C. G. Greig in *EOTH*, pp. 50-75. The German version of these articles may be found, respectively, in Bultmann, *Glauben und Verstehen* (Tütbingen: J. C. B. Mohr), I (2nd. ed., 1954), 313-36; and II (1952), 162-86.

debate into which we shall not enter.[32] If by Marcionist is meant one who would remove the Old Testament from the canon, then Bultmann does not deserve the epithet, for he finds great positive value in the Old Testament and expressly insists that it can on no account be dispensed with.[33] Yet it is not without reason that Bultmann has been taxed with Marcionist tendencies, for his understanding of the Old Testament is such (it has certain similarities to that of Hirsch) [34] that it leads him to accord to it a definitely subsidiary position, by no means on a level with that of the New. Indeed, one may complain that he has rendered the use of the Old Testament in the church's proclamation optional.

In the articles referred to above, Bultmann is concerned to ask if, and in what sense, the Old Testament can be received by the Christian as the Word of his God and a constituent of his faith.[35] He denies that the Old Testament can be revelation for the Christian in a direct sense, as it was—and still is—for Israel. The Christian is not a member of Israel; he does not live under her laws, share her peculiar beliefs and practices, nor can he participate in her history. Israel's history is no more—if no less—a part of his history than is, say, the Spartan band that died at Thermopylae. It is therefore not in a direct sense but only in an indirect one that the Christian hears the Word of God in the Old Testament.[36] Yet this indirect sense is a very real one. Since the Old Testament's understanding of man's existence (*Existenz*), with its sense of the radical claim of God on the total life of man, is the same as that of the New Testament also, the Old Testament exercises the pedagogical function of preparing for the hearing and the understanding of the gospel. [37]

But the Old Testament is not a preparation for the gospel in the sense that it is a *Heilsgeschichte,* a history of redemption, leading on to Christ. Bultmann examines various key Old Testament concepts as they are taken up in the New, and he can see no sign of prophecy moving on to fulfillment.[38] On the contrary, he sees in the Old Testament a history of

[32] Let the reader but examine various of the articles in OTCF, especially those of Carl Michalson (pp. 49-63), who warmly defends Bultmann against such a charge, and of Eric Voegelin (pp. 64-89), who calls Bultmann a Gnostic thinker.

[33] See OTCF, p. 21.

[34] Kraus (*Geschichte* . . . , p. 392) goes so far as to say that Bultmann follows the line taken by Hirsch "to a hair" (*haargenau*).

[35] Here particularly the article in OTCF; see pp. 12-13.

[36] OTCF, pp. 31-34.

[37] OTCF, pp. 20-21.

[38] Here especially the article in EOTH; see pp. 59-72.

shattering failure (*Scheitern*), a history that miscarries at every point, that brought nothing but the disappointment of hope as Israel had conceived it. The Old Testament might be called the prophecy of which the New is the fulfillment only in the sense that it is, as Paul said, a "tutor" (*paidagōgos*) unto Christ (Gal. 3:24).[39] He who reads its history of broken hope and failure, and hears the demands of its law, sees himself as in a mirror and comes to understand the contradiction that belongs to human existence: to be called by God, yet to be bound to earthly history. And as he thus sees in Israel's history the reflection of his own dilemma and the failure of his own false hopes, he is driven to penitence and to the acceptance of justification through faith alone. Since the Old Testament thus places a man in a predicament from which he is able to understand and receive the gospel, it speaks to him in a mediating fashion the Word of God.

The Old Testament thus, in Bultmann's view, is seen as a propaedeutic to the gospel; it has a pedagogical function only. Bultmann, like Hirsch, builds on the classical Lutheran law-gospel antithesis and, again like Hirsch, presses this to the point of making the Old Testament virtually synonymous with law, with the result that the two Testaments, save in their understanding of man's *Existenz*, stand in almost total discontinuity with each other.[40] One cannot accuse Bultmann of wishing to dispense with the Old Testament, for he does not. Nor ought one to quarrel with his assigning to the Old Testament a pedagogical function, for (or at least so I believe) it indeed has such a function. But in that Bultmann limits the use that can be made of it to a pedagogical one and stresses its radical difference from the New Testament revelation, the result is the reduction of the Old Testament to an auxiliary position in the canon. The question then remains: Granted that the Old Testament is useful for the preaching of the gospel, is it really necessary? If all it offers the hearer is an understanding of his existence, is it not possible that this can be communicated to him—and better—by more contemporary means? Bultmann frankly admits that it can. What the Old Testament offers of insight into the nature of man's existence can be found almost everywhere in human

[39] *EOTH*, pp. 72-75.

[40] Bultmann does indeed agree that the Old Testament has a word of grace, and therefore of gospel (*OTCF*, pp. 22-28); but (p. 29) he insists that grace is understood in the New Testament in a fundamentally different way (no longer tied to the destiny of the people Israel).

experience. The preacher will probably use the Old Testament, but he need not do so: it will depend upon the situation.[41] This is at least a modified form of Marcionism. It deals with the problem of the Old Testament along somewhat Marcionist lines. The Old Testament is not excluded from the Bible, but it is effectively deprived of canonical rank and made into a document of subsidiary usefulness which need not be proclaimed in the church.

Bultmann is not the only scholar whose views would, if followed out logically, lead to a reduction of the Old Testament. Indeed, I should say that wherever the law-gospel antithesis is pushed to the virtual equating of Old Testament with law, wherever the discontinuity between the Testaments is stressed to the virtual exclusion of the continuity, wherever the Old Testament is accorded the exclusively pedagogical function of preparing men for the hearing of the gospel, the danger exists that the Old Testament will be reduced to a position of secondary importance. Not a few scholars who have expressed themselves in recent years have run into this danger.

There is, for example, Friedrich Baumgärtel, who has perhaps done as much to stimulate the hermeneutical discussion as any one individual,[42] and Franz Hesse, whose position approximates that of Baumgärtel.[43] Although Baumgärtel's position in some respects parallels that of Bultmann, I feel it to be unfair to use the term "Marcionism" in connection with it and wish explicitly to state that I do not do so. Baumgärtel clearly affirms that the Old Testament is not abrogated for us but concerns us in its totality; he refuses to separate the Old Testament from the New as "less authoritative," and insists that it is essential for our faith.[44] Moreover, he does not view the relationship of the Testaments as one of complete

[41] *OTCF*, pp. 17, 34. Bultmann notes that some of the New Testament writings make little use of the Old Testament.

[42] To list all Baumgärtel's contributions would take a great deal of space. See especially his book, *Verheissung* (Gütersloh: C. Bertelsmann, 1952); in English, see "The Hermeneutical Problem of the Old Testament," trans. M. Newman in *EOTH*, pp. 134-59. For other works, see the bibliography.

[43] See especially F. Hesse, "The Evaluation and the Authority of Old Testament Texts," trans. J. A. Wharton in *EOTH*, pp. 285-313. This article first appeared in *Festschrift Friedrich Baumgärtel*, L. Rost, ed. (Erlangen, *Erlanger Forschungen*, Reihe A. Band 10, 1959), pp. 74-96. See also Hesse, "Haggai" in A. Kuschke, ed., *Verbannung und Heimkehr* (*Festschrift Wilhelm Rudolph* [Tübingen: J. C. B. Mohr, 1961]), pp. 109-34.

[44] See, for example, *EOTH*, pp. 139-40; *Verheissung*, pp. 144-48. Baumgärtel (p. 148) specifically rejects Hirsch's understanding of the Old Testament as the antithesis of the New.

discontinuity, for he sees running through the Old Testament the theme of "promise in Christ," which is also the central concern of the New. Nevertheless, there are dangers in Baumgärtel's approach. In that he repeatedly stresses the differences between the Testaments and repeatedly speaks of the Old Testament as a witness to another religion than the Christian religion, in that he accords to the Old Testament almost exclusively the pedagogical function of preparing for the hearing of the gospel, and in that the hermeneutical principle with which he evaluates its relevance ("promise in Christ") is one that is drawn from the New Testament rather than the Old, I believe that he both seriously limits the use that can be made of the Old Testament and restricts its place in the canon and in preaching to an auxiliary one. The question then raises itself if, under this view, the Old Testament has not been rendered unnecessary.

If the Old Testament is accorded only the auxiliary, pedagogical function of preparing men's minds for the reception of the gospel, then the door is thrown open to Marcionism, whether it is intended or not. If that is the only function the Old Testament has, the question will inevitably be raised if it is really needed. Could it not be dropped, and something else substituted that would serve just as well? The question is a logical one, and it is bound to be asked. And it has in fact been asked, so we are told, in certain of the younger churches—for example, in India, where some have suggested that the ancient Hindu scriptures would provide a better introduction to the gospel for people of that land than does the Old Testament.[45] The suggestion has never, so far as I know, been adopted and Bibles reprinted accordingly. But it is a reasonable suggestion, if the Old Testament is viewed as a propaedeutic to the gospel and nothing more.

5. The scholars mentioned in the foregoing paragraphs by no means exhaust the list of those who have exhibited Marcionist tendencies. But I trust that enough has been said to make it clear that Marcionism has had a long life in the church and still survives. But perhaps the reader will be inclined to ask if this solution to the problem has not been given more attention than it deserves. Granted that Marcionism is an ancient and tenacious heresy and a most protean one, is it really a serious danger to the church, at least in this country? The scholars who have advocated it are

[45] See G. E. Phillips, *The Old Testament in the World Church, with Special Reference to the Younger Churches* (London: Lutterworth, 1942), pp. 14-21; similar suggestions have been proposed in China, pp. 22-28.

redoubtable scholars indeed, but they are relatively few in number (and most of them in Germany, at that). Their views have received no official endorsement among the churches, nor is it likely that they ever will. I know of no movement afoot in any of our churches to remove the Old Testament from the Bible, and it is probable that the average churchgoer would be shocked by such a suggestion. Since this is, then, a minority opinion, held by relatively few and rejected by all major denominations, need it cause us any alarm?

Let us indeed not magnify dangers. But let us not minimize them either, for there is—if I know the situation at all—not a little neo-Marcionism in our churches. It has no official standing—indeed, under that name it scarcely exists at all—but it is unofficially present nonetheless: call it a practical Marcionism, an implicit Marcionism, an inconsequent Marcionism, or what you will. That is to say, there are many of our people who never heard of Marcion and who would be horrified to learn of the company they are in but who nevertheless use the Old Testament in a distinctly Marcionist manner. Formally, and no doubt sincerely, they hail it as canonical Scripture; but in practice they relegate it to a subordinate position, if they do not effectively exclude it from use altogether.

Examples of what is meant leap to the mind. One thinks of the layman or the pastor who is simply troubled by the Old Testament. He finds so much in it that seems to him dull and irrelevant, if not positively unedifying, that he wonders what profit there is in reading it and what authority it could possibly have over Christian faith and practice. And so he gives it up. He does not read it, and—if a pastor—he does not preach from it; he bases his faith—and if a preacher, his preaching—entirely upon the New Testament and treats the Old exactly as if it were not in the Bible. Or there is the preacher who does indeed preach from the Old Testament but only to use it as a foil for heightening the uniqueness of the teachings of Jesus. He portrays the God of the Old Testament as a God of vindictive justice and wrath—a regular "dirty bully," as a certain bishop once put it—who stands in sharpest contrast to the loving and merciful Father revealed in Jesus Christ. He never heard of Emanuel Hirsch, this preacher, but without knowing what he does, he follows his hermeneutic to the letter: he makes of the Old Testament the great antithesis of the New. Or there is the missionary whom I once met, who frankly regretted that the Old Testament had ever been translated into the language of the people with whom he worked; he felt that it confused them and gave support to all sorts of sub-Christian notions and practices. Now this man was not consciously a Marcionist and would have been angered had I taxed him with such a thing. But he felt the Old Testament to be an encumbrance to the gospel; he would like to keep it hidden from his people—in effect, to place it with the Apocrypha (i.e., the "hidden books") —which was just what Harnack suggested. He had, in fact, two Scriptures of unequal value: the one to be proclaimed as normative in the church, the other to be kept aside for the (optional?) use of those mature enough not to be harmed by it.

The tendency to downgrade the Old Testament may be observed too in many of our theological schools, even in some (not my own, I hasten to say) whose catalogs clearly state that the Scriptures of the Old and New Testaments form the foundation of the curriculum. Where the New Testament is concerned, the statement is likely to be taken seriously: Greek will be insisted upon, or strongly urged, and numerous courses provided to give the student adequate grounding in the exegesis, the theology, and the hermeneutics of the New Testament. The Old Testament is in the curriculum too. But it poses a problem; it is like an unwanted guest whom one can neither send away nor entertain properly. It is agreed that some knowledge of it is necessary, but it is felt that in view of all the other legitimate claims on the student's time too many hours cannot be allotted to its study: perhaps an introductory survey course would suffice, with other courses held optional for those who wish them. As for Hebrew, it would be widely agreed that to expect the average student to master it and then to proceed to the exegetical study of the Old Testament is unrealistic, or would at best require an expenditure of time and energy that cannot be justified. This is not the place to engage in special pleading with regard to the value of Hebrew or the importance of Old Testament studies. Moreover, one fully understands the point of absolute saturation which the theological curriculum has reached, which has impelled theological institutions to adopt such a course. Yet let it not be forgotten that it is precisely the course advocated (for other reasons to be sure) by Friedrich Delitzsch. Those who follow it seem to be tacitly saying that while a thorough knowledge of the New Testament is essential to the minister, a thorough knowledge of the Old Testament is not: the Old Testament stands on a level of lesser importance.[46]

[46] Lest I be misunderstood, let me say that were I obliged to choose whether students should be required to master the Old Testament *or* the New, I should without hesitation

Let it be repeated that those who express views such as the above are only in the rarest instances consciously Marcionist. The most of them would not know what Marcionism is and would be shocked were someone to explain it to them. Their attitudes do not, in fact, represent a conscious theological wrestling with the problem at all. It is simply that, evaluating the Old Testament from the side of the New Testament faith and ethics as they do, they have sensed its difficulty and strangeness and, feeling it to be a book that is not fully Christian, have reacted instinctively by ceasing to use it or by refusing any longer to regard it as canonical Scripture in any way comparable to the New. The name of Marcion is seldom invoked. But the fact that such attitudes are so widespread is clear indication that Marcion's answer to the problem of the Old Testament, though long rejected by the mainstream of Christendom, has never lost its attraction.

6. But the church has from the beginning resisted Marcion and must continue to do so. The answer of Marcion is on no account to be accepted. Granted that, if honestly given, it can be an honest answer and that, if drastic, it is at least logically consistent. Granted further that in taking with utter seriousness the differences that exist between the Testaments it comes straight to the heart of the problem. The Old Testament religion is indeed not identical with Christianity, and in no approach to the problem can this be forgotten. Perhaps we should even be grateful to this persistent Marcionist strain for not allowing us to forget it. We cannot "level out" revelation, and we cannot foist the Old Testament—as a whole and without further ado—on the Christian as normative. But the Marcionist answer, in that it elevates the discontinuity between the Testaments to the absolute and makes of the Old Testament a book of another religion, is too consistent, too drastic. Wherever it has been accepted, the result has been irreparable damage to the Christian faith.

The church needs the Old Testament and cannot do without it. She needs it in her liturgy and preaching, and she will always continue to use it. Can one imagine the church being willing to do without the Ten Commandments, which continue even in Christ to speak their eternal imperative to God's people? Or the treasury of the Psalter, wherewith

---

opt for the New. But the choice is a false one. I am confronted with no such choice—any more, I should say, than on sallying forth in the morning I am obliged to choose between wearing my trousers *or* my shirt: the decently dressed man requires both. Just so, the well-prepared minister must know both Testaments.

she sings her praises to God no less than did old Israel, and in which thousands of Christians have found comfort as they passed through the dark valley? And how weakened the church's voice would be in all matters pertaining to righteousness among men if she could no longer read and proclaim the words of the prophets! What a denial of her history, and how impoverished her understanding of her God, if she determined no longer to know anything of his mighty works toward Israel! No, the church will continue to live from the Old Testament and make use of it constantly, and it behooves her never to forget that fact. Moreover, since Christianity had its roots in Judaism, and that in turn in the faith of old Israel, and since no movement can be understood unless it is also understood historically, the Old Testament remains essential for the right understanding of the gospel. Like it or not, it must be accorded its place in the theological curriculum and in the instructional program of the church. The church can never part with the Old Testament.

But it is not enough to say that. After all, what responsible person would question that the Old Testament has abiding values or that some knowledge of it is necessary for the proper understanding of the gospel? Even those who would deny the Old Testament canonical status would admit as much. So we must go a step further and say that not only will we have to retain the Old Testament, *we will have in some way to use it as a part of normative Scripture.* I am quite unable to get around the fact —though Harnack, for example, said he was not impressed by it[47]—that the Old Testament *was* authoritative Scripture for Jesus himself. Jesus knew no Scripture save the Old Testament, no God save its God; it was this God whom he addressed as "Father." True, he used the Scriptures with sovereign freedom, as befitted him. But never once did he suggest that in the light of his work they might safely be discarded. On the contrary, he regarded the Scriptures as the key to the understanding of his person; again and again he is represented as saying that it is the Scriptures that witness to him and are fulfilled in him. At no place did he express himself as shocked by the Old Testament, nor did he adopt what Hirsch would call a polemical attitude toward it (though often enough toward the religious leaders of his day and their interpretations). I find it most interesting and not a little odd that although the Old Testament on

---

[47] *Marcion,* p. 223. Others have expressed themselves similarly. I can only say that I disagree completely.

occasion offends our Christian feelings, it did not apparently offend Christ's "Christian feelings"! Could it really be that we are ethically and religiously more sensitive than he? Or is it perhaps that we do not view the Old Testament—and its God—as he did? The very fact that the Old Testament was normative Scripture to Jesus, from which he understood both his God and (however we interpret his self-consciousness) himself, means that it must in some way be normative Scripture for us too—*unless we wish to understand Jesus in some other way than he himself did and the New Testament did.*

The Old Testament must be retained in the Christian's Bible precisely because it is impossible to be true to the New Testament faith itself while getting rid of it. If there is one point upon which the New Testament is unanimous, it is that Jesus came, lived, died, and rose again "according to the Scriptures." The New Testament writers understood the meaning of his work from the pages of the Old Testament: he is the promised Messiah of David's line, the heavenly Son of man, the servant of God who gave "his life as a ransom for many" (Mark 10:45). And the church fathers resisted Marcion precisely because he cut the link between Old Testament and New, between prophecy and fulfillment. Though we cannot use the argument from prophecy in the mechanical way that the church fathers did, we must, if we would be true to the New Testament faith, take as seriously as they did the bond that binds the two Testaments irrevocably together. To discard the Old Testament is to cut loose from a fundamental factor in the New Testament faith and do it irreparable damage. It is in fact to tear Christianity from its rootage in history and thereby to run the risk of turning it into a system of philosophy or a set of eternally valid principles.

The Old Testament holds the gospel to history. It is its surest bulwark against assimilation with alien philosophies and ideologies, against a flight into a sentimental and purely otherworldly piety, and against that disintegrating individualism that so easily besets it. It is surely no coincidence that Marcion was influenced by the Gnostics, who viewed the teaching of Christ as an arcane knowledge, and that as he essayed to cut away the Old Testament his scissors slipped, so that he cut away a major portion of the New Testament as well. [48] It is no coincidence that Harnack understood the message of Jesus in terms of timeless teachings regarding

---

[48] All except Paul and Luke, and these expurgated of what he believed to be Jewish interpolations. See Harnack, *Marcion,* Ch. IV and Excursuses III and IV for details.

the fatherhood of God and the infinite value of the human soul, the present reality of God's kingdom within the individual heart, and the summons to the higher righteousness of love to the neighbor.[49] It is no coincidence that both Delitzsch and Hirsch were tarred with the brush of anti-Semitism or that the weapons forged against the Old Testament by these scholars and others should have been seized by Hitler and his creatures and turned against the Jews and the church.[50] Nor is it a coincidence, finally, that Bultmann in his concern to interpret the gospel existentially comes dangerously close—or so I think with many others—to dissolving the link that binds the gospel to those *eph hapax* historical events to which it testifies and turning it into a subjective experience.

To loosen the bond between the Testaments seems always to go hand in hand, whether as cause or as effect, with damage to the gospel. We conclude, therefore, that the church must continue to reject Marcion and all his works, in whatever form they may appear. For the answer of Marcion is a wrong answer.

II

But if we cannot dispose of the Old Testament by denying it canonical rank, what shall we say of that other time-honored solution to the problem that it raises, also known since the earliest days of the church—namely, to save the Old Testament by reading a Christian meaning from it?

1. This was the way of the early church fathers generally.[51] They were not unaware of the problem felt by Marcion; they sensed that there is a great deal in the Old Testament which on the surface seems to the Christian strange, if not trivial and morally offensive, and which in no way governs his practice. But their theological instincts were far too sound to permit them to cut loose from the Old Testament. So they got around the problem by recourse to allegory and typology (it is often difficult to draw a clear distinction between the two as the fathers used them).[52]

---

[49] See Harnack, *What Is Christianity*, trans. T. B. Saunders (5th ed.; London: Ernest Benn, 1958), p. 46 *et passim*.

[50] See Kraus, *Geschichte* . . . , pp. 392-94, for a clear statement of the point.

[51] There were differences, of course. The school of Antioch was far soberer in its use of Scripture than was the rival school of Alexandria; but it did not triumph. For the details see the general works mentioned in note 1, particularly that of Farrar.

[52] Properly speaking, allegory refers to the finding of hidden, mystical meanings in the words of the text itself; typology refers to the finding in the events (or institutions, persons, etc.) described in the Old Testament text a deeper, hidden significance prefigurative

Allegory was a method of interpretation widely used in the Greco-Roman world (for example, by the Stoics in interpreting the ancient myths in a manner rationally and morally acceptable to their contemporaries), as well as in Jewish circles (notably by Philo of Alexandria in interpreting the religion of the Jews to sophisticated people of his day). The church fathers—and that includes the overwhelming majority of them: Clement of Alexandria, Origen, Irenaeus, Ambrose, Augustine, and a host of others—took over the method and adapted it to their purposes.

It was generally believed that Scripture had various levels of meaning. Origen popularized a threefold sense corresponding to the supposed trichotomy of man's nature: body, soul, and spirit. There was a literal or corporeal sense (i.e., what the words in their plain meaning say), a moral or tropological sense (i.e., a sense figurative of the Christian soul, which thus gives edification and guidance for conduct), and a spiritual or mystical sense. Later, still a fourth sense was added: the anagogical or eschatological sense. Thus, to give a classical example, the word "Jerusalem" was understood in the Middle Ages as having four senses: literally it referred to the city of that name in Judah, tropologically to the faithful Christian soul, allegorically (mystically) to the church of Christ, and anagogically to the heavenly city of God which is our eternal home. It was possible, albeit not necessary, to understand the word in all four of these senses in a single text. But the tendency was to care far less for the literal meaning than for the spiritual ones, for the true meaning of the text is spiritual. Indeed, some Scripture—so it was held—cannot be interpreted literally, for it tells of things that are immoral and thus unworthy of God (adultery, incest, murder, etc.); and much Scripture is too primitive or too trivial, if taken literally, to be a fit vehicle of divine revelation (lengthy genealogies, rules for animal sacrifice, the dimensions of the tabernacle, etc.). Such passages yield their true meaning only if interpreted spiritually.

The result was a wholesale and uncontrolled allegorizing of Scripture, specifically the Old Testament. This did not confine itself to difficult or morally offensive passages, or to passages that tell of something that seems unnatural or improbable, or to places where Scripture contradicts, or seems

---

of New Testament events (or institutions, persons, etc.). J. Daniélou, *From Shadows to Reality*, trans. Dom Wulstan Hibberd (Westminster, Maryland: The Newman Press, 1960), attempts to distinguish between the two as the church fathers employed them. Undoubtedly they used one as much as they did the other. But a great deal of what Daniélou classes as legitimate typology is so fanciful and so preoccupied with details that it might better be regarded as allegory.

to contradict, other Scripture; it extended itself almost everywhere. Scarcely a text but yielded hidden and unsuspected riches to the interpreter's ingenuity. Examples could be multiplied by the page, many of which became classics and were repeated in various forms by one church father after the other.[53] Thus Moses seated in prayer, his arms outstretched and supported by his companions while Israel battled Amalek (Exod. 17:8-16), makes the sign of the cross of Christ, and it was by this sign that Amalek was overcome by Jesus (Joshua) through Moses (so Ep. Barnabas, Tertullian, Cyprian, Justin, et al.). So too the scarlet cord which the harlot Rahab let down from Jericho's wall (Josh. 2; 6) signifies redemption through the blood of Christ (so I Clement, Justin, Irenaeus, Origen, et al.), while the three (sic) spies (so Irenaeus) were doubtless the three persons of the Trinity; Rahab herself (so Origen) is the church, which is made up of harlots and sinners. In like manner the flood story is a hidden prophecy of salvation in Christ (so, with variations, Tertullian, Cyprian, Chrysostom, et al.): the ark is the church and the hope it brings us (in Justin, it is the wood of the cross); Noah is Christ, the dove the Holy Spirit, and the olive branch the divine mercy (to which others of the fathers add yet further details).

These are but random examples. But they are quite typical and serve to illustrate the exotic jungle of fanciful interpretation into which patristic exegesis strayed. And such interpretations, the rule among the Greek and Latin fathers, remained the rule down through the Middle Ages. The great Aquinas, to be sure, advocated a somewhat saner approach. Although he accepted the theory of the four senses of Scripture and regarded the spiritual senses as useful for edification, he contended that they might not be used to prove points of doctrine; and this view found some official acceptance.[54] But the spate of fanciful interpretations continued to flow unchecked from pulpit and lecturer's desk alike. The meanings that could

[53] It would be tedious and pointless to attempt detailed documentation of the following examples, so often do they crop up. The reader will find all of them, and many others besides, in Daniélou, *From Shadows to Reality*, with a generally sympathetic evaluation; and in Farrar, *History of Interpretation*, with an emphatically unsympathetic evaluation.

[54] See Beryl Smalley, "The Bible in the Middle Ages," in D. E. Nineham, ed., *The Church's Use of the Bible, Past and Present*, pp. 60-61. This article (pp. 57-71) is an excellent summary of medieval exegesis. For a full and definitive treatment of the subject, see Smalley, *The Study of the Bible in the Middle Ages* (Oxford: Basil Blackwell, 1952); more recently and from a Roman Catholic point of view, Henri de Lubac, *Exégèse médiévale: Les quatre sens de l'Écriture* (Paris: Aubier, Vol. I, 1959; Vol. II:1, 1961; II:2, 1964).

be got from Scripture were limited, one might justifiably feel, only by the interpreter's ingenuity. Yet the Old Testament was saved for the church. So interpreted, it presented no problem at all, for it had become wholly a Christian book which in each of its texts propounded Christian truth, had one but the imagination to ferret it out.

2. We moderns are inclined to smile at all this and perhaps to marvel that such fantastic interpretations (for so they seem to us) were ever taken seriously. Certainly we need no lecture to convince us that this is not the way to solve the problem of the Old Testament. It goes against our entire training and the Reformation tradition as well. Whatever their inconsistencies may have been (and they were on occasion inconsistent), both the great Reformers rejected allegory in principle—repeatedly and in the strongest language. In the preceding chapter both Luther and Calvin were quoted in their insistence that it is the duty of the interpreter to arrive at the plain sense of the text intended by its author. Similar quotations, in which they expressed their contempt of allegory, could be adduced almost at will. [55] Luther, whose vocabulary was by no means impoverished, is especially vivid. He declares that Origen's allegories "are not worth so much dirt"; he calls allegory variously "the scum on Scripture," a "harlot" to seduce us, "a monkey-game," something that turns Scripture into "a nose of wax" (i.e., that can be twisted into any shape desired), the means by which the Devil gets us on his pitchfork. He declares (in expounding Psalm 22) that Scripture is the garment of Christ and that allegory rends it into "rags and tatters." "How," he cries, "will you teach faith with certainty when you make the sense of Scripture uncertain?" Calvin is equally stern. More than once (as at Gal. 4:21-26, quoted in the preceding chapter) he calls allegorical interpretations an invention of the Devil to undermine the authority of Scripture. Elsewhere he describes them as "puerile," "farfetched," and declares that one would do better to confess ignorance than to indulge in such "frivolous guesses." The interpreter, he declares, must seek the plain sense, and if that is uncertain he should adopt the interpretation that best suits the context.

It is clear from this that allegorical interpretations have never had a

---

[55] We shall again not trouble with precise documentation of the following. The reader may collect these, and any number of others, from almost any treatment of the Reformers. See, conveniently, Farrar, *History of Interpretation*, Ch. VI; Kemper Fullerton, *Prophecy and Authority: A Study in the History of the Doctrine and Interpretation of Scripture* (New York: The Macmillan Company, 1919), Chs. VI and VII.

legitimate place in the churches of the Reformation, although instances in plenty of preachers resorting to them could no doubt readily enough be found. The Reformers were quite right, as virtually every competent interpreter today would agree. One simply cannot in intellectual integrity interpret the Old Testament in this way or pretend that its texts actually intended such meanings. What is more, its place as authoritative Scripture cannot be defended so. After all, what real authority can the Old Testament have in the church if its texts can have whatever meaning each individual is pleased to find in them? If the Old Testament is to be saved at all, it must be the Old Testament in its plain meaning.

But can the church then find no Christian meaning in the Old Testament? The Reformers certainly were able to.[56] Both Luther and Calvin, to be sure, insisted in principle that Scripture has but one sense, the plain or literal sense. But by this they did not mean precisely what most modern exegetes (who insist on the same thing) would mean. The modern exegete would understand the plain sense as the sense derived from the text by a philological study of it in the light of its historical situation: i.e., what its author intended to convey to those whom he addressed. The Reformers would have meant that too, but they would have understood something more by it. Is not the true author of Scripture the Holy Spirit? The plain sense of a text, then, includes the sense intended by the Holy Spirit, the prophetic sense (*sensus literalis propheticus*), its sense in the light of Scripture as a whole (i.e., Scripture is its own interpreter). And with this understanding of the literal sense the Reformers were able to find abundant Christian meaning in the Old Testament. Luther, giving large play to the polarity of law and gospel and to the pedagogical role of the former, searched the Old Testament for whatever "urges Christ" (*was Christum treibet*) and gave a profoundly christological interpretation of it. Calvin, viewing law and gospel in a rather complementary relationship, and with his massive conception of the sovereign and gracious purposes of God manifesting themselves in the history and institutions of Israel, which foreshadowed their fulfillment in Christ, left generous room for a typological or analogical interpretation of the Old Testament.

---

[56] On the Reformers' use of the Old Testament see, for Luther, Bornkamm, *Luther und das Alte Testament*; for Calvin, H. H. Wolf, *Die Einheit des Bundes: Das Verhältnis von Altem und Neuem Testament bei Calvin* (Neukirchen: Verlag der Buchhandlung des Erziehungsvereins, 1958). The reader will find a useful orientation to the Reformers' hermeneutical principles in T. D. Parker, "A Comparison of Calvin and Luther on Galatians," *Interpretation*, XVII (1963), 61-75.

Christological and typological interpretations, therefore, traditionally occupied a respectable place in Protestant biblical interpretation (the former perhaps more in the Lutheran tradition, the latter more in the Calvinist; but one ought not to generalize), and they continued to do so at least into the nineteenth century. But such interpretations are hard to control, quick to lapse into subjectivism and even fantasy; and too frequently they did so lapse.[57] Sober interpreters came, with justification, to fear them. With the rise of the scientific study of the Bible they fell almost completely from favor. It was generally felt that the exegete had the task solely of setting forth with all possible objectivity the plain, historical meaning of the text as its author intended it, and that to go beyond this would be a betrayal of exegetical integrity and therefore impermissible. And this attitude has remained the dominant one among biblical scholars down to our own day.[58]

3. But can the church rest content with interpreting the Old Testament merely in its historical meaning? If she does so, will not the Old Testament again be seen in its utter strangeness as the expression of an ancient religion not the same as our own? Will not much of it seem irrelevant, or at best of purely historical interest, to the Christian? And what, then, is to prevent the church from falling once more into the arms of Marcion? After all, the allegorists did recognize both the strangeness of the Old Testament in its literal sense and the fact that it is indispensable; and they did save it for the church. And if we reject their methods, must we not still find in the Old Testament a Christian meaning over and above its plain, historical meaning if the church is to retain it as a part of her canon of Scripture? And, more, is not such a deeper, Christian meaning there to be found? There are those who would answer such questions in the affirmative and accordingly insist upon the necessity of an interpretation of the Old Testament that goes beyond the literal sense.

That such sentiments should be expressed in Roman Catholic circles is

---

[57] For an excellent example of a nineteenth-century attempt to define the proper, as over against the improper, use of typology, see Patrick Fairbairn, *The Typology of Scripture*. I understand that this was published in Edinburgh in 1857. It has been reissued by Zondervan Publishing House, Grand Rapids, Michigan, but without indication of the date either of original publication or reprinting.

[58] And not among "higher critics" only, at least where typology is concerned. My own teachers in biblical subjects, when a theological student, held the highest possible doctrine of Scripture and opposed the then-reigning criticism resolutely; but I cannot recall their making any explicit use of typology, or even discussing it as a possible hermeneutical method.

perhaps not surprising, for Catholics (though their scholars today are as committed to grammatico-historical principles of exegesis as are their Protestant colleagues) have by tradition always been more hospitable to "mystical" interpretations than have Protestants. Certain Catholic writers, indeed, have recently declared their sympathy with the fourfold sense as a means of bridging the gap between the Testaments and have found place for allegorical meanings, at least for purposes of edification.[59] A still larger group of Catholic scholars holds that there is a *sensus plenior* in the Old Testament text, a fuller meaning intended by the Holy Spirit which lies within and behind the literal meaning (something not vastly different from the *sensus literalis propheticus* as understood by the Reformers), and that this permits a Christian interpretation of the Old Testament which is in no way arbitrary. The validity of the *sensus plenior*, and whether or not it need have been consciously understood by the human author, has occasioned considerable debate in Catholic publications.[60] Whatever one thinks of these things, they are evidence of a continued grappling with the problem of the Old Testament and the desire to accord it its rightful position in the church.

As for Protestants, although I know of no scholar who has advocated a return to the allegorizing of Scripture in the medieval sense, there have been not a few, especially on the continent of Europe and in Great Britain, who in one way or another would call us back to a christological, or a typological, interpretation of the Old Testament. Karl Barth has undoubtedly exerted a tremendous influence in this connection. It was this distinguished theologian who a generation ago initiated the revolt against the theological liberalism then dominant and the arid historicism in biblical interpretation that accompanied it, and whose career marked

[59] See especially the work of H. de Lubac, mentioned in note 54. Cf. also P. Grelot, *Sens chrétien de l'Ancien Testament* (Tournai: Desclée et Cie., 1962); Grelot speaks (p. 216, n. 3) of the "intemperate allegorizing" of certain Catholic scholars and the "excessive reaction" of others (names and titles listed in both cases). J. Daniélou in *From Shadows to Reality* favors typology rather than allegory; but some of the types he defends as legitimate are, in my view at least, indistinguishable from allegory.

[60] The literature is extensive, and I am by no means familiar with all of it. For a useful summary of the discussion, see R. E. Brown, "The *Sensus Plenior* in the Last Ten Years," *CBQ*, XXV (1963), 262-85. Brown defends the *sensus plenior*; see also, for example, J. Coppens, *Les harmonies des deux Testaments* (Tournai and Paris: Casterman, 1949); P. Benoit, "La plenitude de sens des Livres Saints," *RB* LXVII (1960), 161-96. For a contrary opinion, see the splendid articles of J. L. McKenzie, "The Significance of the Old Testament for Christian Faith in Roman Catholicism" in *OTCF*, pp. 102-14, and "Problems of Hermeneutics in Roman Catholic Exegesis," *JBL*, LXXVII (1958), 197-204; see also B. Vawter, "The Fuller Sense: Some Considerations," *CBQ*, XXVI (1964), 85-96.

a turning point in Protestant dogmatics. As is well known, Barth sees Christ as the true subject of the whole of the biblical revelation and the key to its proper understanding. His interpretation of Scripture—including the Old Testament—is, therefore, strongly christological and goes far beyond a grammatico-historical exegesis of the text. Whatever one says of this, Barth certainly reminded the church that it needs far more from its Bible than mere scholarly objectivity can give. And many of the church's teachers agreed.

Among biblical scholars who have adopted a christological approach to the Old Testament, the name of Wilhelm Vischer stands out.[61] Vischer stands in the Reformed tradition and is apparently quite close to Barth. But he also reaches back to Luther, whom he quotes repeatedly and whose christological interpretations he frequently adopts. Vischer has been the target of a great deal of criticism, even scornful criticism, not a little of which one feels to be unjust. He has again and again been called a typologist, or even an allegorist, and accused of all sorts of irresponsibility in his handling of the text. But this is, I believe, to misunderstand Vischer's intention, for he explicitly disclaims typology (to say nothing of allegory), affirms the validity of grammatico-historical principles of exegesis, and insists that the text is not to be spiritualized but must be interpreted in its plain meaning.[62] But this plain meaning is to Vischer, as to the Reformers, its meaning in the light of God's intention as revealed in Jesus Christ. Vischer has, if I understand him at all, a preacher's concern that the Old Testament be accorded its rightful place in the church's proclamation. For this purpose, he feels that a purely historical exegesis of the Old Testament is not enough, for that would leave the Old Testament a document of an ancient religion of little apparent relevance to the Christian. The Bible, including the Old Testament, must be interpreted in the light of its true intention, its true theme. And that true theme is Christ; "the Bible is the Holy Scripture only insofar as it speaks of Christ Jesus."[63] But if Christ is the theme of the whole of Scripture, then

[61] See *Das Christuszeugnis des Alten Testaments* (Zollikon-Zürich: Evangelischer Verlag, Vol. I, 7th ed., Vol. II:1, 2nd ed., 1946). Vol. I of this work, trans. from the 3rd ed. (1936) is available in English as *The Witness of the Old Testament to Christ*, trans. A. B. Crabtree (London: Lutterworth, 1949); citations from this volume will follow the English ed.

[62] Vischer's principles are set forth in *The Witness of the Old Testament to Christ*, pp. 7-34. For a more recent, and perhaps even clearer, statement see his "La méthode de l'exégèse biblique," *RThPh* X (1960), 109-23.

[63] Cf. *The Witness of the Old Testament to Christ*, I, 14.

an exegesis that examines each of its texts for what they have to say of him is the one that corresponds to its true intention. Vischer therefore reads the Old Testament for its witness to Christ. And he finds that it everywhere testifies of Christ—not in the sense, to be sure, that he is directly to be found in the Old Testament, but in the sense that the Old Testament in all its parts points to him and his crucifixion. Indeed Vischer says that the Old Testament has already told us *what* the Christ is; it remains only for the New to tell us *who* he is.[64] If we do not understand what the Christ is as the Old Testament presents him, we shall never recognize and confess Jesus as the Christ.[65]

On the basis of these principles Vischer provides us with an interpretation of the Old Testament that is fully christological. Many have found it disturbing. Not only does the Old Testament as a whole point to Christ and testify of Christ; in each smallest detail the Christian eye may see some witness to him. Thus the command, "Let there be light" (Gen. 1:3), speaks to us of "the glory of God in the face of Christ" (II Cor. 4:6). Indeed the whole chapter speaks of Christ, for he is the Word who was in the beginning with God (John 1:1-5).[66] The sign of Cain (Gen. 4:15) points to the cross and is renewed in the sign of the cross.[67] Enoch is a sign and witness of the resurrection.[68] The anthropomorphic language of Hos. 11 and Jer. 31:18-20 points to the passion of the Son of man.[69] The prophecy that Japheth would "dwell in the tents of Shem" pictures the church, which includes both Gentiles and Jews.[70] Speaking of the midnight Presence with whom Jacob wrestled at the ford of Jabbok (Gen. 32), Vischer asks who this person was; and he adopts Luther's answer and says, "Jesus Christ is . . . the undeclared name of this man."[71] In Ehud's sword, plunged into the fat belly of the Moabite king (Judg. 3:12-30), Vischer sees "the word of God . . . sharper than any two-edged sword" (Heb. 4:12) unsheathed against God's foes; he finds in the incident biblical justification of the right to assassinate tyrants.[72] Commenting upon Solomon's judgment between the two women in I Kings 3,

[64] *Ibid.*, I, 7.
[65] *Ibid.*, I, 12, 26.
[66] *Ibid.*, I, 44, 51.
[67] *Ibid.*, I, 75-76.
[68] *Ibid.*, I, 87-88.
[69] *Ibid.*, I, 95-96.
[70] *Ibid.*, I, 104-5.
[71] *Ibid.*, I, 153.
[72] *Ibid.*, II, 89.

he remarks that "the true Israel is the true mother of the living child," and then goes on to relate the incident to Mary and the child Jesus in the temple (Luke 2:22-35). [73] Further examples could be added at random, but these will suffice to illustrate Vischer's method.

It is understandable that this approach should have evoked criticism. Does it not represent a complete disregard of grammatico-historical principles of exegesis and an arbitrary imposition of meaning upon the Old Testament text, and does this not in turn throw open the gates to every conceivable vagary of interpretation? I am sure that this is not Vischer's intention. One certainly cannot accuse him of unawareness of the principles of scientific exegesis or want of concern for them. He is an extremely competent scholar who insists upon a historical and philological approach to the biblical text and who is the author of many valuable studies in the best exegetical tradition. But Vischer writes here—or so it seems to me—not as a scholar in his study preparing a learned monograph, but as a preacher and a teacher of preachers concerned to present the Old Testament as the Word of God to the church. In doing this he leaps, almost intuitively as it were, from the text itself to its Christian significance, which to him is its true significance. But so swiftly is this done, and often without indication of transition, that the reader is not always certain just where the leap is taken and might readily gain the impression that Vischer has arbitrarily read New Testament ideas back into the Old Testament texts themselves. To put it another way, in the case of almost every text, historical meaning and theological interpretation are telescoped, with the result that it is not always clear to the reader which he is being offered. Statements that may well be regarded as having dogmatic validity seem to be presented as exegetical statements. The exegesis of the Old Testament is controlled from the side of the New. Or rather, what is actually an interpretation of the Old Testament in the light of the New is so presented that it will appear, at least to the unwary reader, to be proposed as an exegesis of the Old Testament text itself. Vischer certainly deserves thanks for being among the first to remind us that we cannot rest content with a purely historical understanding of the Old Testament but must press on to see it in its Christian significance. But in attempting to do this, we must be careful to hear the Old Testament's own word in its plain meaning. We must not so consistently read the Old Testament from the side of the New

[73] *Ibid.*, II, 295.

that the Old is deprived of its own distinctive witness and made everywhere to echo the New Testament's voice.

If Vischer has been the outstanding biblical scholar to advocate a consistently christological interpretation of the Old Testament, he is by no means the only one to insist that the Old Testament must in some way be read beyond its historical sense, if it is to be saved for the church. Various voices have been raised to similar effect, especially in Great Britain. G. S. Hendry, for example, greeted Vischer's work with enthusiasm and hailed Vischer as "a second Wellhausen" (by which he meant that Vischer, in refusing to interpret only in the historical sense, marked a reversal of the trend established by the Wellhausen school).[74] Hendry attacked the assumption that the historical sense is the only true sense and declared that all exposition of Scripture must be allegorical. This alarming statement is, however, somewhat blunted when Hendry adds that all preaching is allegorical in that it says other things than the literal sense of the text (surely a broad use of the word "allegory"). More recently, R. S. Wallace has defended the right of the expositor to resort to allegory when circumstances seem to justify it.[75] But the word is again used loosely. Wallace does not find hidden meanings in the text but rather observes a correspondence of pattern in God's dealings with men at various times. Thus, for example, he finds an analogy between Elijah being fed by the ravens and Christ feeding us at the Lord's Table; or between Elisha healing the poisoned waters with a sign (salt) and a word, and Christ who heals us with his word and gives us the sign of the sacraments; or between Elisha stretching himself on the body of the Shunammite woman's son and the self-humiliation of Christ.[76] This is not allegory, but imaginative homiletics. But it illustrates the feeling of many that the Old Testament can be meaningful to the congregation only if it can be made to speak to them in some way specifically of Christ.

The above are not isolated examples. Over the years a number of scholars in Great Britain have been calling for a return to a "mystical" interpretation of the Old Testament. Nearly forty years ago Darwell Stone expressed his fear that the church would not long be able to retain the

---

[74] "The Exposition of Holy Scripture," *SJT*, I (1948), 29-47.

[75] *Elijah and Elisha: Expositions from the Book of Kings* (Edinburgh and London: Oliver and Boyd, 1957).

[76] These illustrations will be found in Wallace, *Elijah and Elisha*, pp. 11-12, 95-96, 117, respectively. Others could be added. James Barr, in the foreword, has correctly pointed out that Wallace for the most part interprets analogically.

Old Testament for use in public worship unless it could be interpreted in something more than its literal sense.[77] For example, the story of Jael's murder of Sisera (Judg. 4) is shocking and morally repellent, but it gains real spiritual value if we can see in it, as Augustine did, the church conquering the Devil through the cross. It should be added, however, that Stone—like Aquinas—felt that points of doctrine could be based only on the literal sense. More recently, A. G. Hebert has announced his complete agreement with Stone and expressed his belief that mystical interpretations have their use for illustrative and homiletical purposes, provided that the literal meaning is not invoked in their support.[78] R. V. G. Tasker also cites Stone with approval and declares that the literal meaning of a passage is not always its whole meaning but that there is frequently "a further or allegorical sense" which can be discovered by appeal to other passages where the meaning is clear.[79] Other examples could be added, but these must suffice.[80]

The views of the above scholars—and others—are by no means identical and are not to be grouped hastily under a single rubric. But they have a family likeness in that they spring from a common understanding of the problem. All are alike expressive of the strongly held conviction that, on the one hand, the church needs the Old Testament and cannot do without it and that, on the other, she cannot be asked to "take it straight"; some meaning over and above its plain, historical meaning must be added if she is to stomach it.

4. Let it be repeated that the above scholars are primarily concerned to save the Old Testament for the church. For my part, I share that concern to the hilt. Yet I find it impossible to be happy with the means by which they would achieve this end. However strongly these scholars may insist that interpretation must begin with the plain meaning of the

[77] "The Mystical Interpretation of the Old Testament" in Charles Gore et al., eds., A New Commentary on Holy Scripture (New York: The Macmillan Company, 1929), Part I, pp. 688-96.
[78] The Throne of David (London: Faber & Faber, 1941), esp. pp. 33-38, 256-65; see further Hebert, The Authority of the Old Testament (London: Faber & Faber, 1947), Ch. IX.
[79] The Old Testament in the New Testament (Philadelphia: The Westminster Press, 1947), p. 17.
[80] In particular, the works of L. S. Thornton and A. M. Farrer deserve mention; but space forbids further discussion. See, for example, the remarks of G. W. H. Lampe in Lampe and Woollcombe, Essays on Typology (London: SCM Press, 1957), pp. 18-22, 37-38; or E. C. Blackman, Biblical Interpretation (Philadelphia: The Westminster Press, 1957), pp. 162-65.

text, they too quickly run beyond the plain meaning to expound another meaning, clearly not within the intention of the writer and not deducible from his words. At all costs the plain meaning is to be preserved. The Old Testament cannot be appealed to as authoritative in the church, or proclaimed with authority, unless its plain meaning is adhered to, and adhered to plainly. Once the plain meaning has been abandoned, control over interpretation is gone and Scripture may mean anything the spirit (and who shall say if it be the Holy Spirit or the preacher's?) may see in it. The sky is the limit! If it is permissible to find mystical meanings in the text, then the reader may, I may, and everybody may; and Scripture therewith ceases to be a usable norm, because no agreement as to its meaning is any longer possible. To say that the Old Testament can retain its place in the church only if specifically Christian meanings can be found in its texts comes perilously close to saying that it can be regarded as canonical Scripture only when given a meaning other than the one it plainly intended. To be sure, the Christian must interpret his Old Testament in the light of what the New Testament affirms about it. We shall say more of that later. But the Old Testament must be allowed to speak its own word, not required to produce in a veiled way a message identical with that of the New.

But perhaps someone will say: "Did not the New Testament writers go far beyond the literal sense in their understanding of the Old Testament? Did they not resort to typology? Did they not find in many an Old Testament passage allusions to Christ and his work that were surely not in the original author's mind?" Answer to all questions, "Yes." The New Testament writers repeatedly saw Christ and his work prefigured in persons and events of the Old Testament (in Adam, Melchizedek, Moses, David, etc.), and they repeatedly saw prophecies of him in Old Testament passages that originally had other meanings (for example, Matt. 2:15 refers the words of Hos. 11:1, "Out of Egypt I called my son," to the sojourn of the child Jesus in Egypt, although Hosea himself was clearly speaking of the Exodus). Examples could be multiplied. [81] In the exegesis of such passages this procedure is to be recognized, and the intention of the writer in adopting it as far as possible laid bare. This typological-chris-

[81] On the use of the Old Testament by the New various works may be commended. See, for example, S. Amsler, *L'Ancien Testament dans l'Église* (Neuchâtel: Delachaux et Niestlé, 1960); C. H. Dodd, *According to the Scriptures*; R. V. G. Tasker, *The Old Testament in the New Testament*; L. Goppelt, *Typos* (Gütersloh: C. Bertelsmann, 1939).

tological use of the Old Testament is thus a part of New Testament theology, and grammatico-historical exegesis will be the first to recognize it as such. But this does not give us the right to make typology into an exegetical method. Not only is this procedure on the part of the New Testament writers not exegesis as we would understand the term; it scarcely represents a systematic attempt at exegesis at all, but rather is a more or less charismatic expression of these writers' conviction that *all* Scripture—nay, all that had ever happened in Israel—had come to fulfillment in Christ. Their appeal to the Old Testament was intuitive rather than exegetical, a reinterpretation of its meaning on the basis of the new understanding of God's purpose that had been given them. They found types in the Old Testament not as a result of grubbing through its texts in search of hidden meaning but because they had already seen a new significance in all Israel's history in the light of Christ.

Typology, therefore, cannot be used as a tool for the exegesis of Old Testament texts, nor can it reveal in them levels of meaning not discoverable by normal exegetical procedure. Let us say it clearly: The text has but one meaning, the meaning intended by its author; and there is but one method for discovering that meaning, the grammatico-historical method. If types were intended by the author (and sometimes they were), grammatico-historical exegesis will discover them; if not, then they cannot be discovered by exegetical method at all. Exegesis has the task of discovering, through careful historical and philological examination of the text, the meaning that its author intended to convey, and it can never legitimately go beyond that task. Typology, on the contrary, has to do with the later interpretation of texts—or, better, of the events described in them—and is a way of expressing the new significance that is seen in them in the light of later events.[82] The New Testament writers, of course,

---

[82] It is my strong conviction that the word "exegesis" is best confined to its narrowest connotation—namely, with reference to the task of making clear the precise meaning of the text that is being dealt with. To broaden it so that it becomes interchangeable with "interpretation" invites confusion—as when one hears of "typological exegesis" (there may be a typological *interpretation*, but there is no allowable exegesis save grammatico-historical). The conventional distinction between exegesis and hermeneutics, according to which hermeneutics refers to the theory or art of interpretation, exegesis to its practical execution, is unrealistic, and should be abandoned. I should prefer to regard hermeneutics as denoting the entire interpretive process that lies between the bare Greek or Hebrew text of the Bible and its exposition in its contemporary significance, with exegesis as the first step in that process. For a sketch of the history of these terms see J. M. Robinson in Robinson and J. B. Cobb, eds., *The New Hermeneutic* (New York: Harper & Row, 1964), esp. pp. 1-7.

interpreted the Old Testament in the light of Christ, and in doing so they saw him prefigured and alluded to in many of its texts. Grammatico-historical exegesis of the New Testament (not the Old) reveals this. Now as a Christian one may find this procedure theologically legitimate (it is not an exegetical procedure) and may agree that there is much in the Old Testament that is analogous to, suggests and prepares for, the work of Christ, and that takes on an entirely new significance in the light of that fact. One may even go further and find correspondences between the Testaments beyond those observed by the New Testament writers, and one may, if one cares to, interpret these as divinely given types. But one must be very cautious in this regard lest interpretation of the Old Testament be turned into a game. Typology is a way, and one most difficult to control, of interpreting the Old Testament to the church in its Christian significance. But it is not a substitute method of exegesis. Whatever our zeal to find a Christian significance in the Old Testament, we are on no account permitted to foist meanings upon its text not deducible by grammatico-historical principles, or so to expound them as to convey the impression that they actually contain such meaning. To expound the Old Testament in this way is not to expound the *Old* Testament.[83]

But perhaps some would wish to ask if it is not possible that there may be in the Old Testament text itself a meaning beyond the plain and obvious one, a deeper meaning intended by God, call it a *sensus plenior,* or a *sensus literalis propheticus,* or what you will. If that question is asked, I should, for one, be obliged on theological grounds to answer: In principle, yes. The God of the New Testament is the God of the Old; and who is to place limits upon what he may have intended through the words and deeds

---

[83] It should be evident that none of the foregoing remarks are intended to refer to the typological interpretation of the Old Testament currently advocated in Germany by Gerhard von Rad and others. These scholars specifically disavow any search for hidden meaning in the Old Testament text and insist that its plain, historical sense is to be preserved. But, viewing the unity of the Bible in terms of a *Heilsgeschichte* (or, perhaps better, in terms of the schema: promise-fulfillment), they see the Old Testament as the witness to a series of divine acts which are oriented toward, are analogous to, and derive their ultimate significance from, the definitive divine act of the New Testament. They therefore feel that the saving acts of God in the Old Testament, and the attendant demands and promises, may legitimately be understood *in their plain sense* as anticipating and foreshadowing the final saving act, and thus as being "typical" of it in analogous sense. The adequacy of this approach as a hermeneutical method will concern us in a later chapter. But it is not typology in the conventional sense and has no place in the discussion here. Indeed, it may be questioned if it is wise to call it typology at all, as von Rad himself admits (see *EOTH,* pp. 38-39; also H. W. Wolff, *EOTH,* pp. 181-82, n. 74); other scholars of this same general approach refrain from using the word.

of his ancient servants? Conceded! But that does not change the exegetical task. Whatever fuller sense a text may conceal, if such there be, it lies beyond exegetical control. Exegesis can only by a grammatical analysis of the text in the light of its context determine what the writer meant to convey by his words; if there is some deeper meaning not deducible from his words, exegesis cannot discern it. To put it bluntly but quite fairly, one can make an exegesis of texts, but one cannot make an exegesis of the Holy Spirit's intention. The Holy Spirit is like a wind that "blows where it will," and is not subject to the control of the exegete's tools. By exegesis one can see what the words of a text meant in their original context, and by further exegesis one can now and then discover what they came to signify to later generations, and finally to the New Testament writers. And from this one may learn much of the Christian significance of the Old Testament—and (who shall say?) of God's own intention.[84] But one cannot reverse the exegetical process and read the New Testament's understanding of the Old back into the Old Testament texts. These must be interpreted in their plain meaning, which is the only meaning that can be discovered in them by exegesis.

But can the exegete be satisfied merely to expound his text in its historical meaning? Must he not go beyond that if he would complete his task? Indeed he must. He must if he is also a preacher or a teacher who understands his scholarship as being in the service of the church. A sermon is not an exegetical lecture. Every exposition of the Word before the congregation, every sermon, must go beyond the bare historical meaning of the text and interpret it in terms of something else, specifically in terms of the contemporary situation. But whatever interpretation is given must conform to the historical meaning and be controlled by it and must be a legitimate extension and application of it, else it misrepresents the text. The preacher may not tell himself that he is free to depart from the plain intention of his text and to draw from it whatever lessons he pleases— provided, of course, that these be edifying and in accord with Christian truth generally. This is an attitude that is deplorably common among our preachers; professors of homiletics have been known to defend it. And admittedly, since few preachers actually contradict Christian teaching in their sermons, what results is seldom positively damaging, being for the

---

[84] I think that this is essentially what my Roman Catholic colleague J. L. McKenzie is saying in his criticism of the *sensus plenior*; see the articles cited in note 60.

most part a dreary but harmless moralizing. But the principle is precisely the one that was allowed by the patristic and medieval allegorizers and rejected outright by the Reformers. And it is the breakdown of preaching. Preaching, effectively released from exegetical control, is delivered over to subjectivism. Indeed, it is no longer the biblical word that is heard, but the preacher's superimposed reflections.

Just so, the Old Testament must be interpreted beyond its plain historical meaning in its Christian significance and contemporary relevance. We shall say more of that later. But whatever interpretation is given must develop the plain meaning and be controlled by it. If the Old Testament cannot be saved for the church by finding hidden meaning in its texts through allegory or other means, it cannot be saved by edifying homiletics either. The preacher who can preach from the Old Testament only by moralizing from it, spiritualizing it, or otherwise drawing Christian inferences from it, has in effect resorted to a disguised sort of allegory. He has perhaps not been so unscientific as actually to find a multiple sense in the text: his training has probably been too sound to allow him to do that. But the practical effect is the same. He has consciously disregarded the plain meaning of the text in order to proclaim another and (he thinks) more edifying meaning, perhaps not even tenuously related to the plain meaning, no doubt telling himself that only so can he make the Old Testament acceptable and meaningful to his congregation. The congregation has not been allowed to hear the Old Testament's own word, but something homiletically superimposed. But if the Old Testament can be preached in the church only by disregarding its plain meaning and rushing on to preach some "more Christian" meaning, what reason is there to preach from it at all? The game has been forfeited to Marcion.

III

We have examined the two classical solutions to the problem of the Old Testament which, in one form or another, have been proposed ever since the church's infancy, and we have rejected them. We cannot depose the Old Testament from canonical rank lest we do irreparable damage to the gospel itself and, equally, we cannot essay to save it by imposing Christian meaning upon it else responsible interpretation is at an end and, with it, all possibility of appealing to the Old Testament in matters of faith and practice. But what then? Are we still impaled on the horns of the second-century dilemma, as some insist? [85] Or has some *via media* been found between the classical solutions which would at least allow us to retain the Old Testament in the Bible, while doing no violence to sound exegetical principles? In modern times such a third solution has in fact been proposed. It is one that has seemed satisfactory to many and is widely accepted, though not always consciously, today. This solution, like the other two, takes the New Testament as its point of orientation and views the Old from that perspective. But not to reject it out of hand, and certainly not to spiritualize it. Rather, a value judgment is formed on the basis of New Testament teaching, which is then imposed on the contents of the Old, thereby to separate elements of abiding validity from the ancient, sub-Christian, and outworn.

1. This has been the answer of liberal Protestantism generally. Perhaps it is unfair to identify it so specifically with liberalism, for the imposing of external canons of evaluation on the Old Testament can be observed as far back as the rationalistic thinkers of the eighteenth century and before;[86] and there are many today who follow such a procedure who would emphatically disclaim the epithet "liberal." Still, since this answer found its clearest expression, and was all but universally accepted, in the classical Protestant liberalism of the last century and the early decades of this, the identification is not unjust. Liberal theology, though it sought to retain its footing in historic Christianity, based itself also on modern knowledge and thought and, recognizing the elements of truth contained in each, sought to bridge the gap between them in such a way that Christian truth might be stated in terms rationally acceptable to modern man.[87] It is not our task to discuss liberal theology in general. But its understanding of the Old Testament found its most congenial expression in the approach

---

[85] See, for example, Lampe, *Essays on Typology*, p. 17. Lampe argues (pp. 9-38) for "The Reasonableness of Typology"—by which, of course, he means a legitimate typology that rests upon real correspondences between historical events within the framework of revelation, not upon artificial and unhistorical similarities (but even this last, he feels, has a place in homiletics).

[86] As is well known, Luther employed as his canon of evaluation "what urges Christ," and on the basis of this found certain books of the Old Testament (e.g. Esther) of distinctly inferior value. Would anyone wish to call Luther a liberal?

[87] The definition follows H. P. Van Dusen, "Liberal Theology Reassessed," USQR XVIII (1963), pp. 343-55. Van Dusen's further distinction between "evangelical liberalism" and "modernism" (which took its stand wholly in modern thought and knowledge and then sought to reclaim as much of historic Christianity as it could) is undoubtedly valid; but the line between the two cannot always be sharply drawn. The remarks in this section apply to both, albeit perhaps *a fortiori* to "modernism."

of Julius Wellhausen and his school, an approach which dominated Old Testament studies from the latter part of the nineteenth century until a very short while ago.

That liberalism, to speak in general, operated from a view of Scripture quite different from that of more conservative Protestantism, specifically of orthodoxy, needs hardly to be said. To begin with, it stressed an aspect of Scripture that had been too largely ignored by orthodoxy—namely, its human aspect. The Bible, whatever else it might be held to be, was understood primarily as the religious literature of an ancient people which, like any other human literature, is to be studied by the critical and historical method. Its authors were seen as men of vastly differing perception and depth; but all were men, and all were children of the age in which they lived. The Bible, in a word, was seen as a historically conditioned book. Whatever Word of God might be held to speak through its pages was seen as mediated through the limitations of ancient men in an ancient age. Like all humans, they were fallible. Nor did divine inspiration—whatever place this may have been accorded—guard them from errors of fact or from shortcomings in moral and religious understanding. In addition to this, whereas orthodoxy had stressed primarily the soteriological aspects of Christianity and had looked to the Bible as the infallible source of those doctrines essential for salvation, liberalism—again to speak in general—tended to stress the ethical, moral, and social aspects of religion and to evaluate the various parts of the Bible according to the elevation of their teachings in this regard.

But if one evaluates the Bible from the point of view of its ethical and religious ideas, it at once becomes apparent that it does not all stand on the same level. This is particularly true of the Old Testament, where one may find many levels of moral and spiritual insight from the most rudimentary (from a modern's point of view, at least) to the highest and noblest, great stress on the cult together with hostility to the cult, religious institutions that are highly organized together with religious practice that is simple and spontaneous. As a result of the labors of Wellhausen and his colleagues, it was thought possible to trace through the Old Testament a coherent pattern of development. By ranking the documents of the Old Testament chronologically, in good part on the basis of the level of religious development observable in them, Wellhausen presented Israel's religion as one that had, within the Old Testament period, evolved from lower forms to higher, undergoing a fundamental change of character

97

along the way. It had its beginnings in the primitive polydaemonism of the Hebrew ancestors, subsequently developed into a tribal religion with its tribal God, then into a national cultus, and then through the work of those great creative personalities, the prophets, attained at length to the heights of ethical monotheism before finally solidifying into the law religion of Judaism.[88] Other scholars presented similar reconstructions, all with the watchword "development." To the mind of the day, imbued as it was with notions of unilinear evolutionary progress, this had about it an aura of self-evidence that caused it to be accepted with enthusiasm by virtually the whole of the scholarly world.

With this understanding of its history, theologians came to view the Old Testament as the record of the development of the Hebrew people in the realm of religion and ethics (or, theistically stated, as the record of God's progressive revelation of himself), which led up to and prepared the way for Christianity. The goal and the crown of this developmental process was thus seen as lying beyond the bounds of the Old Testament, in the New. It is here, in Jesus and his teachings, that the highest and best in the Bible is to be found. [89] But whatever authority the Bible may have over the faith and life of the Christian, it goes without saying, must reside in its highest level. In other words, it is the mind and teachings of Jesus that are the Christian's norm, that and nothing else. That is the norm, and the Bible itself is to be evaluated in the light of it. Such authority as it may possess is confined to those parts that exhibit levels of ethics and religion consonant with the teachings of Jesus. All else represents, to a greater or lesser degree, outgrown stages in man's religious development, and is in no way normative for the Christian.[90]

[88] See J. Wellhausen, *Geschichte Israels,* I (Berlin, 1878); trans. Black and Menzies, as *Prolegomena to the History of Israel* (Edinburgh: A. & C. Black, 1885). This book is now available in paperback (New York: Meridian Books, 1957).

[89] It would be tedious to cite instances of this view of the Old Testament. It was, with variations, *the* dominant view among critics and liberal theologians from the latter part of the last century until the twenties and thirties of this. See Kraeling, *The Old Testament Since the Reformation,* Chs. 9 and 12, for example after example from Germany, Great Britain, and America. The reader will find an exceedingly lucid, popular presentation of it in H. E. Fosdick, *A Guide to Understanding the Bible* (New York: Harper & Row, 1938); and see the review by W. Eichrodt (with English summary by W. F. Albright) in *JBL,* LXV (1946), 205-17.

[90] This view of the matter could again be documented endlessly. I know of no clearer expression of it than is found in the concluding pages of F. W. Farrar's book *History of Interpretation,* where, with homiletical fervor, he sums up his own position. See, for example, p. 431: "Is it not enough that, to us, the test of God's word is the teaching of Him who is the Word of God? Is it not an absolutely plain and simple rule that anything

2. Now it is obvious that this understanding of the Old Testament had a bearing upon the problem of its place in the canon. It seemed to answer many of the questions. In that it neither advocated the summary dismissal of the Old Testament nor did violence to sound exegetical procedure, it appeared to avoid the second-century dilemma. Moreover, it provided a plausible means of dealing with those passages in the Old Testament which describe ancient customs and conceptions, vengeful attitudes, immoral actions, bloodthirsty deeds done, perhaps, in the name of God, which had always been troublesome to the Christian conscience. What an embarrassment such passages had been to many a pastor! People continually asked him how such things could be harmonized with the teachings of Jesus, how a Christian could find in them edification and guidance, or if indeed he could receive them as the word of his God at all. And the pastor, too honest to evade the problem, yet having himself no clear answer to it, had been puzzled to know what to say. But here was an answer that relieved him of the embarrassment. How does one harmonize such things with the teachings of Jesus? One doesn't have to! What authority have they over the faith and life of the Christian? None! After all, it is not the Bible as such that is the Christian's norm, but Jesus and his teachings. The Bible itself is to be judged by that norm. As for the Old Testament, since it tells of God's education of his people preparatory to the supreme revelation in Christ, it is only to be expected that it will contain, along with much that measures up to the Christian level, or nearly so, a great deal that does not. But this simply represents, so to speak, the limited comprehension of pupils—perhaps backward pupils at that—in the lower grades of God's school [91] and is to be understood, sympathetically yet critically, as such by the mature Christian.

A logically consistent answer indeed, and to many a satisfying one. Yet it meant that large parts of the Old Testament were seen as of little relevance to the Christian and were as effectively cut from his Bible as if snipped out with scissors. This is not to imply that liberal Christians generally advocated a formal expurgation of the Old Testament. On the contrary, the Old Testament was prized as a document of immense

---

in the Bible which teaches or seems to teach anything which is not in accordance with the love, the gentleness, the truthfulness, the purity of Christ's gospel, is not God's word to us, however clearly it stands on the Bible page?"

[91] The metaphor is borrowed from Leonard Hodgson, who views the matter in this way. See *On the Authority of the Bible*, p. 7.

historical and religious importance, and far too much of value was found even in its less edifying parts for responsible students to wish to see it mutilated by wholesale excisions. But at the practical level the result was much the same: large parts of the Old Testament effectively lost their place in the church's canon. The liberal's canon was actually Jesus himself. And this meant that, for all practical purposes, his Bible tended to become a rather small one: the life and teachings of Jesus and such other passages as might be held, from a moral and spiritual point of view, to stand on a level with them, or approximately so. Much of the Old Testament, of course, did not meet these specifications. Indeed, aside from the Ten Commandments, narrative accounts from which some edifying example or stray moral lesson might be extracted, selected psalms (and how careful one must be in selecting!), and the nobler utterances of the prophets, most of it tended to slip into disuse.

There was, in fact, a certain Marcionist tendency in liberalism, albeit for the most part not consciously recognized or explicitly admitted.[92] That is to say, there was a tendency tacitly to dispense with the Old Testament where matters of doctrine were concerned and to derive the tenets of the faith all but exclusively from the New. Nor was this tendency confined to theologians, for there were many in the rank and file of the church who found little use for the Old Testament and who professed what they more or less vaguely conceived to be "a New Testament religion." It was really inevitable. After all, if the Old Testament is but the record of a long and painful progress preparatory to the coming of Christ, now that we have Christ, what profit is there in retracing these blundering, preliminary steps? Ought not faith and life to be based on the completion, the perfection, on Christ and his gospel alone? The tendency to regard the Old Testament as but a prelude to the gospel, and therefore of secondary importance, has been widespread in the church. To be sure, its importance as background for the understanding of the gospel has never been seriously questioned. But does the busy pastor really have need of so much technical background knowledge? Could that not be left to the scholars, who have time for such unpreachable pursuits? The theological student, appalled

---

[92] It did become explicit in such scholars as Harnack, as it had in Schleiermacher long before; both were liberal theologians, and both declared that points of doctrine could not be based on Old Testament texts. H. Gunkel expressed himself similarly (cf. Kraus, *Geschichte* . . . , p. 333). Other examples could readily be adduced (cf. Kraeling, *The Old Testament Since the Reformation*, ch. 12).

at the narrow gate of Hebrew through which he was told he must enter the garden of the Old Testament, and not altogether convinced of the importance of entering, balked at that gate like a mule and was content thereafter to survey the garden, as it were, from the outside. The preacher left it aside in his preaching—save perhaps for occasional character studies of Old Testament worthies who, presented as moral examples, emerged from the process fearsomely like model elders and deacons. And not a few authorities in religious education, feeling the Old Testament's vivid narratives to be largely unsuitable for the tender ears of children, refrained form presenting them at all, save in a drastically expurgated form.

The liberal's approach to the Old Testament did indeed bring behind it into the church at least the camel's nose of Marcionism. It is in any event an ironical fact that it was precisely in the heyday of the critical, historical, and philological study of the Old Testament so brilliantly set forward by scholars in Wellhausen's tradition that the theological relevance of that study was increasingly called into question. Is it essential to the preparation of the minister? Does it fit him for his pastoral offce? Is it properly a theological subject at all, or ought it to be tranferred to some other department and something else substituted for it? Wellhausen himself seems to have asked these questions.[93] Nor was he the only one to do so. In the minds of many, Old Testament studies came to occupy an ambiguous position within the theological curriculum. And many a professor of Old Testament must have felt his place in a faculty of theology to be likewise ambiguous.

3. Nevertheless, in spite of the fact that liberal theology found its true canon in the New Testament and tended to subordinate the Old to the New, to say that it constructed a New Testament religion would not be strictly accurate. The New Testament was itself involved in the problem. Marcion's scissors always slip! Or to put it otherwise, he who feels free to excerpt from the Old Testament on the basis of a value judgment will feel equally free where the New Testament is concerned. Although there is little or nothing in the New Testament that the Christian would find morally troublesome, there is much there, no less than in the Old, that

[93] See A. Jepsen, *EOTH*, pp. 246-47. Wellhausen in 1882 resigned from the theological faculty at Greifswald and transferred to the faculty of Semitic languages at Halle because, as he himself said, he feared that his approach to the Old Testament was, in spite of all reserve on his part, unfitting his students for the ministry.

THE AUTHORITY OF THE OLD TESTAMENT

the modern, scientifically trained mind finds difficult. One thinks, for example, of its pre-Copernican world view—the three-story universe consisting of a flat earth with heaven arching above and hell lying beneath. One thinks too of its view of this earth as the battleground of angelic and demonic forces; of the frankly miraculous which contravenes natural law as we know it; of eschatological expectations couched in the language of Jewish apocalyptic; of the early church's confidence in the imminent return of Christ on the clouds of heaven—and more besides. The mature believer may indeed not be troubled by these things. But we are blind if we do not realize that for many people they constitute a real difficulty. Can modern man really be expected to believe such things? Must he express his faith in these terms if he would pretend to be a Christian? Since the Age of Enlightenment many have returned a negative answer. It is, therefore, scarcely surprising that scholars who were inclined to see the essence of Christianity in the life, example, and teachings of Jesus should view such things as accretions upon the gospel, the beliefs of a prescientific age which must be peeled away if we would see the gospel in its pristine purity. Nay, it was held necessary to do this. If the Christian is to take Jesus himself as his norm, it must be none other than the unencumbered Jesus of history, not a Jesus obscured by later reflection.

So it was that liberal New Testament scholars of the past century set out on their "quest of the historical Jesus." [94] Jesus must be separated not only from the ancient world view with which the New Testament is burdened but also from the proclamation of the New Testament writers about him, for this sadly misunderstood him. One must get behind the theological assertions of Paul and John and the rest, behind eschatological trappings and messianic expectations, to recover the Jesus who actually lived and taught in Galilee and Jerusalem, for it is he alone who is the source of our faith and the norm of our conduct. It was believed that this operation, if admittedly difficult, was possible. Let one but remove from the New Testament message these extraneous elements so difficult for the modern mind, and there will emerge the figure of the Master who by precept and example propounded eternally valid teachings concerning the

[94] See especially Albert Schweitzer, *Geschichte der Leben-Jesu Forschung* (2nd ed.; Tübingen: J. C. B. Mohr, 1913); trans. W. Montgomery, as *The Quest of the Historical Jesus* (London: A. & C. Black, 1910; reprinted New York: The Macmillan Company, 1948). Schweitzer's critique of this "quest" was devastating and did much to put an end to it (albeit, be it noted, his own view of the historical Jesus was quite as radical in the opposite direction).

fatherhood of God, the infinite value of the human soul, and the present reality of God's kingdom within the hearts of all who have accepted his command to love. This was, with variations, the real Jesus of history as he was widely presented: the great teacher, the prophet, who came to tell men of the love of God and to ask them to live in love with one another. And this Jesus, created by considerable critical ingenuity, became through wide areas of the church—though often in forms hardly more than caricature ("gentle Jesus, meek and mild")—to all intents and purposes the sole supreme authority in matters of faith and practice, and the canon by which the validity of Scripture itself was judged.

4. But perhaps some will wish to ask if we have not been guilty of whipping a dead horse. Has not the approach to the Bible just described, together with the liberal theology that supported it, long since been abandoned in scholarly circles? Is it not, therefore, a bit misleading—not to say unfair—to belabor it as if it were still a live option before the church today? It might seem so. The older liberalism, with its abounding optimism regarding the perfectibility of man and the inevitability of progress, has indeed gone out of fashion—after two world wars and countless other unmentionable horrors so completely so, in fact, that for many years nothing has been safer than to speak patronizingly of its naïveté. In biblical studies too the climate has changed radically.[95] Classical Wellhausenism has vanished from the scene. To be sure, the documentary hypothesis— which Wellhausen adapted and perfected, but did not originate—continues to command the acceptance of the majority of scholars, albeit in a vastly modified form; and many features of the work of that great scholar and his colleagues have stood the test of time. But almost no one today would wish to describe the history of Israel's religion in terms of an evolutionary development in the realm of ethics and of religious ideas and institutions, or would imagine that its essential nature could even remotely be grasped from that perspective. In like manner, the old "quest of

[95] For the best orientation to recent trends in Old Testament studies, see the articles in H. H. Rowley, ed., *The Old Testament and Modern Study* (Oxford: Clarendon Press, 1951); or see H. F. Hahn, *The Old Testament in Modern Research* (expanded ed.), ed. H. D. Hummel (Philadelphia: Fortress Press, 1966). For a much briefer summary, see my own article, "Modern Study of Old Testament Literature" in G. E. Wright, ed., *The Bible and the Ancient Near East: Essays in Honor of William Foxwell Albright* (New York: Doubleday & Company, 1961), pp. 13-31; (paper ed.; 1965, pp. 1-26). For developments in New Testament studies see, for example, Stephen Neill, *The Interpretation of the New Testament, 1861-1961* (London: Oxford University Press, 1964); R. H. Fuller, *The New Testament in Current Study* (New York: Charles Scribner's Sons, 1962).

the historical Jesus" has long since been given up as an impossibility. Indeed, the pendulum has since swung, with Bultmann and others, to the opposite extreme of an almost complete skepticism regarding the possibility of any real knowledge of the historical Jesus at all; and this has, in turn, produced its counterreaction among Bultmann's pupils in the form of a "new quest." [96] Whether this new quest is really new, or is merely a reactivation of the old quest under different presuppositions, the reader must decide. But no one today would suppose it to be possible by a critical operation to isolate in the Gospels a neutral, "nontheological" Jesus, who was the promulgator of timeless ethical and religious teachings. There was, in fact, no such Jesus.

Nevertheless, we cannot pass by the approach of the earlier liberal critics to Scripture as if it were but a temporary aberration in the history of interpretation now happily behind us. It is still very much with us. That is to say, there are still those who appeal to Jesus as their supreme authority and find in him, or at least in their understanding of him, the criterion by which Scripture is to be evaluated and the degree to which it may be regarded as valid and normative determined. Such views have been expressed in theological literature down to the present day. They have been expressed by some who would class themselves as liberals;[97] by others who, I am sure, would disavow the designation;[98] and by still others of whose theological coloration I am personally unaware.[99] Those who take such a position obviously do not all do so on the same grounds. Yet all of them would lead us to a highly selective—and I should add, highly subjective—appeal to Scripture. As for the Old Testament, much of it would be marked down as irrelevant, outgrown, superseded, and thus without authority in the church.

[96] The literature is vast, and growing; see, conveniently, J. M. Robinson, *A New Quest of the Historical Jesus* (SBT, 25; London: SCM Press, 1959).

[97] For example, Van Dusen "Liberal Theology Reassessed," esp. pp. 352-55, who finds the Christian's supreme norm in the mind and faith of Jesus (which the "new quest" seeks to discover).

[98] For example, Nels F. S. Ferré, who sees the normative principle in *agapē* (Christ is *agapē*); he finds much in the Old Testament (and some ideas in the New) that do not measure up to this level. I am not competent to discuss Ferré's theology in detail. But see his article, "Notes by a Theologian on Biblical Hermeneutics," *JBL*, LXXVIII (1959), 105-14; see also the discussion of his position in Johnson, *Authority in Protestant Theology*, pp. 153-61.

[99] See various articles in *Biblical Authority for Today*, e.g. those of C. T. Craig (pp. 30-44) and V. E. Devadutt (pp. 59-81). The latter declares (p. 72) that "Christ is the value judgment on the record of revelation" and regards the various parts of the Bible as authoritative "insofar as they stand the test." Other examples could easily be cited.

But what is far more serious than random scholarly opinion is the fact that this approach to Scripture is the one that is actually employed, albeit for the most part unconsciously, by many of the rank and file in our churches, laymen and pastors alike. Not only by those who like to think of themselves as liberals, either. Not a few who would regard the very word "liberal" as bordering on profanity follow the same procedure. The Old Testament is read, consciously or unconsciously, in the light of a normative principle drawn from the New, usually from the teachings of Jesus, with two deplorable results. On the one hand, large portions of it, apparently because they are felt to have no relevant word for the Christian, are simply ignored; they are not read, not preached, not taught—in a word, are effectively removed from the canon. On the other hand, since the normative principle is essentially an ethical or moral one, there is an irresistible urge to moralize from the rest or to spiritualize it. One hears this endlessly from the pulpit, reads it in denominational literature and in the popular religious press. Thus, for example, the little boy Samuel serving under Eli at the shrine at Shiloh (I Sam. 1–3) is presented to children as an example of helpfulness to one's elders; Isaac yielding his wells to Abimelech (Gen. 26) becomes an example of Christian forbearance; David's care for the lame Mephibosheth (II Sam. 9) teaches us that we should be kind to the weak; Israel's failure to enter the Promised Land because frightened by the report of the spies (Num. 13–14) teaches us that many obstacles in life are purely imaginary, and that opportunity may pass if not boldly seized. Haggai's exhortation to the people to resume the building of the temple reminds us that it is not beginning a work that counts, but finishing it. And so, wearisomely, on and on.[100] And all this without regard to the fact that the texts in question did not *intend* to offer moral examples, and with total disregard of the theology that they did intend to express!

It is, therefore, necessary to say as strongly as possible that this approach to Scripture affords no satisfying answer to the problem with which we have been concerned. Indeed, it is ultimately destructive of any real notion of biblical authority at all. Now I, for one, do not like the indoor sport, currently so popular in some circles, of throwing rocks at the liberals, and I do not propose to indulge in it here. In no way is it suggested that the liberal Christian was contemptuous of his Bible and set out to under-

[100] I could provide precise documentation for each of the above examples, but shall refrain from doing so. I have no wish to engage in controversy.

mine its authority. On the contrary, most of the liberal critics were models of diligence in the study of the Bible, men of impeccable honesty, sincerely devoted to the truth. Their labors conferred on biblical studies gains that must on no account be lost: a concern for exact philological and historical study of the text, the recognition of the Bible's amazing variety and intensely human quality, and much more. Their insistence that the Old Testament is to be heard in its plain, historical meaning, and not arbitrarily harmonized with the New or interpreted in accordance with church dogma, is one that honesty and reverence can only accept. Moreover, they sensed clearly the nature of the problem of the Old Testament, and they essayed to solve it in a way that would both preserve the abiding values of the Old Testament and do justice to the fact that, for the Christian, Christ is the crown of revelation. Their solution, in that it took seriously both the likenesses and the differences between the Testaments, at its best avoided the two extremes of Marcion and of Alexandria. Yet this solution— essentially, as we have said, the attempt to isolate a normative element within Scripture by means of a value judgment—must be marked down as a failure. Where it was accepted, the Bible tended to lose its historic position as the church's supreme rule of faith and practice, with the result that wide segments of the church were left without any *objective* norm to which they might appeal at all.

This is not to allege that liberal scholars intended such a result or that their understanding of Scripture was entirely without merit. Their aim was not destructive, and many of their insights were sound. Their solution was in many respects a plausible and apparently satisfying one. There are indeed ethical and religious insights in the Old Testament that comport fully with those of the New, along with others that seem clearly less than Christian. And Christ is indeed the crown of revelation, in the light of whom the Christian must read and understand his Old Testament. And of course there are degrees of value in the Bible. And since there are, and we are rational beings, value judgments are inevitable. (Let the reader who is inclined to deny this look at his own Bible and see which pages are the most worn, and let him understand that as evidence that he has himself made value judgments.) As for the Old Testament, it is a book from an ancient time, and it is obvious that many of its regulations, institutions, and practices, many of its moral attitudes and religious conceptions, cannot serve as models for the Christian to emulate. Some line has to be drawn between what commands us and what does not if we are to retain the

Old Testament, in its plain sense and without exegetical diddling, as a part of our canon of authoritative Scripture. And since we are Christians, it is very tempting to find in Jesus and his teachings the norm by which Scripture itself is to be tested, and to appeal only to him and to such other parts of the Bible as accord with his spirit, in all matters of faith and practice.

Very tempting indeed! But it quickly becomes a very subjective business. Who is this Jesus by whom all Scripture is to be judged? And by what means is it finally to be determined which parts of Scripture do actually accord with his spirit and thus retain their authority? That will depend ultimately upon the taste and the judgment of the individual and upon his understanding of the nature and significance of Jesus and his work; and that will depend, in turn, upon his critical and theological presuppositions and the resultant picture of Jesus' message and ministry that these allow him to draw. To be sure, the ministry of the earthly Jesus can never be a matter of indifference to the church, and the attempt to reconstruct it, as far as this can be done, is one that must ever and again be made. But that is a subject upon which, understandably, there has never been anything approaching complete agreement, nor is it likely that there ever will be. Jesus is indeed the crown of revelation, and in a true sense the key to the Christian's understanding of Scripture. But to attempt to derive from him a normative principle for testing the validity of Scripture is surely a most subjective procedure. Which Jesus will it be? The Jesus Christ of the New Testament proclamation? The "historical Jesus" of the critics, whether of the old quest or the new? Or some other? And even if this be decided, what objective criteria are there that might serve as a yardstick for measuring the validity of Old Testament texts? Both the framing of the value judgment and its application lie largely within the realm of the taste and critical judgment of the individual interpreter.[101]

Certainly to approach the Old Testament in this way is to do it great violence. It is to find its contribution primarily in its ethical principles, moral values, and religious ideas, and thus to fail to do justice to its true intent. It is to impose upon it an extraneous canon of evaluation of our own making and, in the end, to patronize it by sitting in judgment upon

---

[101] See, for example, the article of C. T. Craig in *Biblical Authority for Today*. Craig clearly recognizes that to appeal to Jesus in this way involves subjectivism and a selective use of the Bible (cf. pp. 34-35), but since he finds this inevitable, he would prefer to speak of the Bible as a "source of guidance" (among other sources of guidance) rather than as an authority.

it when it does not measure up to our Christian ideals. Moreover, the canon of evaluation is not only extraneous to the Old Testament but to the New as well. In spite of the fact that it is derived from Jesus and his teachings, it can claim no precedent in the New Testament, for the New Testament certainly did not read the Old in this way. However freely Jesus and the New Testament writers may have reinterpreted the Old Testament, and however emphatically they may have declared certain of its features (the ceremonial law) to be no longer binding on the Christian, they apparently had not the slightest interest in evaluating it according to the level of its ethical and religious teachings; still less did they appeal to it selectively on that basis. To evaluate the Old Testament from that point of view is to see in it something other—and far less—than the New Testament writers did. It is to hear it neither for what it was itself trying to say nor for what the New Testament understood it as saying. It is, rather, to judge it in the light of our own ethical and moral standards— which is plainly to say that it is our ethical and moral standards that are normative.

The attempt to isolate an authoritative element within Scripture by means of a value judgment leads inevitably to the breakdown of the whole concept of authority. Since a value judgment is by definition an individual matter, it is in the end the individual who formulates his own standard of belief and practice. A subjective norm is substituted for an objective one. And this indeed resulted wherever the liberal approach to Scripture was followed. No longer did men look to the Bible as the church's supreme rule of faith and practice. Rather, the Christian individual in a real sense assumed authority over the Bible to evaluate the validity of its message in the light of his own ethical and religious presuppositions. He could take seriously only those parts of the Bible with which his presuppositions found agreement; and which these would be was a matter of individual judgment. As for the average Christian, since the critical and exegetical operation by which the normative element in the Bible was supposed to be arrived at was quite beyond him in any case, he was obliged, there being no other canon of evaluation, to rely largely on his own feelings, conscience, and native intelligence for guidance in the matter. The result was that the intelligence and conscience of the individual, more or less vaguely informed by the Bible, became in practice the court of final appeal in all matters of belief and conduct. Far from a serious wrestling with biblical doctrine in the church's discussions, one heard hazy talk of Christian principles and Christian attitudes, with the tacit assumption that these are self-evident and that Christians ought to be able to agree on them and pattern their conduct accordingly. In the minds of many, it is to be feared, Christian faith and ethics came dangerously close to becoming a synonym for what is reasonable and good and commends itself to conscience.

To be sure, no man is an automaton. Each responsible individual will have to decide very privately what he can and cannot believe, and even if he can believe the Bible. No authority can relieve him of that responsibility. Moreover, value judgments are both natural and inevitable, and each of us will continue to make them, even with regard to the Bible. But the nature and the content of the Christian faith is not to be decided on the basis of the individual's value judgments or by a free exchange of opinion. The Christian faith is not necessarily what a given individual believes it to be, however sincere he may be in his convictions. The Christian faith is a historical phenomenon: it is what it *was*. And our one primary authority regarding what it actually affirmed and taught remains the biblical record. It is to the Bible, therefore, that all our doctrinal and ethical discussions must ultimately be referred: it is our one objective basis for conversation about such matters. But if we will not take it seriously in its entirety, if we feel free to appeal only to such parts as chime in with our sensibilities, then we are in fact discussing the biblical faith not as it was but as we would like it to have been, and our conversation is once more delivered over to subjective opinion.

So the problem remains, and our dilemma remains. What we have been pleased to call the liberal solution to the problem of the Old Testament is no more to be accepted than are those of Marcion or of the allegorists. If we cannot depose the Old Testament without damage to the gospel, if we cannot impose Christian meaning upon it without surrendering exegetical integrity and opening the floodgates of fantasy, we cannot essay by means of a value judgment to separate the eternally valid in it from the sub-Christian and outworn lest, in allowing our sensibilities to sit in judgment upon Scripture, we place ourselves above Scripture and cease to treat it as authoritative in any final sense at all. Have we, then, reached an impasse? Is there no way out, or is some other solution possible? Certainly we need expect no easy one. But it is clear that, whatever it is to be, it must be sought along other lines.

III

BIBLICAL THEOLOGY AND THE AUTHORITY

OF THE OLD TESTAMENT

We have, then, examined what we ventured to call the three classical solutions to the problem of the Old Testament. These offer us the following options: to take the way of Marcion and remove the Old Testament from the Bible, or deprive it of full canonical rank; to follow a path parallel to that of the church fathers and essay to save the Old Testament by finding a Christian meaning in its texts; or with much of liberal Protestantism to seek, by means of a normative principle derived from the New Testament, to distinguish between those elements in the Old that have abiding validity and those that no longer concern us.

Now it was agreed that each of these solutions reflects a clear understanding of the nature of the problem. Proponents of each have correctly observed that the teachings of the two Testaments are by no means in every case identical and that there is much in the Old that is strange to the Christian and that cannot be, and in fact is not, directly a model for his belief or a law to command his practice. It has been just this observation that through the centuries has forced honest inquirers to raise the question of the canonical authority of the Old Testament, its place in the Bible, and its use in the church. Each of the above solutions represents a consistent attempt to deal with that question. Yet, for reasons already set forth, we were able to accept none of them as satisfactory. If an acceptable solution is to be found, it must be sought along other lines.

But where? What other way is open? Do not the above proposals logically exhaust the possibilities? It is submitted that they do, if we grant the premise that underlies all three of them. As was observed at the outset, all these proposed solutions, in spite of the differences—indeed, the contradictions—between them, have one point in common: All take the New Testament as their point of orientation, and from that perspective they read, understand, and evaluate the Old. All make the assumption that the true text and norm is the New Testament and that the Old is relevant and valid only if, or to the degree that, its teachings accord with those of the New. Whoever approaches the Old Testament with this premise and at the same time takes seriously the manifest differences that exist between it and the New will be obliged, so it would seem, to return some form of one or another of the above answers. No other option is logically possible.

For example, if a man concentrates on those features in the conceptual world and religious practice of the Old Testament that are strange to the Christian, and if he finds these so numerous and so irreconcilable with New Testament teaching that he feels obliged to conclude that the Old Testament is the document of a religion quite other than his own, then he will have no logical course save, with Marcion, to grasp the nettle resolutely and relieve the Old Testament of canonical authority. On the other hand, if a man, while observing features in the Old Testament that seem foreign to Christian thought and practice, yet nevertheless, because convinced that the two Testaments are the revelation of the same God, finds it impossible to believe that any real inconsistency could exist between them, he may then be moved to obliterate the differences through allegorical, typological, or christological interpretations, so that the Old Testament may speak in accord with the New. Likewise, if a man recognizes that there are difficult features in the Old Testament which cannot be harmonized away, yet at the same time finds there abiding values which he cannot consent to let go, then his only logical course is to seek in the New Testament some normative principle by which he may distinguish what is valid for him from what no longer concerns him. These are the only logical possibilities, and none of them is acceptable. In each case the true text is the New Testament. The Old Testament text must conform to it, be made to conform—or get out! In no case is the Old Testament's own witness, in its plain sense and in its entirety, taken seriously as having validity in the church.

So we have reached an impasse and must retrace our steps. Our line of direction must be reversed if an acceptable solution is to be found.

That is to say, we cannot begin with the New Testament and from that perspective proceed straightaway either to pass judgment on the Old Testament or to determine what its true message must be. Rather, we must begin with the Old Testament itself and move with the line of history ahead to the New. In doing this, we are on no account to ignore either the gravity of the problem or the valid insights in the solutions already described. The Old Testament religion is indeed not identical with Christianity and cannot therefore, in its entirety and of itself, serve as a norm for Christian faith and practice. Some line must be drawn between what commands us in the Old Testament and what does not, if we are to use it rightly in the church. And Christ is indeed to us the crown of revelation through whom the true significance of the Old Testament becomes finally apparent. But we are not, for that reason, to make the New Testament's teachings our primary point of departure in dealing with the Old Testament. Rather, we must begin with the Old Testament's own theological assertions and concerns, with the Old Testament's own structure of faith; we must follow that ahead through history to see how it was taken up in the New Testament, and then, from that perspective, we may look back and again understand the Old. How this proposal will work out in detail remains to be seen. But it is here submitted that the key to the solution of the problem is to be found in the theological structure of both Testaments in their mutual relationships—that is to say, through the study of biblical theology.

I

But first let us define our terms. What is meant by biblical theology in this connection? It is always well to begin with a definition of terms, lest we find ourselves talking at cross purposes, and it is doubly desirable in this case, since the term "biblical theology" has been used in such a variety of ways that one is not always certain exactly what is intended by it. Moreover, even among those who understand the term in the sense intended here, there is widespread disagreement regarding the proper task, the method, and even the possibility, of the discipline. A few words by way of clarification are therefore essential if confusion is to be avoided.

1. The term "biblical theology" can, on the surface of it, be used to denote either the theology that is expressed in the Bible itself, or a system of theology which is—or professes to be—in accord with the Bible (as

opposed to other systems of theology which, by inference, are not). Both usages are current today.[1] Understood in the first sense, biblical theology lies within the sphere of biblical studies and has the task of providing a coherent description of the structure of belief actually found in the Bible, Old Testament or New. Understood in the second sense, biblical theology refers to a kind of dogmatics which bases itself upon the Bible as its primary, or sole, source of authority. In this latter sense the term has been widely appropriated in recent years, especially in Great Britain and America, by theologians of neo-orthodox leanings. In addition to these two usages, some would see still a third use current today. Here the term "biblical theology" is used in a sense that lies somewhere between the other two— namely, with reference to the attempt of certain theologians and preachers to expound the Bible in its unity as authoritative in the church.[2]

Such ambiguity in the use of terms has led to endless confusion. Broadsides are fired—but one is never certain at whom the shots are aimed. Thus one may read a sweeping criticism of "biblical theology" and of the bad method followed by certain "biblical theologians" which, oddly enough, touches very few whom one would think of as biblical theologians in the proper sense of the word.[3] Or one sees now and then in the popular religious press a vigorous attack on "biblical theology" which, upon examination, turns out to be directed against certain of the views of Karl Barth and his followers and which has nothing whatever to do with biblical theology as that term is universally understood among biblical exegetes.[4] It is singularly unfortunate that a term should be appropriated for such a variety of purposes and used so ambiguously. Badly aimed shots strike innocent bystanders. The innocent bystander in this case is a legitimate and respectable branch of biblical studies which, whatever its errors and shortcomings, is not deserving of wrath. The term "biblical theology" will

---

[1] On the definition, see for example G. Ebeling, "The Meaning of 'Biblical Theology,'" in L. Hodgson et al. On the Authority of the Bible, pp. 49-67; James Barr, The Semantics of Biblical Language (London: Oxford University Press, 1961), Ch. 9 (esp. pp. 273-74); R. C. Dentan, Preface to Old Testament Theology (Rev. ed.; New York: The Seabury Press, 1963), pp. 15-23, 87-125. I am in complete agreement with Dentan's understanding of the matter.

[2] See J. Barr, The Semantics of Biblical Language, pp. 273-74.

[3] I refer to the book of Barr, just cited. Admittedly, most of Barr's criticisms are well taken and timely. But it is only near the end of his book (pp. 274-75) that he makes it clear that they are directed chiefly at practitioners of biblical theology in the third sense noted above.

[4] As an example of what is meant, see The Presbyterian Journal, October 25, 1961, pp. 5-6, 16-17; also August 5, 1964, p. 12.

here be used only with reference to it. That is to say, it will be used only in the first sense noted above, which, it is felt, is the legitimate and proper sense. Biblical theology as spoken of here is a department of biblical studies, not a kind of dogmatics, whether orthodox, neo-orthodox, or some other.

In the sense just defined, biblical theology was rather a latecomer to the theological scene. It did not, in fact, emerge as a separate discipline until late in the eighteenth century.[5] If the term "biblical theology" was used before that time (and it seems to have made its appearance in the seventeenth century),[6] it was not in the sense of an independent discipline but of one subsidiary to dogmatics, whose task it was to collect proof texts upon which to support orthodox doctrine, or by which to criticize it and purify it of nonbiblical accretions. So far as I can learn, it was Johann Philipp Gabler who was the first to establish biblical theology as a discipline in its own right. In 1787, in the course of his inaugural address at the University of Altdorf, Gabler urged that a clear distinction be drawn between biblical and dogmatic theology and proposed the following definition: "Biblical theology is historical in character and sets forth what the sacred writers thought about divine matters; dogmatic theology, on the contrary, is didactic in character, and teaches what a particular theologian philosophically and rationally decides about divine matters, in accordance with his character, time, age, place, sect or school, and other similar influences."[7] Now one might object to the frankly rationalistic tone of that definition (Gabler was a rationalist) and might feel that the wording could be improved. But the distinction that Gabler drew is, in the opinion of many (and in my own), fundamentally a sound one: it draws the line between biblical theology and dogmatics at the right place.[8]

[5] It is not our task to sketch the history of the discipline, specifically of Old Testament theology, which is our primary concern. For an excellent summary, see Dentan, *Preface to Old Testament Theology*, pp. 15-83; also N. W. Porteous, "Old Testament Theology," in H. H. Rowley, ed., *The Old Testament and Modern Study* (Oxford: Clarendon Press, 1951), pp. 311-45.

[6] See esp. Ebeling in L. Hodgson *et al.*, *On the Authority of the Bible*, pp. 53-57.

[7] *Oratio de iusto discrimine theologiae biblicae et dogmaticae regundisque recte utriusque finibus* (1787). I have never seen this work, but the quotation will be found in most discussions of the subject; mine is taken from Dentan, *Preface to Old Testament Theology*, pp. 22-23. On Gabler's views generally, see R. Smend, "Johann Philipp Gablers Begründung der biblischen Theologie," *EvTh*, XXII (1962), 345-57 (on p. 346 one will find the above quotation in the original Latin).

[8] The fact that Gabler later spoiled a good thing by calling for a further distinction between "true" Biblical theology (i.e., the beliefs of the Bible writers themselves) and "pure" Biblical theology (i.e., the Bible's teachings of abiding validity as distinguished

Biblical theology and dogmatics are thus two separate but complementary disciplines. The first is an inductive, descriptive discipline, synthetic in its approach, which, on the basis of a grammatico-historical study of the biblical text, seeks to set forth in its own terms and in its structural unity the theology expressed in the Bible. The second, while it must base itself upon the theology of the Bible and remain true to it, if it would pretend to be Christian dogmatics, is a logical, systematic discipline, didactic and apologetic in its concern, which seeks to set forth in terms intelligible to the present day the faith of the individual theologian or of the church in whose name he speaks. One of the important functions of biblical theology is thus to provide dogmatics with the material with which it must work.

The task of biblical theology is essentially descriptive. It does not, as biblical theology, have the task of defending the validity of the biblical faith or of setting forth its contemporary significance—although the individual biblical theologian as a teacher and minister of the church may well be, and indeed must be, vitally and unceasingly concerned with just these things. On the other hand, though it must never lose the historical dimension from view, biblical theology does not have the task of tracing the history either of Israel's religion or of primitive Christianity. Its task, rather, is to present a synthesis. Old Testament theology has the function of providing a coherent description of the faith of the Old Testament in its structural unity. It is therefore not concerned to note every ritual practice that may have been observed, and every popular belief that may have been entertained, by the ancient Hebrews. Rather, it is concerned with those features of Israel's faith that were pervasive, constantly present, normative, that imparted to it its distinctive character, that made it both what it was and different from all other faiths. New Testament theology, similarly, has the task of describing the faith of the New Testament writers in its structural unity, as the distinctive phenomenon that it was. And this last, it goes without saying, will include some description of the way in which the New Testament used the Old, claimed it for itself, and reinterpreted it theologically in the light of its Lord and his work.

2. But is there really such a thing as a biblical theology? For that matter, can one rightly speak even of an Old Testament or a New Testament theology? That is to say, is there a sufficient unity of belief in the Bible, or in either of the Testaments, to allow the use of the singular number?

---

from its time-conditioned elements in the light of "the pure religious concepts of our times") need not concern us. See Smend's article, cited above, pp. 348-49.

Before the rise of the critical study of the Bible the fundamental unity of the biblical revelation was generally taken for granted in the mainstream of Christianity. The Bible was regarded on all hands as a compendium of revealed doctrine, given by God, and therefore in all its parts consistent with itself. This resulted, it is true, in a great deal of artificial harmonizing by appeal to the *analogia scripturae* and the *analogia fidei* and, in the case of the Old Testament, by the finding of Christian meaning in the text through methods that sober exegesis cannot condone. Certainly the great variety of belief within the Bible was insufficiently recognized. Nevertheless, theologians were able to view the biblical revelation as a seamless whole and so found little difficulty in drawing the tenets of the Christian faith from all parts of the Bible at will. And this state of affairs prevailed, to speak in general, until relatively modern times.

But the triumph of the critical approach to the Bible brought a fundamental change. For one thing, an almost exclusively doctrinal interest in the Bible was replaced by one that was almost exclusively historical: the Bible was valued by scholars primarily as a source book of history. Most of the leading biblical scholars of the last century, especially in Germany, stood in the tradition of historicism. Their concern was to write biblical history, and the history of the biblical religion, scientifically on the basis of a critical evaluation of the sources, as it actually took place (*wie es eigentlich gewesen*). This approach to history writing had been developed among secular historians of the eighteenth and nineteenth centuries, especially by Leopold von Ranke and his followers, and was taken over by biblical scholars out of an understandable concern to make theology respectable as a historical science. The biblical documents would be subjected to critical analysis like any other historical documents, and biblical history written like any other history, as it actually occurred. The Bible was of interest to these scholars primarily for the historical information that it affords, not for its theology; the fact that the Bible consistently imposes a theological interpretation on history was regarded by not a few as regrettable and a demerit.

As a result of this critical and historical approach, the unity of the Bible was broken up. The triumph of the Wellhausen school in the latter part of the nineteenth century put the seal upon it where the Old Testament was concerned. Wellhausen, as we have seen, basing himself partly on a critical analysis of the Old Testament documents, partly on a theory of dialectical progress in history drawn ultimately from the philosophy of

116

Hegel, demonstrated to the satisfaction of almost the whole of the scholarly world that Israel's religion in the Old Testament period underwent a process of development in the course of which it changed character completely. It had its beginnings in the crude polydaemonism of the pre-Mosaic age, emerged first as a tribal, then as a national cult, and finally, much later, as the result of the work of the great prophets and after the tragedy of exile, evolved into a full ethical monotheism, the values of which were preserved through the centuries within the framework of emerging Judaism. This general view of the matter carried the day so completely that for more than a generation it remained well-nigh an orthodoxy in its own right. Israel's religion was thus set apart into its various stages of development, the later of which bore little or no similarity to the earlier. One could, therefore, speak only of theologies (in the plural). One could discuss the theology of the Yahwist, the Elohist, the Deuteronomist and the Priestly Code, of Amos and Isaiah and Second Isaiah; but one could not speak of Old Testament theology (in the singular), for the Old Testament exhibits not one theology but many.

Still less could one speak of a *biblical* theology. Although a historical connection between Israel's religion and the New Testament faith was of course recognized, and although it was generally agreed that the Old Testament at its highest levels contains many teachings that are fully consonant with Christian belief, the differences were too numerous to be ignored. Manifestly the New Testament faith is not identical either with Judaism or with the religion of Israel at any stage of its development. Nor could scholars trained in scientific methods of exegesis in honesty consent to erase the differences by recourse to a christological or typological interpretation of the Old Testament, as the church had done for so long. They were obliged to understand the Old Testament religion historically and to view the relationship between the Testaments in terms of development.

Nor did the New Testament itself escape the atomizing process. As scholars examined its various documents ever more critically, they were increasingly impressed by the diversity of its witness. How is this to be accounted for? Obviously many momentous events took place—and not a little heart-searching, struggle, and controversy—between Jesus' ministry in Galilee and the establishment of Christian churches in all parts of the Roman empire. Is it not to be supposed that there was also a development in theological understanding, a movement from simpler to more sophisticated forms of belief and practice, in the course of these years? And if so, may one not expect to find this reflected in the pages of the New Testament? Many scholars believed so. Various distinct theologies were isolated in the New Testament which were felt to be expressive of the steps in a process of development and to stand more or less in tension with one another. There was the simple religion of Jesus, which it was thought possible by a critical operation to recover; there was the faith of the primitive Palestinian community; there was the theology of Paul, which was felt to a greater or lesser degree to have overlaid, if not fundamentally altered, Jesus' own gospel; there was the distinctive theology of the Johannine writings—and more besides.

Whatever one's opinion of this approach to the Bible, it brought with it the sudden and almost total end of biblical theology as a legitimate academic discipline. This was not simply that critics of the Wellhausen school were primarily interested in history rather than theology; their critical studies had dissolved the biblical faith into *disjecta membra*, leaving room only for a history of religion.[9] One might write a history of Israel's religion or a history of the rise and development of Christianity, and many attempts to do so were made. But one could not write a theology of the Old or the New Testament, for it was felt that the religion of both lacked the essential unity which the use of such terms implied. It is significant that for approximately a generation after the complete triumph of the Wellhausen school—from the closing decades of the nineteenth century until the third decade of the twentieth, when the masterwork of Walther Eichrodt was published[10]—virtually no attempt was made to produce a theology of the Old Testament.[11] In the English language, between the

[9] Certain scholars of the day said this explicitly. As regards the New Testament, see for example the remarks of G. Krüger and W. Wrede quoted in W. G. Kümmel, *Das Neue Testament: Geschichte der Erforschung seiner Probleme* (Freiburg/München; Verlag Karl Alber, 1958), pp. 387-89. Both these scholars called for the abandonment of New Testament theology and the substitution for it of the history of primitive Christianity. Their remarks are typical of the sentiment of the times, both in Old and New Testament studies: *Religionsgeschichte* had triumphed.

[10] W. Eichrodt, *Theologie des Alten Testaments* (Stuttgart: Ehrenfried Klotz, Vol. I, '6th ed., 1959; Vols. II and III, 4th ed., 1961); Eng. trans. of Vol. I by J. A. Baker, as *Theology of the Old Testament* (Philadelphia: The Westminster Press, 1961). Vol. I of this work first appeared in 1933, Vol. II in 1935, Vol. III in 1939. The 1930's also saw the publication of the shorter, and vastly different, treatments of Old Testament theology by E. Sellin and L. Köhler (the latter also available in English: Philadelphia: The Westminster Press, 1957).

[11] The work of E. König, *Theologie des Alten Testaments* (Stuttgart: Chr. Belsersche Verlagsbuchhandlung, 1922) is practically the only exception to the statement. König was a scholar who all his life resisted the views of Wellhausen and his followers.

posthumous publication of A. B. Davidson's work in 1904,[12] and the 1940's,[13] no book on the subject appeared.[14] Indeed, the subject was omitted from the curriculum of many theological schools. In the case of more conservative institutions this may have been because, it being taken for granted that the church's theology was biblical, no need for the study of biblical theology as a separate discipline alongside dogmatics had ever been recognized. But in other cases it was simply because the validity of the discipline was doubted.

3. Of course a reaction was bound to come and did. In Old Testament studies this coincided quite naturally with the breakdown of the critical orthodoxy associated with the name of Wellhausen. This last came about gradually over a period of years as new discoveries were brought to bear on the biblical record and as new insights were gained in the light of which the Wellhausenist reconstruction of Israel's religious history was seen at essential points to be untenable.[15] As archaeological discoveries brilliantly illuminated the world of Israel's origins, it became clear that a new evaluation of the pentateuchal traditions was required and that the conventional picture of earliest Israel's religion would have to be revised completely; such terms as polydaemonism (or animism) and henotheism were seen not to apply at all. At the same time, studies of shorter units of tradition within the pentateuchal documents in the light of material discovered elsewhere, while leading to no general abandonment of the documentary hypothesis, made it evident that all the documents incorporate much older material, in many instances material that demonstrably reaches

[12] A. B. Davidson, *The Theology of the Old Testament*, ed. S. D. F. Salmond (Edinburgh: T. & T. Clark, 1904). (The shorter work of C. F. Burney, *Outlines of Old Testament Theology* likewise appeared in 1904.)

[13] O. J. Baab, *The Theology of the Old Testament* (Nashville: Abingdon-Cokesbury Press, 1949) was the first full-length treatment of the subject to appear in English since 1904. It had, however, been preceded by the broader, and quite different, work of Millar Burrows, *An Outline of Biblical Theology* (Philadelphia: The Westminster Press, 1946). The 1950's saw the production of still further works on Old Testament theology, as well as the translation into English of the works of E. Jacob (from the French), Th. C. Vriezen (from the Dutch) and L. Köhler (from the German); see Dentan, *Preface to Old Testament Theology* for a review of the literature.

[14] By this is meant no full-length attempt to describe the Old Testament faith in its structural unity. There were, of course, books and articles that dealt with various teachings of the Old Testament, and aspects of its theology; but no theology of the Old Testament was produced. Again see Dentan, *Preface to Old Testament Theology* for details.

[15] To describe all the factors that brought about this change is out of the question here. The reader may gain an idea of current trends in all areas of Old Testament study by a perusal of the articles in H. H. Rowley, ed., *The Old Testament and Modern Study.*

back to the beginnings of Israel's history. This placed the documentary hypothesis in an entirely new light. It was realized that the date of a document by no means determines the date of its contents or passes verdict on its historical value and that, because of this fact, the documents themselves could no longer be used to support a neat pattern of evolutionary development. Further, as the nature of the early Israelite tribal league and its institutions was more clearly grasped and as the place of the cult in Israel's religion was better appreciated, it became apparent that the prophets, far from being spiritual pioneers, bitterly anti-cultic, who imparted to their people new ethical and moral insights, were actually men whose preaching was deeply rooted in the sacral traditions of Israel's formative period.

As these insights—and many others—were assimilated, it became increasingly evident that Israel's religion did not evolve slowly from lower forms to higher but had already in all essentials assumed its normative form in the earliest period of Israel's life as a people and that, in spite of obvious and manifold developments, it did not thereafter fundamentally change its character. Whatever their disagreements in their understanding of Israel's history (especially in the earliest period), it became impossible for scholars to view Israel's religion in terms of an evolutionary process, as the older critics had done.

Parallel with the above developments, a great revival of interest in the theological study of the Old Testament took place. If one were pressed to set a date for the beginning of this, one might go as far back as 1921 and refer to an address given by Rudolf Kittel before a meeting of Orientalists in Leipzig that year.[16] In this address Kittel, himself an outstanding historian, called for a break with the tyranny of historicism and a return to a more theologically oriented study of the Old Testament. Kittel's remarks won considerable acclaim and began gradually to bear fruit as others expressed themselves similarly.[17] This was undoubtedly in part because Old Testament scholars, themselves ministers of the church, felt a responsibility to the church for their discipline and desired to see it reestablished as a theologically, and not merely a historically, relevant discipline—a position which it had, in fact, all but lost. But there was also the growing realization that the Old Testament does not itself intend to

---

[16] "Die Zukunft der alttestamentlichen Wissenschaft," *ZAW*, XXXIX (1921), 84-99.

[17] Notably Carl Steuernagel, "Alttestamentliche Theologie und alttestamentliche Religionsgeschichte," *BZAW*, XLI (1925 [*Festschrift Karl Marti*]), 266-73.

provide us with historical and philological data or with information regarding the development of religious and ethical concepts, however legitimate it may be—and is—to examine it for what it can teach us about such matters. Rather, the Old Testament intends to make theological statements. Can the exegete, then, be content to mine it for all sorts of information that it did not intend to give, while paying insufficient attention to what it is really trying to say? Scholars more and more felt obliged to answer that question in the negative and were moved to devote more attention to the study of the Old Testament's theology. Moreover, as the developmental pattern imposed on the history of Israel's religion by the Wellhausen school was seen to be fallacious, it became increasingly apparent that there is actually more unity in the Old Testament faith than had previously been supposed. The conviction entrenched itself that the Old Testament faith can legitimately be spoken of in the singular and that it is theologically relevant to describe its structure and content.

In any event, biblical theology (for similar developments took place in the realm of New Testament studies also) has experienced nothing less than a renaissance in recent decades. As evidence of that fact one need only point to the numerous volumes that have appeared in almost every modern European language in the past thirty or so years bearing the title *Old Testament Theology* or *New Testament Theology*, to say nothing of literally scores of monographs and articles on almost every phase of the subject. There is, to be sure, wide disagreement as regards the task and method of the discipline, as anyone who is even remotely familiar with the literature knows. Indeed, one has only to compare, say, treatments of Old Testament theology by two such outstanding scholars as Walther Eichrodt and Gerhard von Rad[18] (or those of New Testament theology by Bultmann and almost any other) to see that disagreements in this regard are at times so great as to appear irreconcilable. Nevertheless, the validity of the task itself and the relevance of the attempt to discharge it would be all but universally conceded today.[19]

[18] W. Eichrodt, *Theologie des Alten Testaments*; G. von Rad, *Theologie des Alten Testaments* (Munich: Chr. Kaiser Verlag, Vol. I, 1957; Vol. II, 1960); Eng. tr. by D. M. G. Stalker as *Old Testament Theology* (New York: Harper & Row, Vol. I, 1962; Vol. II, 1965).

[19] Of course, there are those who contest it, and their number seems to be increasing. Recent expressions of this point of view, culled at random from my reading, include: P. Wernberg-Møller, "Is There an Old Testament Theology?" *Hibbert Journal* LIX (1960/61), 21-29; C. F. Evans in *On the Authority of the Bible*, pp. 70-71; W. L. King, "Some Ambiguities in Biblical Theology," *Religion in Life*, XXVII (1957/8), 95-104;

4. We shall not attempt to describe the various ways in which the task of biblical theology has been conceived and executed in current treatments of the subject, still less to referee between them. That would lead us too far afield. [20] But surely Old Testament theology has the task in one way or another of describing the faith of ancient Israel, and New Testament theology that of describing the faith of the New Testament church, each in its structural unity; and both together have the task (although it may fall more specifically within the realm of New Testament theology) of grasping the theological relationships that exist between the two.

But here a word of caution is necessary. In discharging the above task, the diversity within the biblical witness is by no means to be ignored. There is great diversity within the Bible, and within each Testament, and no honest student will ever seek to gloss it over. Israel's faith had a history, and in the course of that history it expressed itself in a variety of ways. It is both legitimate and necessary to trace that history and to examine each expression of faith for its unique witness. The beliefs and practices of the Mosaic age cannot be made to walk on all fours with those of the second temple. Nor can the theology of the Yahwist simply be identified with that of Isaiah, and both treated as if they differed not at all from that expressed in the Holiness Code. Likewise, there is a great deal of history between Jesus' teaching in Galilee and the extension of the church to all parts of the Roman world; and in the course of that history men expressed their faith in their Lord in many different ways. The various "theologies" to be found in the New Testament—those of Matthew, Mark, Luke, Paul, John, and the rest—are by no means artificially to be harmonized with one another: scholarly integrity forbids it. No treatment of the faith of either Testament that does not do justice to its amazing variety will do for a moment.

So then the diversity within the Bible is not to be harmonized away but expressly recognized. But recognition of diversity does not prevent us from asking after unity. The faith of Israel did indeed have a history in the

---

S. H. Hooke, *Myth, Ritual and Kingship* (Oxford: Oxford University Press, 1958), pp. 1-21. In so far as these scholars are protesting an oversimplification that erases diversity their criticisms are justified. But the fact of diversity does not eliminate the possibility of an overarching unity, either in the biblical faith or any other; see further below.

[20] The reader will find review articles dealing with nine of the most significant recent treatments of the theology of the Old and New Testaments, respectively, in the issues of *The Expository Times* for Sept. 1961 through March 1962, and for July 1962 and April 1963.

course of which it found many forms of expression. But what *is* this that so had a history and so expressed itself? Is there not, behind all the development, an entity that so developed? Can we not, in spite of the infinite variety of belief which the Old Testament exhibits, nevertheless discern in its pages a phenomenon that is unique and is to be spoken of in the singular, the faith of Israel? Equally, can we not discern in the New Testament, for all the diversity of its witness, a phenomenon that must likewise be spoken of in the singular, the New Testament faith? Finally and still further, is there not, in spite of the manifest differences between the religion of the two Testaments, nevertheless a theological as well as a historical link that binds the two together within the same heritage of faith? These are reasonable questions, and they are to be answered in the affirmative.

Certainly development and diversity within the framework of unity is something with which we are familiar enough in other areas. For example, there is a remarkable development in the life of any individual from infancy to childhood, to adolescence, to maturity, to middle age, and perhaps on to senility. There is growth and change; the thoughts expressed and the concerns felt by the man in middle life will differ completely from those of the child, or even the adolescent. But can a biographer be satisfied with pointing out the obvious differences between the toddler at his play, the boy setting out for school, the middle-aged executive behind his desk, and the broken old man? Must he not also ask after the person who so grows and changes, yet remains the same person, himself and no other, hinged to the same bones, surrounded by the same skin? In like manner, an ocean of history has rolled over the church. She has developed amazingly since her beginnings; in organization she has become incredibly complex, in belief exceedingly diverse. But are we for that reason able to do no more than note the differences between our developed denominational organizations and the simple community that met in an upper room? Can we not affirm, are we wrong in so affirming, that in spite of all development we are still the same church? And are we so bankrupt that in spite of all theological differences, in spite of the variety of creedal expression within Christendom, we cannot speak of *the* Christian faith, as opposed to all other faiths? There has been development, and there is diversity; but there is also unity.

And so it is within the Bible itself. It was a long way from Moses to the Maccabees, and along that way Israel's faith expressed itself in ways exceedingly diverse; and this diversity can neither be erased nor ignored. There are indeed many different "theologies" in the Old Testament, if one wishes to put it so, just as there have been many theologies written within Christendom. Augustine and Aquinas, Luther and Calvin, Schleiermacher and Ritschl, Barth and Tillich, are not identical. No more do the documents of the Old Testament express everywhere an identical theology. But in each case these "theologies" have a family likeness which is more striking than the differences; in both cases they belong together as expressions of the same religion. For all their diversity, the various theological expressions of the Old Testament belong together because all are rooted in a commonly held structure of belief, in common traditions, common commitments, in a common sense of peoplehood—in short, in a common faith. And this was a very distinctive faith, one marked by certain characteristics which made it both what it was and different from all other faiths. In like manner, there is a diversity of witness in the New Testament also, many "theologies" if you wish. But these too belong together and have quite properly been bound together within a single canon of Scripture. All are expressive, albeit in different ways, of a single, commonly held faith which was distinct from all other faiths and absolutely unique.

Biblical scholarship cannot therefore rest content with an analysis of the distinctive message of each book and document and a rehearsal of the Bible's witness in its diversity—in the case of the New Testament, say, with a description of the witness of each book (or group of books) to Christ or, in the case of the Old, the witness of the various documents to Yahweh's actions in history. This indeed has to be done if each segment of the Bible is to be heard in its uniqueness and the differences not simply suppressed. It is, moreover, to expound in all its variety a central feature—perhaps *the* central feature—in the Bible's message, and one not always sufficiently stressed. But it is not to complete the task of biblical theology—any more, I should say, than the theology of a given denomination could be adequately described merely by reviewing the messages of its leading preachers: some summation is called for. Biblical theology must press on behind the various different witnesses to lay hold of the structure of belief that underlies and informs them, and of which they are all in one way or another expressions.[21]

[21] It is not intended to discuss specific works on Old Testament theology here. But it will be apparent that I find the general approach followed, for example, by Eichrodt more

Manifestly there are dangers here. Such a structure of belief is not presented in systematic form, or even in the form of an articulated complex of concepts, anywhere in the Bible. The danger exists that the theologian, in attempting to present the material in an orderly fashion, will force it into the Procrustean bed of a scheme of organization foreign to its nature—say the conventional rubrics of dogmatics (God, man, salvation, etc.)—with the result that what is presented is not biblical theology but something abstracted from it. And whatever principle of organization is used—and some must be—there is always the risk that pertinent material will be overlooked or slighted because it fits badly. Yet the risk must be taken. We cannot be content to view the biblical message only in its diversity. If we are rightly to understand the Bible, we must also grasp the unifying structure of belief that undergirds it both in the Old Testament and in the New.

The fact that the religion of neither Testament is systematically articulated makes the task of biblical theology a difficult one. Perhaps it will never be performed to absolute perfection. But it is not on that account to be written off as impossible. If biblical theology is an inductive, descriptive discipline that seeks through an examination of the biblical records to determine and set forth in its own terms the essential and normative content of the faith of the Old Testament and the New, respectively, as distinct from other faiths and as distinct from transient, peripheral, aberrant, and incidental features within their own structure, then its task ought not to be regarded as impossible, for surely it is possible to present a coherent and orderly description of the essential beliefs of a religion even though these may never have been formally systematized. Certainly such a thing is possible where other religions are concerned. It is possible to a significant degree, for example, in the case of the pagan religions of ancient Israel's environment. Compared with Israel's faith, these religions seem to present somewhat of a still life picture; they convey the impression —though this is deceptive—of remaining static and hardly developing at all. On the other hand, their cultus and myth are so bewilderingly variegated as

---

satisfying than that of von Rad (see works cited in notes 10 and 18, respectively). Von Rad's exposition of the kerygmatic witness of the various Old Testament documents is so masterly, and I have myself learned so much from it, that I hesitate to enter a criticism. Yet it seems to me that what von Rad has given us is an analysis, and a most penetrating one, of each of the various "theologies" (theological expressions) found in the Old Testament, rather than a theology of the Old Testament. My evaluation parallels that of Dentan, in *Preface to Old Testament Theology*, pp. 79-80.

to seem to defy all classification; and they never articulated their beliefs in any systematic way. Yet scholars are able by an analysis of the extant texts to reconstruct with some success those distinctive patterns of belief and ritual practice which made each of these religions, in spite of mutual similarities, a phenomenon unto itself. The numerous books entitled *Egyptian Religion, Mesopotamian Religion,* or the like, may be taken as evidence of that fact.

But if such a thing is possible where other—and much more poorly documented—religions are concerned, surely it should be possible in the case of the faith of the Old and the New Testaments. In spite of all the diversity that may be observed, there is an overarching unity in both Testaments. Israel's religion developed and changed and expressed itself in a variety of ways. But underneath all change and variety there was an entity, the faith of Israel, that stubbornly preserved its identity. It is the task of Old Testament theology, while never forgetting its diversity, to describe it in its structural unity. There is a marked diversity of expression in the New Testament too; but there is also amid the diversity an entity, the faith of the New Testament church, which is essentially one and is unique. It is the task of New Testament theology to set forth its essential content. And, in spite of the manifest differences between the Testaments, and in spite of one's horror of reading New Testament doctrine into the Old, there is nevertheless a theological as well as a historical connection between the two, if only because the New Testament faith saw such a connection. The fact that it saw it draws the Old Testament within the orbit of Christian theology. We have the right to affirm, as the New Testament affirmed, that the true conclusion of Israel's history, and the fulfillment of her faith, lies in Christ and his gospel—not in the Talmud. But that is to say that there is in a true sense a biblical theology, embracing both Testaments.

II

But what is the nature of this structure of theology that undergirds the Old Testament? What is its essential content? How is it taken up in the New? Many large books have been written on the subject, and it is manifest that we cannot pretend to deal with it adequately in a few short pages. All that we can attempt to do is to suggest certain broad outlines, in the hope that this will suffice to make the point at which we have been driving at least tolerably clear.

1. That Israel's faith was a unique phenomenon, a thing *sui generis* in the ancient world, would be denied by no informed person today. This is, of course, not to imply that it developed in isolation from its cultural environment, independently of it and untouched by it. To the contrary, Israel was throughout her entire history culturally and politically a part of the larger world around her, and it would be surprising indeed if her religion had not been affected by that fact. And indeed it was. Not only did practices of foreign origin repeatedly infiltrate the structure of Israel's religion, as the Bible makes abundantly clear; many of the forms through which her own distinctive faith found expression are so closely paralleled among neighboring peoples that they may be assumed to have been borrowed from outside or passed down from a common cultural heritage.

Examples of this could be multiplied. One thinks of Israel's legal tradition with its numerous likenesses to the Mesopotamian legal tradition as represented by the Code of Hammurabi and its predecessors. Or one thinks of her sacrificial system which in various of its details was similar to that of the Canaanites. The temple in Jerusalem where she worshiped her God was, in its architectural pattern, of a type at home in the surrounding world, and much of its symbolism was apparently adapted from abroad. Again, Israel's poetic forms, her psalms and her wisdom, all had their parallels among neighboring peoples. The phenomenon of prophecy, though absolutely unique as it developed in Israel, was nevertheless in some of its manifestations not without parallels elsewhere. Israel's notion of the physical universe, her science (such as she had), was that of the ancient world generally. In a word, Israel again and again expressed the deepest things of her faith through categories shared with others.

But this in no sense cancels the uniqueness of Israel's faith, which remained, in spite of all similarities and all borrowing, a phenomenon quite without parallel among the religions of the pagan environment.[22] To speak in general, Israel borrowed only what she could assimilate. Features in the religions of her neighbors, as well as features inherited from her own pre-Yahwistic past, which were felt to be out of harmony with her distinctive faith were either rejected out of hand or were combated and,

---

[22] For a more extended discussion of points made in this and the ensuing paragraphs, the work of G. E. Wright, *The Old Testament Against Its Environment* (SBT, 2; London: SCM Press, 1950), is highly recommended.

in the course of time, sloughed off. And what was borrowed was adapted to Yahwistic faith, "baptized" as it were into Yahwism, undergirded with a new theological rationale, and not infrequently subjected to a radical inner transmutation in the process. Features shared with the religions of the pagan environment simply do not get us to the heart of Israel's faith. Such features are numerous enough and evident enough, but they tend to lie near the surface; beneath "there is a great gulf fixed."

For one thing, Israel's God was of a type absolutely unique in the ancient world. The ancient paganisms were all polytheisms, with dozens of gods ranged hierarchically in complex pantheons, each with his cult, his priesthood, and his images. The will of no one god was supreme. Clashes of will in the world of the gods were thought to be as much the rule as they are here on earth and, indeed, were thought to affect the outcome of earthly struggles. The gods were for the most part identified with the heavenly bodies, with cosmic functions and natural forces; they were in and of nature and, like nature, without any particular moral character. To the pagan, nature was, if one may put it so, alive with gods: it was not an "it," but a "thou." [23] The pagan understood the functions of nature in terms of the doings of the gods. Through the myth he sought to comprehend the ultimate realities of his universe—the rhythmic pattern of the cosmos, which seemed unchanging, yet was liable to violent and inexplicable upheavals—to which the life of earthly society must adjust itself. In the cult, in mimetic ritual, the myth was reenacted, for it was believed that by this means a renewal of the powers of nature was effected and a measure of control over them gained. The pagan conceived of his gods as beings who were perhaps benign, perhaps malign, but certainly capricious. Though he had no doubt that they both could and did act in events (they could bring victory or defeat, famine or plenty, good fortune or ill), any notion of a purposive guidance of history by the gods was lacking. The gods were expected, when approached through the appropriate ritual, to confer tangible benefits upon their worshipers and to maintain the orderly balance of the cosmos, upon which the well-being of the existing order depended.

Israel's God was of a radically different type. Unlike the pagan gods, he stood quite alone. No pantheon surrounded him. He was the one God

[23] For an introduction to the ancient paganisms and their understanding of the world, see H. Frankfort *et al., The Intellectual Adventure of Ancient Man* (Chicago: University of Chicago Press, 1946; reprinted in paperback with the title, *Before Philosophy*).

who alone might be worshiped; worship of other gods was illegitimate and not to be tolerated. Moreover, any attempt to provide an image of him, or to depict him in any visible form, was at all periods strictly forbidden. Nor was Israel's God identified with any heavenly body or natural function. To be sure, he was conceived of as controlling the heavenly bodies, restraining the watery chaos of the oceans, working in the rainstorm and the sun, the earthquake and the wind, and conferring the blessings of fertility. But no one of these aspects of his activity can be said to be more characteristic of him than any other, so that we might classify him as a sun-god, a storm-god, or a fertility god. Though nature was by no means conceived of as lifeless in Israel's faith, it was nevertheless "undeified," demythed; it no longer reflected the activity of gods but was the sphere of activity of the one God who was Creator and Lord of all nature and who ruled all things in accordance with his sovereign will. Israel's faith emancipated her from the world of pagan myth. Since her God was one God, without sex and without progeny, myth was alien to her. She created no myth and took over none save to devitalize it.[24] And, in sharpest contrast to the pagan religions, which were keyed to the rhythm of nature and without exception "nonhistorical," Israel's faith had a lively sense of history: her God was one who works through the events of history for the accomplishment of a purpose.

And so Israel conceived of her God from earliest times onward. To say this is not to suggest that Israel's understanding of God remained static through the Old Testament period, for obviously it did not, but rather broadened and deepened enormously with the passing years. Nor is it to suggest that all Israelites at any time had an equally clear comprehension

---

[24] Perhaps the reader has been puzzled to note that while some scholars speak freely of myth in the Bible (and perhaps suggest "demythologizing"), others, equally competent, declare flatly that the Bible contains no myth. It is a question of definition into which we need not go here. Suffice it to say that myth as we know it from the ancient pagan world (Egypt, Mesopotamia, Canaan, Greece, and Rome) is absent from the Bible save perhaps in the form of vestigial survivals. The Bible adapts material and uses language that had its origin in myth, and contains allusions to mythical characters and events, but its thinking is not mythopoeic. Myth, in the sense in which the word is used here, is properly at home in a polytheistic nature religion—which the biblical religion is not. On the question of the definition of myth, and the applicabilty of the term in the case of the Bible, see *inter alia*, C. Hartlich and W. Sachs, *Der Ursprung des Mythosbegriffes in der modernen Bibelwissenschaft* (Tübingen: J. C. B. Mohr, 1952); B. S. Childs, *Myth and Reality in the Old Testament* (SBT 27; London: SCM Press, 1960); J. L. McKenzie, *Myths and Realities* (Milwaukee: The Bruce Publishing Co., 1963), Part III (esp. "Myth and the Old Testament," pp. 182-200).

of the nature of their God and an equally strong commitment to him. Of what religion has such a thing ever been true? The Bible tells us explicitly that Israelites again and again hankered after other gods, made images of them, and worshiped them; and it repeatedly lets us see Israelites whose attitudes and actions betray that their understanding of their God was little better than pagan. But one learns little of the true nature of a religion from the superstitions and aberrant behavior of its less instructed and less committed adherents. In spite of such things, and in spite of a general development of concepts through the years, the God of Israel's normative faith was at all periods unique in the ancient world. Israel did not in the course of her history exchange one type of God for another. There was development to be sure; but this was not an evolution from lower forms of religion to higher but rather the unfolding of features that were present from the beginning and stubbornly constant.

2. But Israel's faith did not center upon an idea of God, nor did it consist in an articulated complex of religious and ethical teachings of any sort. Were such the case, one might readily see more diversity than unity in it. There is indeed a great refinement of ideas through the pages of the Old Testament, together with the widest divergencies in moral and theological understanding, as we have said. And it was no doubt in good part because of its penchant for examining the Bible primarily for its religious and ethical teachings that the older liberalism was led, in view of its philosophical and critical presuppositions, to describe the biblical religion in terms of evolutionary development. But the genius of the Old Testament faith does not lie in its idea of God or in the elevation of its ethical teachings. Rather, it lies in its understanding of history, specifically of Israel's history, as the theater of God's purposive activity. The Old Testament offers a theological interpretation of history. A concern with the meaning of history, and of specific events within history, is one of its most characteristic features.[25] It records a real history, and it interprets

[25] James Barr has recently challenged what he calls the almost universally accepted notion that in the biblical faith history is seen as the one supreme channel of revelation; see "Revelation through History in the Old Testament and in Modern Theology," *Interpretation*, XVII (1963), 193-205; reprinted in M. E. Marty and D. G. Peerman, eds., *New Theology, No. 1* (New York: The Macmillan Company, 1964), pp. 60-74. Barr's remarks are a needed caution against over-much glibness, but they do not, I believe, affect the position taken here. The Old Testament of course does not view history as the sole vehicle of revelation. On the contrary, it knows of (and Old Testament theologies usually point out) many media of revelation including, not least, God's direct word to his servants the prophets. Indeed, the *bruta facta* of history by themselves could scarcely be considered

every detail of that history in the light of Yahweh's sovereign purpose and righteous will. It relates past events—the stories of the Patriarchs, the Exodus, the covenant at Sinai, the giving of the Promised Land—in terms of his gracious dealings with his people, his promise to them and its fulfilment. It continually sets forth the response that Yahweh requires of his people, and interprets their fortunes in the midst of events, in terms of their obedience or disobedience to his demands. And it announces what Yahweh will yet do, in the judgment of Exile and beyond, for the accomplishment of his purpose. The Old Testament consistently views Israel's history as one that is guided on to a destination by the word and will of her God.

The Old Testament's understanding of and witness to, God's action in history is indeed diverse in its expression, and it can by no means be reduced to a harmonious system of doctrine. But it is not, for all that, a cacophony of discordant voices. Behind it and informing it in all its variety of expression there lies a commonly held structure of believing, an understanding of reality, that was both constitutive of it and characteristically Israelite. And this understanding of reality remained, in spite of all developments and shifts in emphasis, essentially constant throughout the Old Testament period.

It is out of the question to attempt a comprehensive description of this distinctive structure of belief here. We can at most suggest only a few of its essential features. Among these, that complex of beliefs which we associate with the word "election" stands out. Wherever one looks in the Old Testament, one encounters the stubbornly held conviction that Yahweh has in his sovereign grace called Israel to himself, delivered her from bondage, and given her the Promised Land, and that Israel therefore occupies a peculiar position among the nations of the earth as his chosen people.[26] It is true that the distinctive terminology used to express this concept seems to have been fixed only at a relatively late period. [27] But the belief that Israel had been in a peculiar sense the recipient of Yahweh's

---

revelatory. Yet the fact remains that the divine word in the Old Testament, whatever the medium of communication, characteristically has to do with events, what is to happen or has happened, rather than with propositional truth.

[26] For discussion of the place of this concept, see H. H. Rowley, *The Biblical Doctrine of Election* (London: Lutterworth Press, 1950); also G. E. Wright, *The Old Testament Against Its Environment*, esp. pp. 46-54.

[27] In the Deuteronomic literature (7th and 6th centuries); cf. Th. C. Vriezen, *Die Erwählung Israels nach dem Alten Testament* (Zürich: Zwingli-Verlag, 1953). But the terminology is also evident in certain psalms (cf. K. Koch, "Zur Geschichte der Erwählungs-

favor and stands under his special protection as his chosen people is in evidence as far back as we can go. It is reflected in certain ancient poems which date to the tenth century or before (e.g. Exod. 15:1-18; Num. 23:9; 24:8-9; Deut. 33:26-29).[28] It is expressed in the preamble of the Decalogue ("I am Yahweh your God, who brought you out of the land of Egypt, out of the house of bondage"). It is to be seen in certain creedal confessions which seem to reach back to the earliest period of Israel's life as a people (Deut. 6:20-25; 26:5-10; Josh. 24:2-13).[29] And it is the central theological concern of the ancient account of the Yahwist (tenth century), who tells how God called Abraham and fulfilled the promise made to him by bringing Israel out of Egypt into the Promised Land. Belief in Israel's election is one that pervades the whole of the Old Testament, both early and late. Nowhere in the Old Testament is it not tacitly assumed or confidently asserted that Yahweh has called Israel out of all the nations of the earth to be his chosen people. And nowhere is it really doubted that this relationship is an enduring one that will last for all time to come.

Equally prominent is Israel's understanding of the sovereign and exclusive lordship of Yahweh over his people, of the demands that he has laid upon them and the response that he expects of them if they are to continue in his favor: in short, that whole understanding of reality that expressed itself in the concept of covenant.[30] This again was a primitive feature in Israel's faith. Indeed, Israel first emerged into history as a covenant society. When those fugitive slaves who had experienced the Exodus deliverance entered into covenant with Yahweh at Sinai, a new society was formed where none had been before: a league of clans united

---

vorstellung in Israel," *ZAW*, LXVII [1955], 205-26), and was almost certainly at home still earlier in the official cult of the Jerusalem temple. On the subject, see G. E. Mendenhall, *IDB*, II, 76-82.

[28] On the date of these poems, see W. F. Albright, "The Oracles of Balaam," *JBL*, LXIII (1944), 207-33; F. M. Cross and D. N. Freedman, "The Song of Miriam," *JNES*, XIV (1955), 237-50; and Cross and Freedman, "The Blessing of Moses," *JBL*, LXVII (1948), 191-210. There is a considerable further technical literature on these and other ancient poems in the Old Testament, but it need not be cited here.

[29] See G. von Rad, *Das formgeschichtliche Problem des Hexateuchs*, BWANT, IV (1938); reprinted in *Gesammelte Studien zum Alten Testament* (Munich: Chr. Kaiser Verlag, 1958), pp. 9-86. The antiquity of these pieces has been disputed, recently by Th. C. Vriezen, "The Credo in the Old Testament" in *Studies on the Psalms* (Die Ou-Testamentiese Werkgemeenskap in Suid-Afrika, 1963), pp. 5-17. We cannot debate the question here.

[30] See esp. W. Eichrodt, *Theology of the Old Testament*, Vol. I, for an understanding of the central importance of the covenant in Israel's faith.

through common allegiance to the same God. In its form, the Sinaitic covenant follows the pattern of a suzerainty treaty of the Hittite empire.[31] The Israelite clans, having in effect acknowledged Yahweh's benevolent acts in their behalf, accepted him as their (divine) suzerain and bound themselves to live in sacred truce with one another under his overlordship. The notion of the kingship of God over his people, which runs like a thread through all the Bible, has its beginnings here. By its very nature as a suzerainty treaty—which was anything but a pact between equals—the covenant imposed rigorous stipulations. In particular, Israel was forbidden to have dealings with any other overlord (i.e., god) save Yahweh and was obligated to conform to the demands of his law in every aspect of her life, whether public or private. Failure to comply with these stipulations constituted breach of covenant and invited the Overlord's wrath. One sees from this that law, although it did not occupy in early Israel the absolute position that it did in postexilic Judaism, was nevertheless an essential feature in the structure of Israel's faith from the beginning.

This understanding of reality in terms of covenant found its classic expression in the organization and the institutions of the early Israelite tribal league; but it remained normative even after the tribal league had vanished. To be sure, all its features underwent great development, and many vicissitudes, with the passing years. The notion of the kingship of Yahweh in time assumed dimensions of which early Israel could never have dreamed; and there were also times when it came close to being forgotten altogether as Israel "went a-whoring" after other gods. Covenant law was at times flagrantly disregarded; yet the covenant stipulations continued to be recited and reaffirmed as normative. The legal tradition continued to develop as new precedents were laid down to care for new situations as they arose and as new formulations of law were undertaken. Law assumed an ever more important position, till in postexilic Judaism it became well-nigh the organizing principle of religion. The understanding of covenant itself underwent many changes, especially as the old tribal order gave way to the monarchy. By some the covenant was made virtually into a guarantee of the national safety; by others its stipulations were regarded as a mortal

---

[31] See esp. G. E. Mendenhall, *Law and Covenant in Israel and the Ancient Near East* (Pittsburgh: The Biblical Colloquium, 1955); also "Covenant," *IDB*, I, 714-23; similarly, K. Baltzer, *Das Bundesformular* (Neukirchen: Verlag der Buchhandlung des Erziehungsvereins, 1960); W. Beyerlin, *Origins and History of the Oldest Sinaitic Traditions*, trans. S. Rudman (Oxford: Basil Blackwell, 1965). There is a considerable further literature on the subject which we need not cite here.

threat to the sinful nation's existence. Yet, through crisis and beyond, it continued to be clung to as Yahweh's gracious provision for his people, which he would never finally abandon. In spite of all development, Israel's understanding of her existence in terms of the covenant relationship remained a central feature of her structure of belief. At no time did her normative faith cease to look to Yahweh as the divine Overlord of his people, whom alone they must worship, upon whose favor their life depends, and whose commands they must obey.

A note of promise, a confident expectation for the future, is likewise a characteristic feature of Israel's faith at all periods. To be sure, an eschatology in the proper sense of the word developed relatively late (just when is a question of one's definition of eschatology).[32] But a lively confidence in what God would do in the future, which is the seedbed of eschatology (however defined), is to be observed as far back as the very earliest period. Assurance of his continued protection and blessing is a prominent note in various of those ancient poems noted above (Exod. 15:1-18; Num. 23–24; Deut. 33; Gen. 49, etc.).[33] The theme of promise moving on to fulfillment positively dominates the thought of the so-called Yahwist as he tells the story of the Patriarchs, the Exodus, the Wilderness wandering, and the giving of the land, and it was almost certainly present in the still older material with which he worked. Indeed, one may believe that the confidence that they had been promised abundant land and a great posterity was an original feature in the religion of those northwest-Semitic seminomads who were Israel's remotest ancestors.[34] Promise for the future is, moreover, implicit in the nature of the Sinaitic covenant itself. If this covenant imposed stringent stipulations enforced by the threat of dire penalties in the event of disobedience, it also carried with it

---

[32] If one understands eschatology only in suprahistorical terms (a doctrine of the last things, the end of the age, etc.), as S. Mowinckel, for example, does (see *He That Cometh*, trans. G. W. Anderson [Oxford: Basil Blackwell, 1956] *passim*), then Israel had none until well on in the postexilic period. If, however, one allows the term to include the expectation of a consummation within history toward which God's purpose is moving, then eschatology made its appearance at least as far back as the eighth century, with its roots farther back still. I should prefer the latter alternative as being more proper to the thought of the Old Testament. The future hope of the classical prophets was an eschatology of a kind.

[33] See note 28 above.

[34] First pointed out by Albrecht Alt, *Der Gott der Väter*, BWANT, III (1929); reprinted in *Kleine Schriften zur Geschichte des Volkes Israel* (Munich: C. H. Beck'sche Verlagsbuchhandlung, 1953), I, 1-78.

the assurance that, if its demands were met, the Overlord's favor would be endlessly continued.

This note of promise, characteristic of Israel's faith from the beginning, underwent spectacular development through the pages of the Old Testament and expressed itself in a variety of ways. At first it was perhaps little more than confidence in the continued possession of the land and the assurance of divine blessing and protection from enemies round about. Under the monarchy in Judah it found expression in the theology of the Davidic covenant, with its assurance that God had promised to David a dynasty that would rule forever and triumph over all its foes.[35] There was also the hope of the Day of Yahweh, which was firmly entrenched in the popular mind at least by the eighth century (Amos 5:18-20) and which eagerly awaited Yahweh's imminent intervention when he would come to the aid of his people, demolish their foes, and triumphantly vindicate them in accordance with his promises.[36] With the classical prophets, promise was pushed into a yet farther future and began to assume eschatological dimensions. In the immediate future the prophets saw judgment, not promise; but beyond the catastrophe that they knew was coming, or that had come, they envisioned the time when Yahweh would once more act, rescue his faithful people, and triumphantly establish his rule. This hope took many forms: the expectation of an ideal king of David's line (beginning with Isaiah); the reestablishment of the Mosaic covenant, which the people had so grievously broken, on a new and deeper level (especially in Jeremiah, but also in Hosea); a national resurrection and the confirmation of the covenant with David (notably in Ezekiel, e.g. ch. 37); a new Exodus march out of the wilderness of exile and the turning of all nations to Yahweh (especially in Isa. 40–55); the coming of the Son of man on the clouds of heaven (in Daniel and intertestamental literature)—and more besides. But all these forms, diverse as they are, witness to the unshakable confidence that Yahweh is sovereign in power, faithful to his promises and

[35] See esp. II Sam. 7 and the Royal Psalms, e.g. Pss. 2, 18, 20, 21, 72, 89, 110, 132, etc. For a convenient introduction to these psalms and the significance of their theology, see Keith R. Crim, *The Royal Psalms* (Richmond: John Knox Press, 1962); see also A. R. Johnson, *Sacral Kingship in Ancient Israel* (Cardiff: University of Wales Press, 1955); H. J. Kraus, *Gottesdienst in Israel* (2nd ed.; Munich: Chr. Kaiser Verlag, 1962), Ch. V [Eng. trans. by Geoffrey Buswell as *Worship in Israel* (Oxford: Basil Blackwell, 1966]).

[36] On this concept, see the theologies of the Old Testament, esp. Eichrodt, *Theology of the Old Testament*, I, 459-62; also G. von Rad, "The Origin of the Concept of the Day of Yahweh," *JSS*, IV (1959), 97-108.

saving purpose. Characteristic of the Old Testament faith is its forward look, its straining ahead toward God's future, the triumph of his kingly rule in the earth.

The above features, and others that might be mentioned, run through the whole of the Old Testament and inform all its parts. Israel's witness to history, as well as her understanding of her own existence within history, springs from this structure of theology. Her law is an expression of it, her piety is the piety of men nurtured in it; the prophets' attack upon the nation's sin, their announcement of the judgment, and also their hope, are rooted in it. To be sure, some parts of the Old Testament are far less obviously expressive of Israel's distinctive understanding of reality than are others. Indeed, some parts (and one thinks of such a book as Proverbs) seem to be only peripherally related to it, while others (for example, Ecclesiastes) even question certain of its essential features. Yet nowhere can Israel's normative faith be said really to be absent, for in one way or another it underlies all parts of the Old Testament. Even where its central themes are not explicitly developed (as in Proverbs), the place of Israel as Yahweh's people, bound to live under his law, is clearly taken for granted; and where there is outright questioning (as in Ecclesiastes), it is *this* understanding of reality—and no other—that is questioned.[37] The Old Testament in all its diversity hangs together about a coherent, though never systematically articulated, structure of belief, either to express some facet of it (perhaps in some cases a very minor one) or, on occasion, to enter into debate with it. It is in the light of this structure of belief and its overarching themes, let it be said by way of anticipation, that all preaching from the Old Testament is to be done.

3. The Old Testament, then, both records a real history and provides a theological interpretation of it. It understands the events of that history and the vicissitudes of Israel's fortunes in the course of it in terms of the gracious and purposive dealings of God and his sovereign demands. As has

[37] The place of the Wisdom Books in the theology of the Old Testament has always constituted a problem. Thus, for example, Proverbs contains chiefly canny, prudential instruction and has nothing explicitly to say of God's guidance of history, or of election or covenant. Nevertheless, it clearly assumes both that Israel is God's people and that the true measure of wisdom is the law of God, who is the source of wisdom. Proverbs is indeed peripheral to Israel's faith, but it does not stand apart from it or conflict with it; rather it expresses in its own way a limited, albeit a not altogether unimportant, aspect of it. The theological rootage of wisdom becomes more apparent in later books such as the Wisdom of Solomon and Ecclesiasticus. For discussion of the point, see conveniently, G. E. Wright, *God Who Acts* (SBT 8; London: SCM Press, 1952), pp. 102-5.

been said, it was believed that this history was moving toward a destination, the triumphant establishment of God's rule on earth and the fulfillment of his promises.

But if this be so, the Old Testament is an incomplete book, a history with no ending. It announces a conclusion, but it never arrives at it. It is a book in which hopes are often dashed, always deferred, at best only partially realized. It is a history of God's redemptive purpose, a *Heilsgeschichte;* but it is also a most human history, the history of an ancient people and the disappointment of their hopes—and of God's judgment upon their history. The Old Testament itself makes this plain. It was the business of the preexilic prophets to tell their people that hope as they had conceived it would never come to pass. The people, they declared, have served all possible false gods, have kicked and crowded their covenant brother, and in so doing have spat on covenant law and made mockery of Yahweh's overlordship. They are, therefore, living in a fool's paradise in assuming that Yahweh, through his covenant with David, is irrevocably committed to their defense. Their confidence that he will always protect them and will guide their national history to a triumphant consummation is a false confidence. They have by their sins broken covenant with Yahweh, and the covenant promises cannot be made good to them. All their busy religion, their sacrifice and ritual, is of no avail. Doom on them!

That doom fell, and the Old Testament tells of it. The Israelite nation was destroyed. It would be impossible adequately to describe the shock, the disillusionment, and the suffering both physical and spiritual that this catastrophe entailed. To many an Israelite it seemed that God had failed. Yet Israel survived. A new community rose out of the ashes of the old and, rallying around the law, stubbornly perpetuated itself as a people. Nor were the mighty constants of Israel's normative faith ever surrendered— though all, perforce, underwent adaptation. Still Israel held fast to her status as the chosen people of Yahweh; still she acknowledged no God but him, recited his past mighty acts, and looked forward with heightened intensity to his definitive intervention in the future. Meanwhile the law, massively developing and exalted to a position of absolute authority, continued to lay down before her the lines that she must follow if she would live in covenant with her God as his holy people and be heir to his promises. Down to the end of the Old Testament period, Israel marched toward the future, looking for the final consummation when hope would be fulfilled and promise become fact.

But the Old Testament knows of no such fulfillment. The expected *eschaton* did not come; on its own terms it would not and could not come. No messianic deliverer appeared to demolish the tyrant power and usher in God's rule of righteousness and peace. No apocalyptic overturn took place to put an end to the present evil age and to inaugurate the new age of God's triumphant kingdom. Consummation of hope lies beyond the bounds of the Old Testament. The Old Testament does indeed relate a *Heilsgeschichte,* a history of redemption; but it is a strange *Heilsgeschichte,* a *Heilsgeschichte* that does not arrive at *Heil,* a broken *Heilsgeschichte,* a truncated *Heilsgeschichte.* The Old Testament is a book that is theologically incomplete; it points beyond itself and ends in a posture of waiting. Down to its very last page it must speak of the fulfillment of promise in the future tense: the God who acted in the days of Exodus and Conquest, and through great David, *will act again* one day.

4. It is just this fulfillment of unfulfilled promise, this completion of incomplete history, that the New Testament is principally concerned to affirm. It has the boldness to announce that the long-awaited eschatological event, and the turning point of all history, has taken place in Jesus Christ: the God who acted in Israel's history *now has acted decisively* in him. To make this announcement is the New Testament's central theological concern. The New Testament simply does not center upon a higher code of ethics or a more exalted conception of God, as so many people seem to think. Granted that the ethical teachings of Jesus have never been surpassed; granted, further, that Christendom unanimously affirms that the perfect revelation of God has been given in him; the fact still remains that the uniqueness of the New Testament does not consist in its ethical teachings or its idea of God. He who tries on such grounds to commend the merits of Christianity to his Jewish friend will be unhorsed—and for his ignorance will deserve to be. Jesus did not come to say to his fellow Jews that a better ethical code or a loftier notion of God was now available, but to tell them that *their* God had "in the fulness of time" acted to fulfill *their* law and *their* prophets.

The New Testament's theology, like that of the Old, centers upon events and affirmations regarding the significance of those events; it does not consist in ethical or religious teachings but is a gospel (i.e., good news). Where the Old Testament expects, the New announces: It has happened! "The time is fulfilled, and the kingdom of God is at hand" (Mark 1:15); Jesus is the Christ (Messiah), the promised deliverer of David's line; he is

138

the servant of God foretold by the prophet (Luke 4:16-21); and he has done his sacrificial and saving work and is now exalted to highest heaven (Phil. 2:5-10); he has given to his followers the new covenant promised by Jeremiah (Jer. 31:31-34) when, "on the night when he was betrayed," he distributed to them the bread and the wine and said, "This cup is the new covenant in my blood" (I Cor. 11:23-26). The New Testament, indeed, reaches back to the eschatological hope of the Old and claims it in all its variety for Jesus Christ, thereby drawing eschatology into the present. It is concerned to affirm that all the hope of Israel, all that her prophets had envisioned and all that her law had tried to do, has been given in Christ, in whom God's final redemptive act has been done.

At the heart of the New Testament's theology there lies, thus, a procla-mation, a kerygma. This kerygma, examples of which may be seen in certain apostolic speeches recorded in Acts and elsewhere, seems to have been the burden of the preaching of the earliest Christian community.[38] The gist of it is something like this: The long-awaited Messiah has come, and he is none other than this Jesus, who was born of the lineage of David, attested of God by his mighty works; who was crucified, whom God raised from the dead and elevated to sit at his right hand in glory until all creation bows at his feet; let men therefore repent, acknowledge him as Lord, and receive the remission of their sins, that they may be delivered from the present evil age and may share in the blessings of God's new age which has dawned.[39] Diverse as its witness is, the New Testament finds unity in this kerygmatic affirmation. In all its parts its principal concern is to announce what has happened in Jesus Christ, and to expound the significance of this both in history and beyond; no part but shares this concern and is animated by it. Thus the teachings of Jesus are not proposed as ethical principles, but as a summons to that radical commitment which the now-intruding kingdom of God demands and a suggestion of what that commitment entails. The death of Jesus is not set forth as a heroic martyrdom or a tragic misadventure, but as God's decisive act for man's redemption, the climax of his struggle with the evil

[38] See esp. C. H. Dodd, *The Apostolic Preaching and Its Developments* (2nd ed.; London: Hodder & Stoughton 1944). Passages in question include Acts 2:14-40; 3:12-26; 10:34-43; 13:16-41; cf. I Cor. 15:1-11; Rom. 1:1-4, and others. It is possible that Dodd's views require some modification, but we cannot discuss the point here; see the remarks of J. M. P. Sweet in *ET* LXXVI (February, 1965), 143-47. Certainly these speeches can be regarded only as skeleton outlines of what may actually have been preached.

[39] It will be realized that any summary of the kerygma is a composite. Not all of these features will be found at any one place.

powers of this world, which issues on Easter morning in total victory. The theology of Paul is not the result of abstract doctrinal or philosophical reflection but rather represents the attempt to express the significance of the kerygmatic affirmations in language intelligible to Jew and Greek alike. His instructions to the churches which few of his letters are without —these are no arbitrary rules of conduct, still less moralistic casuistry, but are a summons to the new life in Christ and a suggestion of what that may mean in the tangible situation.

Viewed in the light of the New Testament's affirmations, the Bible as a whole is seen to possess a profound and by no means artificial unity. It is the unity of the beginning and the affirmed completion of a single redemptive process. The New Testament is, in fact, a reinterpretation of the Old in the light of Christ. It takes up the great central themes of the Old Testament's theology—God's gracious election of his people, his covenant with them and kingly rule over them, his purposes for them and promises to them—and gives these a new significance in the light of what Christ has done. As God through his grace once called Israel out of bondage, so now through his grace in Jesus Christ he summons to himself his new Israel, the church, redeemed from the bondage of sin and death. As God gave his covenant at Sinai, binding Israel to live under his law, so now through Christ he has given his promised new covenant, committing his church to the lordship of Christ and to the service of his purpose in the world. As God through his prophets promised to Israel the triumph of his kingly rule in earth, so now through Jesus, who is the Christ (Messiah), he has brought that kingdom to pass and has promised its final victory. Everywhere the New Testament seizes hold of the key themes of the Old and gives them a new meaning in Christ. In doing this, it both completes the Old Testament's incompleteness and binds it irrevocably with itself within the canon of Christian Scripture. This, and no less than this, is the assertion that the New Testament makes: The redemptive purposes of God, begun in Abraham and the Exodus, have come to fulfillment in Jesus Christ—and this is the whole meaning of God's history with his people, nay, of history altogether.

III

The foregoing section has admittedly offered no more than a sketch; only the broadest outlines have been touched upon. But perhaps enough has been said to allow us to make the point at which we have been driving. It is submitted that this structure of theology which undergirds the whole of the Old Testament and informs each of its parts, and which is then taken up in the New Testament and reinterpreted in the light of Christ, has the greatest bearing upon the problem of the authority of the Old Testament with which we have been concerned, indeed provides us with the key to its solution.

1. Our problem has been essentially that of laying hold upon the normative element in the Old Testament, of defining the sense in which it remains authoritative over the Christian. We have seen the gravity of that problem; let us briefly review it. That the Old Testament cannot be, in all its parts, directly normative for the Christian is obvious. It contains much—ancient laws and customs, ancient institutions and ways of thinking —that cannot serve as a model for Christian faith and practice, as well as attitudes and actions that are not safe guides for the Christian conscience to follow. We cannot foist every feature of the Old Testament, just so, upon the Christian as a law. Yet we have refused to evade the problem either by deposing the Old Testament or by arbitrarily forcing it to speak with a New Testament voice; we have insisted that the Old Testament must be retained in the Bible with full canonical status and that it must be allowed to speak, and must be taken seriously, in its plain sense. But how can it be appealed to as authoritative Scripture when, read in its plain sense, it contains so much that is not obviously, or obviously is not, a model for Christian faith and practice? That is the problem. Manifestly some line must be drawn in the Old Testament between what commands us and what does not, between what is normative for our faith and what is not.

But—and it cannot be repeated too often—this line must not be drawn in such a way that we are betrayed once again into a selective or one-sided use of the Old Testament. The problem of the Old Testament is not to be solved by subtraction. We cannot undertake to declare this passage fully inspired, that less so, and the other expressive of no more than the thoughts and beliefs of ancient men. We have no scales for weighing such matters save the rigged scales of subjective taste. By the same token, we cannot impose upon the Old Testament a normative principle drawn from outside—whether the New Testament's ethics, its idea of God, the principle of *agapē,* or whatnot—thereby to separate the Christian from the sub-Christian, the eternally valid and authoritative from the ancient and

141

outworn. This is again to plunge into subjectivism, for such distinctions can only be made on the basis of a value judgment; and value judgments are by definition subjective. It is also tacitly to undermine the Old Testament's authority, for the value judgment is given priority over the material. For the same reason, we are not permitted to nominate this or that feature in the Old Testament itself—whether the "prophetic faith," the law, its witness to Christ, its understanding of *Existenz*, or whatever it may be—as alone of decisive concern, while dismissing the remainder as of little theological interest, if not irrelevant. This is also to impose an external—and ultimately subjective—canon of evaluation on the Old Testament, and seriously to limit its witness.

Let it be said as plainly as possible: We cannot rightly speak of the authority of the Old Testament if we allow ourselves to appeal to it selectively, as it pleases us. We must be willing to confront its witness *as a whole,* even those parts of it that offend us, and make our peace with it. We may not on the basis of a value judgment make selections from it and then call the result thus subjectively arrived at its normative teaching. It is, of course, obvious that parts of the Old Testament have greater importance and stand on a higher level ethically and morally than do others. And because this is so, it is both legitimate and inevitable that the reader should form judgments with regard to those passages that are to him spiritually the most meaningful. But if any real notion of the authority of the Old Testament is to be maintained, value judgments must be made with recognition of the *validity* (i.e., the authority) of the whole. Either we accept the Old Testament as a valid document of our faith or we do not. If we do, we will no doubt continue to find some parts of greater value than others, but we will listen to it all and will not be tempted to discard any part as valueless, for the whole has been accepted as valid (i.e., normative Scripture). [40] We must take the Old Testament seriously

---

[40] The question of validity must precede the question of value if the latter is to be theologically meaningful. To illustrate: a $100 bill obviously has more value than a $1 bill, but both have value since both are valid currency. On the other hand, a $100 Confederate note has precisely the same value in the marketplace as a $1 Confederate note—nothing; neither will purchase anything since the entire issue is invalid. Just so, I apply value judgments to the Old Testament, but I find value in all of it, because I accept the whole as valid (normative) for my faith. I also apply value judgments, say, to the Koran or the Hindu scriptures; but here the question of value is theoretical and theologically irrelevant, since I do not regard these writings as having validity for my faith. The above illustration is adapted from Franz Hesse, "The Evaluation and the Authority of Old Testament Texts," trans. J. A. Wharton, *EOTH,* pp. 285-313; see esp. pp. 289-91.

in its entirety, just as we must the New. If we will not do that, then we cannot properly speak of its authority over us; we have advertised that we are willing to listen to it only insofar as its teachings happen to coincide with our own presuppositions.

But it is just here, it is submitted, that biblical theology may come to our rescue. We have agreed that there is much in the Bible, specifically the Old Testament, that is not directly normative for the Christian, and that somehow a distinction must be made between what commands his faith and practice and what does not. But if we cannot separate the divine from the human in the Bible, if we cannot by some value judgment separate the eternally valid from the sub-Christian and outworn, we can through the discipline of biblical theology hope to distinguish the normative from the incidental and transient, the central from the peripheral, *within the biblical faith itself.* That is to say, we can hope to discern the essential structure of the biblical faith, which is visible behind the ancient forms and institutions through which it found expression, as distinct from much of which the Bible tells that is peripheral to that faith. We may hope to detect behind every biblical text (for there are no nontheological texts in the Bible) that facet of theology which expresses itself there, and which, though it cannot be abstracted from the text, is nevertheless antecedent to the text, in that it caused it to be said (written) and said (written) as it was. It is further submitted that this overarching structure of theology, which in one way or another informs each of its texts, constitutes the essential and normative element in the Old Testament, and the one that binds it irrevocably to the New within the canon of Scripture. To delineate this distinctive structure of faith is the task of Old Testament theology and is the first step toward the solution of the problem of the Old Testament.

2. What has just been said touches upon something inherent in the very nature of Scripture. Whatever one's view of its inspiration, the Bible is at one and the same time the religious literature and the historical record of an ancient people; and it is the normative (canonical) document of the faith of Israel and of the Christian community which regarded itself as the true heir of Israel. Viewed as the first, it contains many things that belong to the ancient situation and cannot in any direct way serve as a model for Christians today. Viewed as the second, it is the primary record of the faith which we claim as our own and, as such, remains the court of final appeal in all discussions regarding the nature of that faith. By

virtue of the Bible's twofold character, it is possible to approach the biblical religion in more than one way. Because the Bible tells of a history, and because the biblical religion underwent many vicissitudes in the course of that history, it is possible to approach it "lengthwise," along the line of chronology, with the aim of reconstructing Israel's religious history or the rise and development of Christianity. This would be the approach of the historian of religion. But because the Bible, Old Testament or New, presents us with a faith which, in spite of vicissitudes, remained at all periods a distinctive and definable entity, consistent with itself, it is possible to approach it in "cross section," with the aim of setting forth those characteristic and normative features which impart to it its structural unity. This would be the approach of the biblical theologian.

It is evident, therefore, that the historian of religion and the biblical theologian will present differing pictures of the biblical religion, coming at it as they do from differing points of view. They have the same body of evidence at their disposal, but their fields of interest differ. The historian of Israel's religion is concerned to examine objectively all available evidence relating to the history of that religion, in order that he may describe how it came into being, how it adjusted to new situations, and how it developed through the course of the centuries. He is interested in aberrations of belief as well as in normative affirmations, in peculiar customs of occasional incidence as well as in normative cultus, in infractions of law as well as in the purest expressions of ethics, in idolatrous practices as well as reaction and reform. His aim is to present the history of a religion; like any historian he must deal with all known phenomena relating to his subject of study.

The Old Testament theologian, on the other hand, has a rather more restricted, if no less difficult, task. His concern, as we have said, is to set forth in orderly fashion the normative beliefs and practices of the Old Testament faith, those all-pervasive and constant features that impart to it its structural unity and distinctive character. While he must work as objectively as does the historian and on no account disregard pertinent evidence, and while he must not allow himself to gloss over variety and change or in any way to ignore the dimension of history, his task is to present a synthesis arrived at by induction. It is not his duty to describe every custom that Israelites may at one time or another have observed, or every popular belief that may have been entertained, whether distinctively

Yahwistic or not.[41] Still less is it his business to analyze every event that may have affected the fortunes of Israel's religion. His concern is with the essential and normative features of the Old Testament faith; and these he seeks to set forth within the framework of terminology proper to that faith.

The point just made might be illustrated by comparing the functions of the church historian and the Christian theologian. The former is concerned to describe the history of the church as it actually unfolded. He must, therefore, deal not merely with normative Christian belief but with every significant phenomenon relating to the history of organized Christianity: with religious wars and controversies, with schismatic and heretical movements, with Christians burning one another at the stake *ad majorem gloriam Dei*, with conduct on the part of professing Christians—and even ecclesiastical authorities—utterly in contradiction to the teachings of the gospel. He would take note of the fact that Christians have believed in witchcraft and have executed "witches"; he would take note of such things as Grandfather and the matter of slavery.[42] All these things belong to the church historian: they happened. But they do not belong to normative Christian theology. Slavery is again an excellent case in point. It was for many centuries practiced, and even defended on theological grounds, by Christian people, and at times it became a subject of controversy in the church. It therefore belongs to the history of Christianity at certain times and places. But it is no part of Christian theology—which does not include, but ultimately excludes, a "doctrine of slavery"—and it in no way directly concerns the church theologian, whose task it is simply to set forth and to defend the normative tenets of the Christian faith.

In the light of what has been said, it is apparent that there are many things in the Old Testament that are of the greatest interest to the historian of religion but that have no place, or no central place, in normative Old Testament theology. Some of these were actually extraneous to the faith of Israel and are rebuked in the Old Testament itself. One thinks above all of foreign beliefs and practices that from time to time infiltrated

---

[41] It seems to me that those who deny the possibility of an Old Testament theology on the grounds that there was no one religion of Israel (see note 19, above) tend to think of any religious belief or practice on the part of ancient Israelites as Israel's religion. If one does this, one will of course observe little unity in the religion of Israel. But would anyone think of identifying all the actual beliefs and practices of professing Christians as normative Christian theology?

[42] See Ch. I, pp. 49-51, above.

Israel, such as the cult of the Tyrian Baal in the reign of Ahab and Jezebel, or the worship of the heavenly host in the Assyrian period (II Kings 21: 1-9). Or one thinks of the practice of the occult arts, witchcraft and divination, which, though never countenanced by normative Yahwism (e.g. Exod. 22:18; I Sam. 28:3; Isa. 2:6, 8:19), seems to have been endemic in Israel, as it was among neighboring peoples. Such things belong to the history of Israel's religion, but they are obviously no part of Israel's faith. The same can be said of various tribal and social customs which Israel had in common with her neighbors and which may be assumed to have been inheritances from a common cultural environment. Examples could be multiplied: the practice of polygamy, customs regarding marriage and the inheritance of property, the institution of slavery, the custom of blood vengeance, and many others. Social institutions such as these were regulated under Yahwistic faith by means of its covenant law; but they were not themselves integral to the structure of that faith, nor did they impart to it its distinctive character.

Moreover, such customs and institutions were not in every case permanent features in Israel's religious history, for one can point to not a few of them which seem at one time to have been quite widely practiced but which in the course of the years—whether because felt to be not fully compatible with Yahwistic faith or because of changes in social patterns —seem to have fallen into desuetude or been suppressed. For example, the practice of blood vengeance, the clan vendetta, was apparently quite common in the earliest period and had to be regulated by the provision of cities of refuge to which the slayer who had taken life unintentionally might flee (Num. 35; Deut. 19; Josh. 20), but seems to have been progressively suppressed with the rise of a stable political order. Or the ḥerem (the wholesale sacrificial destruction of the defeated enemy), which was practiced in the holy wars of Israel's earliest period but which, although idealized in the Deuteronomic corpus (Deut.–Kings), especially in the book of Joshua, seems not to have been a characteristic feature of Israel's military policy after the demise of the tribal league. The holy war, to be sure, occupied an important position in Israel's thinking and continued to exist as an ideal and a future expectation until a very late period;[43]

[43] It becomes a feature of later Old Testament eschatology (cf. Ezek. 38-39; Joel 3 [ch. 4, H]; Zech. 14, etc.). After the end of the Old Testament period, the people of Qumran looked forward to the eschatological holy war (see, *The War of the Sons of Light against the Sons of Darkness*); and the symbolism of holy war is used in the New Testament to describe the eschatological struggle (in which the Christian is even now engaged).

but the *ḥerem* itself was neither distinctive of Israel's faith (it was also practiced by her neighbors) nor was it a permanent feature of her practice. Things such as these belong to the history of Israel's religion, but none of them is integral to the structure of Old Testament theology.

3. The Old Testament, then, presents us with both history and theology. It is the record of a real history—is indeed virtually our sole source of knowledge of a certain ancient people: its political fortunes, its institutions, its customs and religious practices. At the same time, it consistently presents that history and understands every facet of life within it in terms of theology—of certain convictions and affirmations regarding the purposes of God, his relationship to his people, his demands and his promises. But what is of primary concern to us in the Old Testament, what is normative for us as Christians, lies precisely in its theology —not in the details of Israel's history or in the historically conditioned forms in which Israel's faith found expression.[44]

This is emphatically *not* to say that the study of Israel's history, and of her religion as an historical phenomenon, is of no interest to us theologically. To the contrary, it is only through that history and those ancient forms of expression that we know anything of Israel's distinctive faith. We cannot abstract the biblical faith from history and present it as if it were no more than a complex of religious beliefs without robbing it of its essential character. Nor can we, in approaching a faith so essentially concerned with the interpretation of events, ever regard the events themselves as a matter of indifference.[45] The study of Israel's history and the history of her religion therefore remains essential to theological science. But what is of primary concern to us in the Old Testament is neither the details of Israel's history nor her religious institutions and practices, but the theology that expresses itself in the texts that tell of these things. Or, rather, it is this theology that makes us interested in Israel's history; with-

---

[44] The point made in these paragraphs is similar to that of A. Weiser, "Vom Verstehen des Alten Testaments," *ZAW*, LXI (1945/48), 17-30; reprinted in *Glaube und Geschichte im Alten Testament* (Göttingen: Vandenhoeck and Ruprecht, 1961), pp. 290-302; see esp. pp. 20-22 (pp. 294-95).

[45] The question of the relationship of revelation (faith) and history in the Old Testament, especially as raised by the work of von Rad (*Old Testament Theology*), has evoked a considerable literature, mostly in German, which we cannot attempt to list here (see the Bibliography for selections). It is a most important subject, but it must lie outside our present concern. The English-speaking reader will get some idea of the issues from various articles in *EOTH*, especially those of W. Pannenberg, F. Hesse, and von Rad himself; see also the criticisms of von Rad in W. Eichrodt, *Theology of the Old Testament*, pp. 512-20.

out it the Old Testament's history would not be very significant—indeed, it would never have been recorded.

Israel's history is not, in itself, normative for us. Although it affords us many an example and warning for our edification, it is an ancient history that can never be repeated; it runs parallel to our situation only occasionally, broadly and by coincidence, and it furnishes us with little direct guidance as we seek to make our political and ecclesiastical decisions. Nor can the forms through which Israel's faith found expression be our forms, or directly normative for them: they belong to the ancient world and are expressive of a culture and a way of thinking not our own. We cannot go back to live in that ancient society or express our faith in terms of its peculiar institutions. What concerns us first and last in the Old Testament is not its historical information as such, but its understanding of the words and deeds, demands and promises of Israel's God in this history, which in one way or another underlies each of its texts.

This last is relevant and normative for us precisely because the New Testament affirms that this history found its terminus, and this theology its fulfillment, in Jesus Christ. The New Testament faith did not break with that of the Old or deny its validity, but rather announced its fulfillment. In so doing, as we have indicated, it took over the great theological constants of the Old Testament faith, reinterpreted them, and gave them new depths of meaning in Christ. Indeed, one can go so far as to say that the *structure* of the New Testament's theology is essentially the same as that of the Old, but with the *content* radically transformed in the light of what Christ has done. Since this is so, the Old Testament is both essential to the proclamation of the gospel and indivisibly linked with the New in the canon of Christian Scripture. The theology of the Old Testament takes on new significance in the light of the New; the theology of the New is filled out and clarified by the Old.

We shall return to this subject in the next chapter. Suffice it here to make the point that it is through its theology, not its ancient forms and institutions, that the Old Testament speaks with relevance and authority to the church. Thus, the covenant made at Sinai is in its form and essential features a thing of the ancient world, as is the Israelite tribal organization which it brought into being; as an institution the Christian might find it of purely historical interest, since it was made with Israel and neither he nor his ancestors were parties to it. But the theology of covenant, resumed in the new covenant that he has received from Christ, remains valid for him; it both tells him of the dealings of his God in the past and clarifies for him the nature of his own relationship to his Lord and to his Christian brother. Just so, the stipulations of Old Testament law are relevant to the Christian not in themselves (they are the laws of an ancient society quite different from his own) but in their theology. The theology of the law, resumed in the New Testament, speaks to him of the fact that he—no less than Israel—is summoned to respond to the grace that he has received in specific acts of obedience, reminds him that the righteousness God demands is something that he can never—no more than Israel—produce, and drives him anew to understand that his justification must be by faith alone. Again, the institution of animal sacrifice is abrogated as a cultic form, but it is theologically relevant, both because the atonement and peace with God it sought to secure have been given us in Christ and because we too need the reminder that it gives of the gravity of sin, and of the fact that we stand daily in need of atonement and forgiveness. The eschatological hope of Israel is couched in ancient and time-bound forms. But it is only as we grasp its theology that we can begin to appreciate what the New Testament has claimed for Christ; and at the same time, because the Old Testament's hope is to such a large degree our common human hope, it points us out beyond ourselves and our possibilities—toward Christ.

In fine, the Old Testament's forms of belief and practice cannot be our forms, or directly a model for them. Indeed, in many of its texts the Old Testament seems in its plain meaning to have little to say to us as Christians. But it is as we examine these ancient forms and ancient texts, lay hold of those theological concerns that inform them, and then see what the New Testament has done with that theology in the light of Christ—it is then, through its theology, that the Old Testament speaks its authoritative word to the church.

4. It should be added that the situation is not essentially different where the New Testament is concerned. To be sure, the problem is much less acute here, for the New Testament was from the beginning a document of the church and its primary witness to the work of the Lord and its significance; as such, it addresses the Christian with a directness and an authority that is unquestioned. Nevertheless, there is much in the New Testament that belongs to the ancient situation and to the history of primitive Christianity, rather than to normative New Testament theology.

The New Testament writers were all men of the first century. They presuppose a notion of the physical universe which was that of the ancient world generally but far different from that entertained in this modern age of science. They phrase their message in terms of concepts which were at home in Judaism or the Greco-Roman world, but which are in many cases foreign to the thinking of modern man. They address men facing the situation of the first century and living in its cultural environment, which is not at all the situation and the cultural environment that the church faces today; not a few of their admonitions and directives, so desperately relevant then, seem on the surface scarcely to apply to our situation at all. We are men of the twentieth century, and we cannot pretend that we live in the first century, nor can we be asked to turn first-century customs and ways of thinking into absolute norms for our faith and practice. But the authority of the New Testament does not reside in these things but in its theology—its gospel. This gospel, as we have seen, undergirds the whole of the New Testament and animates each of its texts. The New Testament cannot be abstracted from the first century, but through its gospel it addresses all centuries. And it is this gospel that is supremely normative in the church.

To revert to an example already alluded to,[46] the church as we see it in the pages of the New Testament cannot be turned into an absolute norm for the churches of today. To be sure, we must maintain our continuity with it, and it is proper for us to seek in it precedents for our forms of government and worship; but we cannot beyond a certain point model ourselves upon it, and none of our churches today actually succeeds in doing so. To mention but one thing, what did the New Testament church know of the ecclesiastical machinery, the burgeoning boards, agencies, and executive offices so characteristic of almost all the churches today? Perhaps we could do with less of this. But who feels obliged, or would think it wise, to dispense with such machinery altogether because the New Testament church had none? We cannot, twenty centuries later and in a wholly different situation, slavishly imitate the first-century church. Indeed, since it was composed of sinful and fallible men like ourselves, there were features in its life (read Paul to the Corinthians) that we should not wish to imitate. But this one thing commands us: There is in the New Testament a doctrine, a theology of the church, that is and must ever remain our norm. Whatever our outward forms of government and worship may be, and however different from those of

[46] See Ch. I, pp. 36-37, above.

the New Testament church, we must, if we would be the church at all, strive to make that theology actual in our corporate life.

So it is, too, with so many of Paul's directives to the churches, such a prominent feature in most of his letters. These were clearly of urgent relevance for the situation then existing. But to what degree are they to be taken as binding upon conduct in all ages? To what degree do they even concern us? Some of them seem hardly to touch the life of the church as we know it today: do not be drunk and disorderly at the Lord's Table (I Cor. 11:17-22); do not eat meat that has been offered to idols (I Cor. 8); let women keep their heads veiled in church at all times (I Cor. 11:2-16); celibacy is to be preferred to marriage (I Cor. 7:8-9, 25-40). Whether, or to what degree, such rules are to be taken as binding on Christians today may well be debated (Paul himself offers some of them as no more than his own opinion). Some of them seem scarcely relevant in that they relate to issues that no longer trouble us. But this much is clear: The theology that informs these directives is both relevant and binding. All of them spring from the apostle's conviction that the Christian has been called to a new manner of life in Christ and from his concern that this exhibit itself in all areas of deportment, to the end that Christ be glorified in the church and before the world. This theology is normative, and we too must ever seek to give it tangible expression in whatever moral instruction we offer our people.

IV

The key to the Bible's authority, then, lies in its theology. But if this be so, then it follows that *no part of the Bible is without authority*, for all parts reflect in one way or another some facet or facets of that structure of faith which is, and must ever remain, supremely normative for Christian faith and practice.

1. Perhaps that statement requires clarification, for it may seem to the reader too strong. It certainly does not intend to say, let it be repeated, that there are no degrees of value in the Bible. Manifestly there are. Each of us tacitly admits as much by the fact that we read certain parts of the Bible over and over again till the pages are soiled and worn, while reading other parts seldom or never. Nor does it mean to say that all parts of the Bible are of equal theological importance. This, again, cannot be maintained. It would surely be no irreverence to say that the Ten Com-

mandments are of greater theological importance than the genealogical lists of I Chron. 1-9, Isaiah than Esther or the Song of Solomon, Romans than Philemon, the Gospel according to John than Jude. But that merely says that some parts of the Bible stand less close to its central theological themes than do others. In some books, indeed, the essential features of the biblical faith are scarcely developed at all but are, one feels, simply taken for granted (so, I believe, in books such as Proverbs or Esther). In others, we find theology expressed negatively, as it were, by individuals who are in debate with it (so notably in Ecclesiastes). There are indeed degrees of theological importance and value in the Bible. But all of it is *valid* for us, for each of its texts in some way reflects or expresses some aspect of its structure of theology and thus shares in the normative authority of that theology. There are no nontheological texts in the Bible. We will continue to use some parts more than others; but it is not a question of selecting certain passages as valid and discarding others, but of laying hold in each passage of that theological concern that informs it.

The point can better be illustrated than argued. Let us then take as examples certain passages from the Old Testament which many people would regard as of peripheral importance if not positively irrelevant to the Christian or, alternatively, as posing serious difficulties from a rational or moral point of view. No attempt will be made at this point to discuss the hermeneutical principles that govern, or should govern, the use of such passages in the pulpit. We shall return to that subject in the chapters that follow. All that is suggested here is that the abiding relevance of these passages, and their authoritative word for the Christian, rests in the theology that informs them. Indeed, it is only through their theology that some passages, ancient and strange as they are, can speak any meaningful word at all.

First, then, an example from the Old Testament law: the laws regarding the transfer and redemption of real property, indebtedness, etc., as these are found in Lev. 25. The chapter can scarcely be called one of the high points of the Old Testament. Indeed, the regulations described therein are obviously so little applicable to the modern situation that the preacher might be pardoned if he told himself that the passage contains no relevant message for his people whatever. It stipulates, among other things, that if a man should be forced because of debt to sell a part of his inherited property, his next of kin was obligated to redeem the land in question, thus keeping it in the family (vs. 25). But land was not in any event to be sold in perpetuity (vs. 23) but must revert to its original owner at the year of Jubilee, the price being adjusted according to the length of time between the date of sale and the next such year (vss. 13-17, 27-28).

Now the intent of that law is clear, and it is a worthy one: to prevent the amassing of large estates in the hands of a few, while poor peasants were crowded from their land. But the law is manifestly not one that serves directly as a norm for us. How could it ever be applied or enforced in a complex society such as our own? Indeed, it is an open question whether Israel was ever able actually to apply it or not. So let us say it: The law, as law, is ancient, irrelevant, and without authority. But what of the theology of the law? That the entire chapter is undergirded by, and expressive of, a very definite theological concern is obvious to all who read it carefully. It seeks to tell us that the land is God's and that we live on this earth as aliens and sojourners, holding all that we have as it were on loan from him (vs. 23); that God narrowly superintends every business transaction and expects that we conduct our affairs in the fear of him (vss. 17, 36, 43), dealing graciously with the less fortunate brother in the recollection that we have all been recipients of grace (vss. 38, 42). And that is normative ethics! It speaks with an eternal relevance to the Christian, whose Christ is the righteousness that has fulfilled the law, and who is summoned in each of his actions to obey Christ's commandment of love to the brother. The law we cannot obey; but we are enjoined in all our dealings ever to strive to make the *theology* of the law actual.

As a further example, let us take a historical narrative: the story of David and Bathsheba (II Sam. 11-12). The story is well known and is most lucidly told. But it is an altogether sordid tale of lust, adultery, treachery, and murder, and many a reader has been shocked by it. How can such a story possibly be said to speak any authoritative word to the Christian with regard to his faith, or in any way to furnish guidance for his conduct? Certainly it provides him with no example to follow—unless it be an example of what he ought under no circumstances to do. Well, perhaps we could wring an example from it in that David, when confronted with his sin, expressed repentance—and so ought we. Or, maybe, an example in that Nathan was bold enough to denounce sin even in the highest places—and so ought we to be. Quite so. But if all we can do is to salvage a few stray morals from the story, we are helpless before it. We have succeeded only in drawing from it something its author had no intention of giving, for it was simply not his aim to present either David or Nathan as an example to follow. Indeed, if all we wish of the Bible is edifying lessons, we would do well to skip this story (and many another in the Old Testament), for it is not edifying. The story seems on the surface to tell us nothing save that the incident happened and that it was regrettable that it did.

But what of the theology expressed in the story? Nathan leaps to the eye. What were the theological convictions—for such they emphatically were—that emboldened this man to march right up to the steps of the throne, level a finger at the king, and say in effect, "Your majesty, you are a murderer"? The answer is plain. Nathan's rebuke clearly moved from the theology of the Mosaic covenant, according to which all Israelites—the king no exception—stood equally under the overlordship of the Divine King and subject to his law, and which viewed any crime against the brother as breach of covenant and *lèse-majesté*. And what of the theological concern of the unknown author who has given us all these stories about David? He is willing to depict David with pitiless clarity as the all-too-human man that he was. But he is also concerned to make it clear that this same David is God's chosen and designated king, to whom his sure promises have been given, and through whose line his gracious purposes for his people will be set forward. And through both these facets of its theology the old, unedifying story speaks its word to me, who through Christ—the fulfillment of the promises to David—have received eternal promises, and who live in covenant with Christ. Through Nathan it condemns me, drives me ever to confess my sin against the brother as a sin against Christ, reminds me that nothing—nothing—that I can do can erase the wrong that I have done, and impels me in helpless penitence to seek some righteousness, some justification, through no merit of my own. At the same time, I hear the author of the story as he seeks to tell me that God's sure purposes are set forward not necessarily through saints but through ambiguous men like David—and perhaps like myself—and that because he so wills it.

As a final illustration, let us take a portion of the primeval history: the creation account in Genesis 1–3. Critical and exegetical details cannot concern us here. But every pastor knows what a source of difficulty these chapters have been to so many Christians, especially perhaps to young people who have begun to be introduced to the physical sciences in school. Perhaps a youth will come to him and say: I have been taught to believe

BIBLICAL THEOLOGY AND THE AUTHORITY OF THE OLD TESTAMENT

the Bible, but what am I to make of such a story? Does it not contradict the findings of science? How can I accept it as true? Really now! Creation in seven literal days, with light before there was ever sun or moon! Man created when God took a lump of clay and breathed into it the breath of life—and woman formed from one of his ribs while he slept! The whole tragedy of history beginning when a snake tempted the woman, and she the man, and they ate a bit of fruit! Can I in honesty, in view of all that I have learned, really believe that? Isn't it (so this lad may say if he is sophisticated) a myth? And if I cannot accept this story as true, what does that say about the truth of the rest of the Bible?

Serious questions, these, and every pastor has heard them. And truly the ancient story does present problems from a scientific point of view. We cannot attempt to discuss them here. To be sure, they are problems that arise only when one persists in putting to the Bible scientific questions, while failing to see the questions it asks us to confront. Nevertheless, for those who feel them, they are real problems. But whatever difficulties the creation account may present from a scientific point of view, I for one have no difficulty whatever in affirming its theology. Indeed, I should go so far as to say that the Christian can accept no other *theological* explanation of his universe: that God created all things by his word and found his creation good; that as the crown of his creative activity he made man, in physical form a superior animal, yet no animal but a creature formed in God's own image, summoned to live in communion with his Maker and in obedience to him; but that man has, in a rebellion reaching back through all generations to his primeval origin, chosen his own autonomous way and said No to his God—and that is the whole trouble with him. Call that what you will as science, as theology it is normative; it is far more true than if it were merely scientifically true. It is the story of the race in the figure of its primal representative. As I read it, I learn of man's high calling and destiny, of his abysmal failure and his alienation from God, and of the death in which he continually lives. Moreover, I see myself as identified with Adam, a child of Adam's brood, locked up in Adam's sin and dead in it. And it is as I so see myself that my ears come open to the hearing of the gospel, which has somewhat to say of a New Adam in whom many are made alive (Rom. 5:12-21).

We have no space for further illustrations. But perhaps these will suffice to make the point clear. The normative element in the Old Testament, and its abiding authority as the Word of God, rests not in its laws and customs, its institutions and ancient patterns of thinking, nor yet in the characters and events of which its history tells, but in that structure of theology which undergirds each of its texts and which is caught up in the New Testament and announced as fulfilled in Jesus Christ.

2. It might be added here by way of postscript—for we cannot pursue the subject at length—that what has been said has the greatest bearing on the problem of the canon, to which we alluded briefly in an earlier chapter.[47] As is well known, the canon both of the Old Testament and of the New came into being through a long and gradual process. We need not attempt to trace the history of that process here. But the result of it was that out of all the literature of ancient Israel and of early Judaism on the one hand, and out of all the writings of the early church on the other, certain books which had come to be regarded as having peculiar authority were selected as canonical Scripture. Humanly speaking, this selection was made on the basis of a judgment of value, in the case of the Old Testament by the Jewish rabbis, subsequently by the church fathers in the case of the New. The considerations involved in this judgment—why certain books were included and others excluded—are not in every case altogether clear. But, again, we need not discuss the point. Enough to say that the church simply took over the Jewish canon of the Old Testament (though not everywhere in the same form) and that where the New Testament is concerned those writings seem to have been selected which commended themselves to the church as embodying the firsthand apostolic witness to the Lord and his gospel. But whatever factors may have been involved, the result was that certain books, though not composed by their human authors with any such intention in view, came to be regarded (and who shall say that the Holy Spirit was not at work in this?) as sacred Scripture and, as such, were recognized as authoritative in the church in all matters of belief and practice.

Since the canon came into being through what was essentially a judgment of value, the question of its dimensions is one that has always remained open. There has never been complete agreement on the point within Christendom. For example, the Roman Catholic Church includes in her Bible (the Latin Vulgate) and accords canonical status to certain books—by Protestants generally called the Apocrypha—which are found in the Greek version of the Old Testament (the Septuagint), but which do

[47] See Ch. I, p. 38, above.

156

not appear in the Hebrew Bible. Some Protestant churches (the Lutheran, the Anglican) customarily print these books in their Bibles (they were in the King James Version of 1611), but with the notation that, while useful and good to read, they are not to be regarded as having the same binding authority that the other books have. Other Protestants, notably of the Reformed tradition, flatly declare them to be without divine inspiration and no part of the canon at all. For my part (and I am sure that my inherited presuppositions are showing!), I feel the Reformed position to be far the safest one.[48] But that is neither here nor there. The point is that the line between canonical and noncanonical is at many places a fine one and a somewhat fluid one. Certain noncanonical books, by any objective test, can be said to stand as high from a spiritual point of view as some canonical ones, if indeed not higher. Who shall say that the Word of God is not to be heard from them? [49] One could argue endlessly. Why should not the Wisdom of Ben Sira (Ecclesiasticus) or the invaluable historical narrative of I Maccabees be included? Are these books not at least as valuable as Esther, which does not even mention God, and exhibits a most vengeful spirit, or Ecclesiastes, which is openly skeptical, or the Song of Solomon, which probably needed to be allegorized in order to get in? It is well known that centuries after the canon was officially closed men continued to express value judgments with regard to certain of its books. Luther's opinion of James ("a right strawy epistle") and of Esther (he wished that it did not exist) are classic examples.

It is quite understandable, in view of this, that the canon should present a problem in most discussions of biblical authority. If one is going to appeal to the Scriptures as authoritative, which Scriptures does one mean? What are the limits of Scripture, and how is this to be decided? By what standard of evaluation is a line to be drawn between those books that have canonical authority and those that do not? Can any line be drawn that would not cut into the canonical books themselves? Since certain of the so-called Apocryphal books, as well as other noncanonical writings, contain teachings as exalted as are some of those of the Bible, why should they not be added

[48] For an excellent discussion of the whole subject, see F. V. Filson, *Which Books Belong in the Bible?*

[49] John Bunyan confesses that he found God's comfort in the words, "Look at the generations of old, and see; did ever any trust in the Lord and was confounded?" But, try as he did, he could not find the verse in the Bible. He finally discovered it at Ecclesiasticus (Ben Sira) 2:10, and blessed God for his word. I thank H. Cunliffe-Jones (*The Authority of the Biblical Revelation*, p. 68) for reminding me of this illustration.

to the canon? On the other hand, why should not certain of the less exalted and less important biblical books be eliminated? After all, some of them were admitted to the canon in the first place only after considerable discussion. But if no clear line consistently separates canonical writings from noncanonical, with what justification are certain books declared to be authoritative, while others—perhaps equally elevated in their teachings— are denied that status? Is not the whole notion of a closed canon arbitrary? Why should we not add to it certain of the writings of the apostolic fathers and even the outstanding Christian classics of subsequent centuries? Surely some of these have as much to give us of instruction in the faith, edification, and guidance as do, say, Ecclesiastes or the Song of Solomon. Short of this, is there any course open to us save to take the canon on faith? But in that event, again, which church's canon?

So stated, the problem of the canon is a serious one and perhaps an insuperable barrier to any unambiguous notion of biblical authority. But coming at the subject of authority as we have done, it seems to me that the sting of the problem is removed. We have argued that the normative element in the Bible, though by no means to be abstracted from the verbal meaning of its texts, does not reside mechanically in certain books or certain texts *per se*, but in the structure of theology, the gospel, that undergirds the whole of the Bible and in one way or another informs, and expresses itself in, each of its texts. It is through its theology that the Bible speaks its authoritative word. Since we have in the writings universally accepted as canonical a wide enough field of evidence for determining what the normative theology both of the Old Testament and the New was, it little affects the problem whether further books are drawn in or not. The normative biblical theology having been established, the question of the deuterocanonical becomes less pressing. Thus, for example, if we were by some unthinkable accident to lose a minor prophet, or one of the pastoral epistles, we should be immeasurably poorer; but the total picture of the theology of the Old or the New Testament would not be seriously altered. On the other hand, were we to find in some yet undiscovered Qumran an authentic new minor prophet, or a new apostolic epistle, we should be enriched; but, again, the total picture of the Bible's theology would not be essentially changed. Indeed, the normative theology of the Bible, as derived from the books universally accepted as canonical, is precisely the standard by which any conceivable new candidate for canonicity would have to be judged. It is also the test of the value to the church of the "disputed" writings. It is my own conviction that the Masoretic canon of the Old Testament and the accepted canon of the New cannot be improved upon. But add a book or two—and nothing essential is added; leave them off—and nothing essential is lost.

What has been said also makes it clear why the canon cannot be expanded by the addition of later Christian classics, even though their teachings may be as thoroughly Christian and as elevated as those of the Bible itself. If the biblical faith consisted of abstract teachings regarding God, man, and the proper conduct of life, there would be no reason in principle why the canon should ever be closed. Teachings as noble, insights as profound—indeed, fresh insights, yet clearer formulations of Christian truth—might conceivably emerge in any age, wherever the Holy Spirit is active. But the Bible's theology does not consist of timeless, abstract teachings. Rather, it is concerned with events, with the interpretation of events, and the meaning of life in the context of events: the events of a specific history in which, it is asserted, God acted for man's redemption. The Old Testament concentrates upon the great events of Israel's history, and it points to the promised eschatological event. The New Testament announces that eschatological event as present in Jesus Christ and promises his universal victory. Of this event the New Testament is the primary record and witness. The canon, therefore, *must* be closed: there can never be a primary witness to *this history* again. Great Christian classics have been written, and no doubt will yet be. And they will nurture the church. But they can be called Christian classics precisely because, and to the extent that, they are derivative from Scripture.

The Bible's word speaks to us through its theology, and there its authority resides. That is not an easy authority to handle, perhaps not the sort that we had wanted. We are given no rule book which we may thumb in search of ready-made answers to every question the church may turn up. To expect such an authority of the Bible is a false expectation; a virile church will not expect it. The answers the Bible gives are ancient answers to ancient problems, and they cannot in every case be applied directly to our problems; often the Bible is unaware of the specific problems that vex us. It becomes, therefore, our task to examine its ancient answers and to discern the theology that expresses itself through them, so that we, praying at every step for the Holy Spirit's guidance, may give that theology

159

a new expression in the answers we seek to give. To do that is never easy and is often difficult in the extreme. It involves an attention to hermeneutical method in our study and our preaching which few of us have troubled with and which we have not yet ventured to discuss. It is to that subject that we must now turn.

IV

THE OLD TESTAMENT IN THE CHRISTIAN PULPIT:

GENERAL HERMENEUTICAL CONSIDERATIONS

ᛁᚹᚱᛟᛁᚲᚱᛁ

In what sense is the Old Testament to be regarded as authoritative Scripture and an integral part of the church's supreme rule of faith and practice? That is the problem with which we have been wrestling through the pages of this book. It is a difficult problem and not one that can be brushed aside with an easy answer. In the preceding chapter the suggestion was ventured that the authority of the Old Testament resides in that structure of theology which in one way or another undergirds and informs each of its parts and which is, in its major features, taken up and re-interpreted in the New. By virtue of this fact—so it was argued—the Old Testament is indissolubly linked with the New within the canon of Christian Scripture and, like the New, speaks an indispensable and authoritative word to the church.

But the subject has a more practical side which we have so far not touched upon. How does what has been said bear upon the task of preaching from the Old Testament? Any discussion of biblical authority must in the end concern itself with biblical preaching. Biblical preaching is the practical, week-by-week expression of the doctrine of authority. To say that the Bible is the church's supreme rule of faith and practice is to say that it both can and must be proclaimed as such in the church. It is meaningless to hail it as authoritative if this is not done. The pastor who does not consistently base his preaching on the biblical text does not, whatever his doctrinal position may be, take the authority of the Bible

161

seriously; it is to him a theological password and little more. By the same token, it means little to declare that the Old Testament is an integral part of canonical Scripture if it is not so interpreted and proclaimed in the church that the people hear and receive it as the Word of *their* God and an authentic expression of the faith they claim as their own.

But how is one to go about doing this? What principles are there to guide the preacher in dealing with an Old Testament text? How is he to proclaim it as a word that is binding upon the faith and life of the church without in many instances doing violence to its meaning? These are important questions, and I fear that our entire discussion will be of little practical help to the preacher if it does not make some attempt to grapple with them. The task of preaching from the Old Testament is not always an easy one, nor is its performance something that can be left to the preacher's intuition: attention to hermeneutical method is required. The pages that follow make no pretense to completeness, still less do they seek to provide a master key that will unlock every text. There is no such master key; and the problems of hermeneutics are too numerous and many-sided to be dealt with in a single chapter.[1] All that can be attempted here is to suggest the nature of the problem to be faced, the steps to be negotiated, and the hermeneutical considerations to be kept in mind, if proper and rounded preaching from the Old Testament is to be done.

I

But first a plea—and perhaps a rather homiletical one—that ought not to be necessary, but unfortunately is: a plea for a return to biblical preaching generally, which is to say, to preaching based in the authority of the biblical Word. The overriding concern in this entire discussion, and the one that caused it to be undertaken in the first place, has been that such preaching be done. The strength of the church lies in the gospel it proclaims—thus in its preaching—today, as it always has. And since the church stands under the authority of the Word, it follows that the best preaching—nay, the only proper preaching—is biblical preaching. Only biblical preaching carries with it the authority of the Word. If, therefore, the Christian pulpit is ever to regain the power and respect which rightfully belongs to it, it will be through a return to biblical preaching.

[1] On the whole subject, see K. Frör, *Biblische Hermeneutik*. I understand that an English ed. of this work is planned.

1. But has the pulpit in our land actually departed from biblical preaching? To make any such sweeping accusation would be both an unwarranted generalization and, from one point of view at least, decidedly unfair. Moreover, it would be arrogant. No sniping at hard-worked pastors for their alleged failure to preach the gospel is intended. Certainly it is not suggested that ministers by and large no longer accord the Bible a unique position, no longer study it, or feel any compulsion to preach from it. This is doubtless true of some, but by no means, I am convinced, of the majority. Most ministers conscientiously take their texts and, however badly they may fail, suppose it to be their duty to proclaim a biblical message. And, if by biblical preaching one means preaching that is in accord with biblical truth, or at least does not contravene it, most of the sermons that one hears can be called biblical.

Nevertheless, it is to be feared that biblical preaching in the strict and proper sense of the word is, by and large across our country, the exception rather than the rule. By biblical preaching is meant the exposition of a biblical text or of some segment of the Bible's teaching, and the proclamation of that as normative for Christian faith and practice. And this one hears too seldom. It is hard to say just why this is so. Is it that the ghost of the authoritarian preaching of yesterday haunts us and makes us uneasy lest we should unintentionally conjure it up? Is it that we fear that an exposition of a biblical text would be too technical, unrelated to contemporary issues, and therefore boring? Is it that we proceed on the assumption—surely a false one—that our people are already familiar with the biblical teachings and need only to be guided in applying them in their daily living? Or is it that we really do not see that it matters whether the sermon is exegetically based or not, so long as it accords with Christian principles? Whatever the reasons may be, one again and again hears sermons that, having taken a text, thereafter say very little about it, if they do not disregard it altogether. One hears sermons that are oriented upon some personal problem, some question of current interest, and only superficially upon the Bible. Or, one hears sermons that, in spite of an honest effort to expound the biblical word, are so poorly executed that they do not get to the heart of the matter. One hears, in short, sermons that are based vaguely on the Bible, that are generally in accord with the Bible, perhaps are illustrated from the Bible, that are Christian in tone and advocate Christian attitudes. But the proclamation of the Word with authority—I would go far out of my way to hear it. This is said in no critical spirit, and with the painful awareness of personal failure. Yet the feeling will not down that much of our preaching is rather thin as regards its content; one could listen to it regularly without gaining any clear idea of what the Christian faith essentially affirms and demands.

It may be partly for this reason that there is a tendency abroad today to discount the importance of preaching altogether. Preaching such as ours perhaps is *not* very important. To be sure, preaching still occupies a central place in the corporate life of the church. Each week the minister spends a good part of his time in the preparation of sermons. And each Sunday the Scripture is read and the text taken and, for some twenty or thirty minutes, a sermon is preached. Yet preaching scarcely occupies the exalted place it once did. Many a pastor feels constrained to place more stress upon his role as a counselor, as an administrator, as one who directs his congregation in its various worthy undertakings, than upon his function as preacher and teacher of the Word. Even in the service of worship the place of the sermon is played down. In the minds of many, the measure of good preaching has become a decent brevity. Indeed, the trend seems to be to enrich the order of worship at the expense of the sermon, by adding interludes, anthems, and liturgical responses until, in some churches at least, little time is left for the sermon at all. One even hears it said that the future of the church no longer lies in her preaching, and that if she cannot find some better way of making her witness she will soon become irrelevant—if, indeed, she is not already.

2. Whatever the reasons for it may be, this is a dangerous trend, and one that is to be resisted, for it bodes no good for the church. The church lives, let it be repeated, in her preaching—always has, and always will. Granted that the church's mission does not consist merely in the formal preaching of sermons. That should be obvious. The church must also witness to the gospel through her manner of living, through the contact of person with person, and through doing the works of Christ in the world. Granted, also, that each generation must adapt its methods to new situations and that our conventional ways of inculcating the faith—Sunday school and morning worship, youth groups and conferences, revivals and preaching missions—may not in every case prove adequate for the challenge of our day, and new techniques and new avenues of service may have to be found. But the church must still live in her preaching. By whatever means it is done, to preach the gospel is her major commission. If a church is faithfully and intelligently discharging that commission, one simply

cannot say that it is irrelevant—unless one wishes to assert that the gospel is itself irrelevant. If the church is at all open to the charge of irrelevancy, this may be in good part precisely because of her failure at preaching, because through the shallowness of her preaching she has conveyed the impression that the Christian faith has nothing significant to say.

No church can be greater than the message it proclaims. Since this is so, it behooves us to strengthen the quality of our preaching, and that as a central feature of our regular services of worship. True, we want no unhealthy overstress on preaching. We have no need of pulpit pyrotechnics, nor ought we ever to evaluate a minister's effectiveness solely on the basis of his homiletical skill. We advocate no return to the full-bodied, hour-long sermons of yesteryear: our people would not endure it, and we are perhaps not worth that much time. The preacher and his sermon ought not to dominate the order of worship. Most of us would do well, indeed, while resisting aimless "prettifying" of the service, to devote more attention to whatever liturgical heritage is proper to the tradition in which we stand. Yet the place of the sermon in our regular services of worship must at all costs be protected. It must be protected because, in Protestant theory, the reading and the exposition of the Word is an integral and indispensable part precisely of the service of worship—to some of us, indeed, its culmination. It must be protected, too, because—at least in this country—it is then that we have the ear of the people. For the present and the predictable future, the regular Sunday service provides most of our pastors with their best opportunity for addressing their people with the claims of the gospel and instructing them in its meaning; with some of the people it is their only opportunity. How long we will continue to have the ear of such large numbers if we persist in our shallowness, no one can say. But not forever.

3. It is incumbent upon us, then, while yet there is time, to strengthen the quality of our preaching. But this means a return to biblical preaching. We shall never have strong preaching, or even really edifying preaching, until our pastors, Sunday in and Sunday out, consistently base their sermons in the authority of the Word. The reasons for this have already been suggested. The minister preaches of a Sunday for no other purpose than to expound the Christian faith, to invite men to accept it and live in a manner consonant with it. He is not in the pulpit to present his reflections on the meaning of life or the secrets of successful living, or to propound his opinions on religious, moral, and social issues. He has, of course, a right to his opinions (precisely as much right as anyone else), and these may be

per se well worth hearing. But if he has only his opinions to offer, let him reflect that his hearers will have theirs too, and that, as opinions disagree, preaching becomes a *conversation between men.* Manifestly the preacher cannot suppress his opinions without making of himself a cipher; but his concern in the pulpit is not with his opinions, but first, last, and always with what the Christian faith teaches and affirms, promises and demands. Each sermon must deal with some aspect of that subject or be marked as a failure: at best it is a bit of helpful advice, at worst an unwarranted intrusion on the hearers' time.

There can, therefore, be no substitute for biblical preaching. Biblical preaching is the only kind that carries with it authority. And the preacher needs an authority. He proposes to be a teacher and advocate of the Christian faith. But how can he be sure that his personal understanding of that faith and its claims, if that is what he presents to his people, faithfully represents its actual teachings? What authority has he to insist that it does and, on that basis, to undertake to rebuke and correct his congregation? What, really, can he say more to those who may disagree with his views than "Well, it seems so to me"? The very fact that he undertakes to set forth the teachings of a historically held faith makes it imperative that he base his statements about that faith and its claims upon some authority. And that authority—so the church has always affirmed—is supremely the Bible; and rightly, too, since it is only from the Bible that it can finally be learned what the Christian faith originally was and, by extension, is. Granted that the minister, being only human, may through ignorance or carelessness misinterpret the biblical teaching. Granted, in any case, that the time will probably never come when all his hearers, without exception, agree with everything that he says. But, if we are truly sons of the Reformation, such disagreement ideally ought not to be a mere clash of free opinion, but an objective question of the correct interpretation of a commonly recognized authority. And since that recognized authority is for us the Bible, it is biblical preaching or no preaching with authority. And, let it be added, since the Old Testament remains an integral part of the Bible, there must be preaching from it also, or there will be no complete and rounded biblical preaching.

Biblical preaching does not, of course, necessarily imply a specific type of sermon. There are many ways of presenting the biblical truth, and it would be foolish to insist that one technique, and one alone, is the correct one. Nor would one, however great one's zeal for biblical preaching, go so far as to suggest that each and every sermon must be an exposition of a specific text. There is a real and necessary place for preaching on the doctrines, creeds, and symbolism of one's church. And there are times when the pastor feels obliged to address himself specifically to some issue that is agitating his congregation, or some cause that deserves their attention, and—there being no single, applicable text—is forced to preach a topical sermon. Speaking for myself, I have to say that I regard the topical sermon as a great snare and a device to be resorted to as seldom as possible. Topical sermons can be biblical, but they very rarely are. They tend to be far more preoccupied with *our* problems and concerns than with faith's affirmations and almost never are adequately based in the biblical teaching. At the same time, it must be said that a sermon is not biblical merely because the preacher has taken a text. He may depart from his text or egregiously misuse it; he may draw stray lessons from it, make random comments based upon it, while utterly failing to bring it to word. And even the preacher who regularly and efficiently expounds his text may misrepresent the Bible by preaching only from favorite passages, while ignoring the rest (he would do well to discipline himself by following a lectionary). No style of preaching is biblical by virtue of itself. But all preaching can and should be biblical in the sense that, whatever the type of sermon and however executed, it can and should make itself a faithful expression of the biblical word.

Nevertheless, to voice once again my own firm conviction, there can be no substitute, Sunday in and Sunday out, for preaching that expounds the biblical text itself. This is the preaching that is most sure to confront our people with the claims of the faith and to build them up in sound instruction. It is also a preaching that carries with it an unusual authority. As individuals, what we say carries little weight. But if in our preaching we seriously attempt to expound the biblical text, we will find that the Bible's own word is speaking again through us with its own peculiar authority. Indeed, it is no longer we who speak, but a heritage of believing four thousand years old that speaks through us. Men may still disagree with what we say: that is their privilege. But if we have rightly set forth the biblical faith, it is no longer we with whom they disagree, but the biblical faith itself. And that is a very stout authority for a little pastor to have behind him. He can, in fact, have no stouter.

II

Our concern in this chapter is primarily with the problem of preaching from the Old Testament. But we must first say a few words about what is involved in biblical preaching generally. Leaving aside the practical problems of sermon construction, which we cannot undertake to discuss here, how does one go about preaching from a biblical text? What procedure does one follow? It seems to me that at least three distinct steps are involved.[2] I have no advice as to how they should be accomplished in the preparation of a particular sermon. The actual execution will no doubt depend in large degree upon the individual, his exegetical training and style of preaching, upon the sophistication of the audience he expects to address, and indeed upon the text that is being dealt with. Though we shall take them up seriatim, they are not in practice actually so, but interlock. But none may be skipped or scamped in the preparation of a sermon, if that sermon is intended to be biblical.

1. Biblical preaching, it should not have to be said, must begin with the biblical text. That is to say, it must begin with exegesis. Whoever would preach a biblical sermon must first of all trouble to find out as exactly as is humanly possible the precise meaning of the text he intends to expound. Not what he had always thought it meant, not what he would prefer it to mean, not what it may seem on the surface to mean, but what it actually means. There can be no biblical preaching if the text is not taken with utmost seriousness. If the preacher feels free to disregard his text, if he allows himself to twist or slant its meaning in order to have it support some point he wishes to make, or if he is content to derive incidental lessons from it while ignoring what it principally intended to say, he should give up all pretense of doing biblical preaching. Biblical preaching is a preaching that aims to bring the text's own word to bear on the contemporary situation; it must therefore begin with the text's own words. It demands that the preacher make a manful effort to ascertain as precisely as he can what the text intended to convey to those to whom it was originally addressed. If he will not trouble to do that, he can derive no legitimate message from the text for his congregation. His sermon may be interesting, perhaps even edifying; but let him not advertise it as the authentic biblical word to his people. It represents no more than his

---

[2] I believe that L. E. Toombs, who suggests four steps, is actually saying much what I do here, since I mean to include his first two steps under point one, below; see Toombs, *The Old Testament in Christian Preaching*, pp. 15-21.

own words, his own reflections, perhaps as these were suggested by the biblical word, and he ought frankly to admit it.

Biblical preaching, then, begins in exegesis. And exegesis, as we have said before, follows the grammatico-historical method: it seeks to understand the language of the text (grammar) in the light of the situation in which it was first written or spoken (history). That, admittedly, is no easy task. The language, unfortunately, is Greek or Hebrew. And the critical and historical studies necessary for its proper understanding are time-consuming, deadly dull—and virtually unpreachable. Many a hard-pressed pastor has complained that it is unrealistic to expect him to perform such a task and has asked to be excused from it. Can he really afford the time—even granting that he had the skill—that the proper performance of the task would require? Is this journey into tedium really necessary? Is there not some shortcut? Now, it is of course not to be expected that every pastor should become a specialist in biblical studies: he simply hasn't the time. Indeed, the average pastor, harassed by multifarious duties, beset behind and before, has to struggle manfully to maintain even that level of exegetical competence gained in seminary. Few indeed remain fluent in Greek and Hebrew, if fluent they ever were. One understands this perfectly. To suggest, therefore, that biblical preaching can be done only by highly skilled exegetes would be conducive to despair—and snobbish. It would, in effect, be to write off biblical preaching as a practical impossibility for most of our pastors. And that we must never do.

Still there can be no shortcuts. No one who wishes to do biblical preaching can bypass or scamp the exegetical task. Knowledge of the original languages is invaluable equipment for this task. But the preacher who is without such knowledge is not for that reason excused from it; it is his proper task, and he must undertake it. Making use of such commentaries as are available to him and such other helps as are within his command, he must week after week do his very best to arrive as nearly as possible at the precise meaning of his text.[3] Whatever one's level of knowledge, be it high school diploma or Ph.D., all attempts at biblical preaching

---

[3] By consulting as many commentaries as possible one gains an idea both of the history of the exegesis of one's text and of the possibilities of interpretation that are open. The preacher cannot come at his text as if he were the first one ever to do so; by seeing how others have interpreted it, he benefits from the wisdom (and perhaps also the folly) of the past, and is restrained from over-hasty conclusions. On the importance of this, see Frör, *Biblische Hermeneutik*, pp. 64-68. I have heard Professor James T. Cleland make this point orally on more than one occasion.

must invariably begin with a serious attempt to understand the text. Perhaps one will often feel that precious time has been squandered in attention to inconsequential detail. Perhaps, in any event, relatively little of one's exegetical labors will be obvious in the Sunday sermon; certainly they ought not to be paraded there. But an honest attempt to understand the meaning of the biblical text must precede every sermon. Slovenly exegesis and biblical preaching can no more coexist than God and Baal. He who shirks exegesis advertises in a loud voice that he does not really care what the Bible says but only wishes to *use* it insofar as it supports the clever points that *he* wishes to make. Such a man cannot possibly do biblical preaching, for he will not begin seriously with the Bible.

2. But biblical preaching requires not only an exegesis of the text that brings out its precise verbal meaning; it involves one also in what we shall call theological exegesis. The term is admittedly a loaded one and, I fear, open to misunderstanding. But I know of no better one to use. Let us make it clear, then, that by theological exegesis is *not* meant a special kind of exegesis, for example, an exegesis that is in some way controlled by the exegete's own theological presuppositions.[4] Still less is it implied that one is permitted to read one's own theological convictions back into the biblical text. May Heaven forfend! Rather, by theological exegesis is meant an exegesis of the text in theological depth, an exegesis that is not content merely to bring out the precise verbal meaning of the text but that goes on to lay bare the theology that informs the text. It is an exegesis that seeks to discover not merely *what* the ancient law required but also the theology expressed in the law; not merely *what* abuses Amos attacked but the theology that caused him so to attack them; not merely *what* directives Paul gave to this or that church but the theology that moved him to give them. All biblical texts are expressive of theology in that all are animated, if at times indirectly, by some theological concern. It is incumbent upon the interpreter to seek to discover what that theological concern is. To do this is no violation of sound exegetical principles. Rather, it is the completion of the exegetical task.[5]

[4] The term is so used by Karl Barth and various of his followers. For discussion, see Frör, *Biblische Hermeneutik*, pp. 31-34; Oscar Cullmann in J. Boisset, ed., *Le problème biblique dans le Protestantisme* (Paris: Presses Universitaires de France, 1955), pp. 131-32. In my opinion "exegesis" is the wrong word here. What Barth offers is a theological *interpretation* of Scripture, rather than an exegesis in the proper sense of the word; there is but one legitimate kind of exegesis—the grammatico-historical.

[5] In other words, to expound the theological content of the text is included in the task of grammatico-historical exegesis. For a similar understanding of the matter, see, for example,

Amos was just mentioned. Let us use him as an illustration. The message of Amos—what he said, the abuses he attacked—is, in general, plain enough. The most cursory exegetical study—indeed, even a single attentive reading of the book without benefit of Hebrew or critical commentary—will give one a reasonably clear idea of *what* Amos said. It is clear that he assailed those unscrupulous members of the wealthier classes of his day who gouged the poor, the venal judges who connived in their dastardly schemes, and the elaborate cultus by which these villainous creatures sought to "square it all" with God, and so on. It is also clear that he pronounced God's judgment upon the nation because of its crimes. Very good! But what considerations—religious, ethical, or personal—moved Amos to speak in this way? Was he a revolutionary, filled with a burning hatred of the privileged classes, who desired the overthrow of the existing order? Was he a reformer, inspired by lofty ideals of justice and brotherhood, whose aim was a program of social action? Was he a spiritual pioneer who had arrived at the insight that Yahweh is a God who desires justice rather than ritual, and who sought through his preaching to impart this insight to his contemporaries? Caricatures? But Amos has been understood in all these ways. We cannot pause to expound the theology that motivated Amos. But it is clear that until we understand it, until we understand that his preaching was rooted in the ancient traditions of his people, in the recollection of Yahweh's grace toward them in the past (e.g. Amos 2:9-10) and his election of them (e.g. Amos 3:1-2), we shall never succeed in understanding Amos' message at all.

An exegesis that stops short of the theology of the text is an incomplete exegesis. (And here, it seems to me, many of our commentaries fail the preacher by providing him with too little guidance at this essential point.) The preacher does not go into the pulpit merely to explain the verbal meaning of an ancient text, from which he may then proceed to draw random lessons. Still less is he there to parade his knowledge of Greek and Hebrew—if any—in order to impress the congregation. His aim is to expound and interpret the mind of the Bible writer in such a way that his word may once again speak through the text to the congregation. In order to do this, the preacher needs to understand not only what the text

---

K. H. Bernhardt, *Die gattungsgeschichtliche Forschung am Alten Testament als exegetische Methode* (Berlin: Evangelische Verlagsanstalt, 1956), pp. 14-16; cf. also A. A. van Ruler, *Die christliche Kirche und das Alte Testament* (Munich: Chr. Kaiser Verlag, 1955), pp. 20-21.

says, but also those concerns that caused it to be said, and said as it was. His exegetical labors are, therefore, not complete until he has grasped the text's theological intention. Until he has done this he cannot interpret the text, and may egregiously misinterpret it by attributing to its words an intention quite other than that of their author.

It is very easy to fail here, and many preachers who conscientiously begin with their Bibles do so. Indeed, this may be one of the reasons why everything some preachers touch seems to turn into a dreary moralizing. For example, the text is taken from I Cor. 1:10-17, and the congregation is told what Paul said to the Corinthians about party strife—and they are begged not to indulge in party strife. Or, the text is taken from II Cor. 8, and it is explained to the congregation what Paul said to the Corinthians about stewardship, using the liberality of the Macedonians as an example—and they are exhorted to give liberally. All very true, of course. The Christian ought not to indulge in party strife and ought to give liberally: so said Paul, and so ought we to do. But what of the theology that caused Paul to exhort his people so? All his instruction to the churches is undergirded and motivated by the gospel he had been commissioned to proclaim, and this shines through the very texts in which he gives it. Yet it is strange how often it is missed. And when it is missed the sermon, because it lacks theological depth, tends to degenerate into a shallow moralizing that does little more than recommend Christian attitudes and chide the congregation for its shortcomings.

Every preacher who has thought seriously about his job is aware of this pitfall. Let him preach, for example, on the parables of Jesus without attention to the theological concerns that undergird them, and they become little more than wise moral instruction. One hears this on every hand. The parable of the wise and foolish virgins emerges as a canny teaching on the virtues of preparedness. The parable of the good shepherd teaches how kind Jesus was to the lost and straying—and so ought we to be. The parable of the good Samaritan—that inculcates the grace of neighborliness. All very true as far as it goes, of course; and the congregation that is subjected to such preaching will not be left unaware of its Christian responsibility. But it is scarcely the beginning. All that the Gospel writers have to say about Jesus is informed by certain affirmations about him and the imminence of God's kingdom in his person; all the parables have something to say about the nature of that kingdom and convey something of its challenge to radical response. Miss it, and the gospel of the parables is

172

missed and, therewith, all that matters is missed. An exegesis of the parables that does not grasp and expound them in theological depth is manifestly an incomplete exegesis.

One can even go so far as to say that certain parts of the Bible are well-nigh irrelevant unless presented in theological depth, for it is only through their theology that they speak to us at all. Let us take just one obvious example, precisely because it is obvious. In I Cor. 8, Paul discusses the question of eating meat that has been offered to idols. He declares that since idol gods have no real existence, and since righteousness before God is not measured by one's diet, it is a matter of indifference to him whether one eats such meat or not. But, he says, since he knows that certain weaker brothers will be offended if they see him doing so, thinking that he has compromised with paganism, he will eat none; and he urges his hearers to eat none. Now as a specific directive that is irrelevant to us. Eat no meat that has been offered to idols? We are not tempted to. No one does. No such meat is on sale at the butcher's. Since the problem is no longer a live one, what Paul had to say about it is of no direct concern to us, one way or the other. But we do not need to waste words pointing out that Paul's theological concern—to indulge in no practice or habit, however harmless in itself, that may cause damage to the faith of some weaker brother "for whom Christ died"—is as relevant as it ever was. Through its theology the passage addresses us and reminds us of our responsibility in a thousand areas of personal demeanor.

In this case the point is so obvious that we take it for granted. But it holds good throughout the Bible. The Bible's word is an ancient word, addressed to an ancient situation quite different from our own. Its message to that ancient situation may, in its verbal meaning, have little to say to us. But the theology of the biblical word is able to address all situations, since as Christians we stand under that theology, and since the human situations to which it was addressed are in a real sense "typical" of our own human situation. It is, therefore, precisely through its theology that the biblical word to the *then and there* of an ancient age speaks to us in the *here and now*. Since this is so, our exegesis of the text must always be a theological exegesis, else it is incomplete.

3. But, finally, biblical preaching is the communication of the gospel to men of the present day. That is to say, it requires that the word of the text be translated into the idiom of today and so presented that it is clearly seen to address the situation of today.

This we know well. But it is not an easy thing to do. It seems to me that much of our preaching tends to run to one or the other of two extremes. On the one hand, there is the preacher who bases himself upon his text and faithfully expounds its meaning. But where the congregation is he wots not. He makes it clear what Isaiah said to Ahaz, or Paul to the church in Corinth, and he even shows awareness of those theological convictions that moved the prophet or the apostle to speak as he did. But what Word of God Isaiah or Paul may have for the people sitting before him is not clear, nor were such questions as the text may have raised in their minds ever dealt with. In short, his preaching is biblical but irrelevant. At least, it seems irrelevant to his hearers, because they were never made to see in what way what was said concerns them.

On the other hand, there is the preacher (and his name is Legion) who is apparently convinced that his people would not listen to a solid biblical exposition and so, disliking above all things to lose their attention, makes no attempt to provide one. He is determined that his preaching will be relevant, or at least interesting. So he has recourse to illustrations, anecdotes, and various attention-catching devices; he devotes his time to dealing with the personal problems of his people and to the discussion of contemporary issues, and he makes little reference to Scripture at all beyond the courtesy taking of a text. And he has some success: he is tolerably listenable. But it is such thin gruel! There is much that is of interest, but little that matters; and faith's affirmations are seldom spoken. Such a preacher has betrayed his people. They needed of him bread, and he gave them, if not a stone, the very stale bread of his interesting conversation. Too often he has confronted them only with *themselves*.

Now it must be insisted that neither of these is proper biblical preaching. The second, of course not: it scarcely tries to be. The first is far better, for it is based in the biblical text, not the preacher's reflections. But if it fails to be relevant, and to the degree that it so fails, it cannot be called satisfactory, for the biblical word is a relevant word and demands to be preached with relevancy. To be sure, we must be careful how we talk of "making the Bible relevant." The biblical word *is* relevant, no thanks to us; it is not up to us to *make* it relevant. When we attempt to do that, we usually succeed in cheapening the Bible. On the other hand, we certainly do not wish to make the Bible irrelevant! We cannot be satisfied with the sort of preaching that strikes no one, involves no one; and this is something that is all too possible. The biblical word was *address* then—

address to certain specific individuals or groups (or the address of men to God)—and it must be *address* today. That is to say, it must so be proclaimed that it addresses its present-day hearers in their situation and involves them, just as it did its ancient hearers. If this is not done, they will remain passive spectators to the word; they will not hear it, but only hear about it. It does little good to explain the text and affirm that it is relevant, if it cannot be got through to the hearers, if it cannot so be presented that it is seen to be relevant. Until it has so been presented, it has not yet been *preached,* nor is the full impact of its authority likely to be felt.

We have to face the fact that the Bible is an ancient book, an unfamiliar book even to many Christians, and one that in more than one sense speaks an ancient language. How very hard it is to make it real, or even understandable, is known to every pastor who has at all tried to take his teaching function seriously. It addresses ancient situations of which the average man in the pew knows nothing. What is far more serious, its message is couched in ancient thought patterns which are not the thought patterns of modern man. Its view of the physical universe is pre-Copernican, presupposing a flat earth with the vault of heaven arching above and with Sheol and the watery chaos beneath. It takes for granted the possibility of the miraculous, which may at any moment interrupt the normal course of things. It has no doubt of the reality of angelic and demonic beings, who are locked in cosmic conflict one with another. It sees history as moving on to a final judgment, which is described in the language of Jewish apocalyptic. And much more. Whatever the preacher's convictions may be, he knows that this is all very strange to the average man today. Even the stock theological terms: sin, judgment, atonement, justification, salvation—the whole language of *Heilsgeschichte* and kerygma—are scarcely in the vocabulary of a great many of his people. How shall he interpret this ancient book to them in such a way that they understand it and hear it as the Word of their God?

Biblical preaching, therefore, must issue in translation—the translation of the text from that situation to this, from that idiom to this. In attempting this, we must never allow ourselves to take liberties with the text. Communication is not to be secured at the price of the substance.[6] Nor is it

---

[6] On the point, see D. Müller, "Die Sprache als Problem der praktischen Theologie" in W. Schneemelcher, ed., *Das Problem der Sprache in Theologie und Kirche* (Berlin: A. Töpelmann, 1959), pp. 85-111.

up to us by our cleverness to "sell" the text to our hearers; we shall perhaps have to leave that to the Holy Spirit. But pious reliance upon the Holy Spirit does not absolve us of our best efforts to translate the text and present it in such a way that it can be heard and understood. To proclaim the biblical word without translation, it matters not how accurately, is to run the risk of speaking a foreign language. And the gospel *will* be preached in the vernacular—that is, if Pentecost be come. Biblical preaching therefore begins with an exegesis of the text which presses beyond the bare words to grasp the theology expressed in them. It must then take the word of the text, couched in an ancient idiom and addressed to an ancient situation and, without wresting its meaning, so translate it into the modern idiom that the ancient word may speak again as the relevant word that it is. Each sermon thus becomes at once a theological and a psychological exercise (what someone has called an exegesis both of the text and the congregation),[7] which seeks to present the text in such a way that the modern hearer knows himself to be addressed by it and involved in it.

This means, of course, that the preacher must learn to ask the right questions, both of his text and about his people. He cannot be content merely to explain what his text meant in its original setting and leave his hearers to make of it what they can. He must preach the text *to them*. Since it is the text that he must preach, he must ask questions of it. Who was the speaker of this word, and as whose word is it to be heard today? To whom was it originally addressed, and who is the corresponding addressee today? For what purpose was this word uttered then, and what did it intend to convey? And what ought it to convey to its proper addressee today? And so on. But the preacher must also ask questions about his people, since it is to them that he must preach. In particular, he must ask what their reaction is likely to be when this word is presented to them, for that will condition his entire procedure. Will it be a failure to understand? Then he must take time to explain and clarify. Are there likely to be questionings and doubts? Then he must honestly attempt to deal with them, so that the word may be heard and received, or at least not rejected because of needless misunderstanding. Will there be intellectual assent and no more? Then how can it be brought home to this people that this word is of desperate concern *to them*? Or will there be enthusiastic and committed acceptance? Then perhaps the task will be primarily one

---

[7] I believe that I came across this expression somewhere in the files of *Evangelische Theologie*, but I have been unable to locate it.

of guiding the people toward the responsible implementation of the word in action. This phase of the preacher's task is enormously difficult—perhaps the most difficult thing about preaching. How shall one ever be sure that it has been done rightly? Nevertheless, it has to be undertaken if the biblical word is to confront and address men today with full immediacy. And it is as men are confronted with the biblical word in our preaching that our preaching takes on authority—becomes, indeed, an instrument of God's saving act in Christ.

4. The problem involved in attempting to communicate the gospel to the modern mind deserves a far more extended discussion than we can give it here. It is easily one of the most crucial problems confronting the pulpit today. Nor is it merely a problem of practical homiletics, but one that leads to the very heart of the current theological discussion, for it was precisely his concern for the communication of the gospel that led Rudolf Bultmann to his radical demythologizing of the New Testament —and the reader knows what a flutter in the theological dovecotes that has occasioned. It is not my intention to enter the debate with Bultmann here. Literally scores of books and articles have been written on the subject.[8] Indeed, so much has been written, and from every conceivable point of view, that one has the feeling that the subject has been exhausted and that the debate ought either to be suspended or shifted to other grounds (as, indeed, it has been in the so-called new hermeneutic developed by certain of Bultmann's pupils, who see themselves as moving beyond their teacher's position).[9] It would be difficult to think of anything significant to say on the subject that has not already been said, and said repeatedly. Nevertheless, since the question of the communication of the gospel— which is the focus of the whole debate—is certainly a proper one, and since no discussion of it can ignore the issues that have been raised, one is compelled to take some position with regard to the matter, if misunderstand-

[8] Even to list a skeleton bibliography would take pages. The best firsthand introduction to the debate probably remains H. W. Bartsch, ed., *Kerygma and Myth,* trans. R. H. Fuller (London: S.P.C.K., Vol. I, 1953; Vol. II, 1962). There are three other volumes that have not been translated.

[9] See esp. J. M. Robinson and J. B. Cobb, eds., *The New Hermeneutic.* I became aware of this approach when the present book was already in semifinal form, and I am not yet prepared to offer a considered evaluation of it. But if I understand what its proponents are trying to say (and some of them express themselves with an extraordinary want of clarity), I have severe reservations. To impose an external (and existential) hermeneutical principle on the text, as it seems that they do, and to claim that by doing so the true intention of the text is recaptured, must be regarded as a very questionable procedure. I believe that most of the remarks below apply to it, as well as to Bultmann's views.

ing is to be avoided. We shall attempt to do this briefly and, as far as possible, in a positive way, and without engaging in specific debate. What will be said here makes no claim either to originality or completeness.[10]

(a) First of all, it is submitted that the problem of interpretation is not primarily one of demythologizing and, moreover, that the widespread use of the word "myth" in this connection only serves to muddy the waters and create confusion. To begin at the practical level, "myth" is an unhappy word because it is certain to be misunderstood—so certain, in fact, that one is reluctant to use it in public discussion lest needless offense be given. To most people myth suggests a fable, a fabrication, a story that is not true. To be sure, this is not what the word properly means, nor is it at all what Bultmann and his followers intend by it. But one may be quite sure that the average person will so understand it. The pastor who suggests to his people that the Bible must be demythologized will only succeed in angering great numbers of them, who will understand him as having said that the Bible must be purged of untruth. If myth is the right word, we shall of course have to use it. But a word so certain to create misunderstanding is one that we would do well to avoid unless, in honesty, we cannot.

But is myth the right word? Is it an accurate designation for the problem we face in the Bible, or even applicable in that connection? The answer will depend upon the meaning that one assigns to the word. There is little agreement on the point. This explains why, at one and the same time, one can hear a call from some scholars for the demythologizing of the Bible and from others, equally competent, the assertion that the Bible contains no myth in the proper sense of the word. What is this myth that is at once an obstacle to the understanding of the Bible and not in the Bible at all? A word so variously, and often so vaguely, defined is bound to give rise to confusion.[11] Bultmann, of course, defines myth very broadly. He says that myth "is the use of imagery to express the otherworldly in terms of this world and the divine in terms of human life, the other side in terms of this side."[12] Now if that be an acceptable definition, then the Bible is full of myth, for it consistently speaks of God and his activity in

---

[10] My position at essential points closely parallels that of G. E. Wright; see *God Who Acts* (London: SCM Press, 1952), pp. 116-28; and Wright, "From the Bible to the Modern World," in A. Richardson and W. Schweitzer, eds., *Biblical Authority for Today*, pp. 219-39.

[11] See Ch. III, p. 129, and n. 24, above.

[12] See *Kerygma and Myth*, I, 10, n. 2. Bultmann's definition is that of the so-called History of Religions school, as he himself points out.

the world in personal, even highly anthropomorphic, terms ("in terms of human life") which, under the definition, would fall into the category of myth. But this is certainly a remarkable extension of the term. So defined, myth would seem to embrace not only the ancient world view of the Bible, and such of its concepts as may have had their background in mythopoeic thinking, but virtually the whole of the Bible's central theological structure as well. Indeed, one might ask if it is possible to make any meaningful statement about God at all save in terms of what is here called "myth," since we have no language in which to express ourselves save the language of "this world."

How to interpret such features in the Bible to the modern mind is one question; whether they ought to be classified as myth or not is another. Certainly such a definition blurs the distinction between what we have in the Bible and myth as we know it elsewhere. The Bible contains no myths such as we find in the literature of Egypt, Babylonia and Canaan, Greece and Rome. To be sure, it affords vestigial survivals of myth and various allusions to mythical figures and events. Moreover, it not infrequently employs concepts and imagery originally at home in the pagan environment as vehicles for the expression of its own distinctive theology. But the Bible is really quite free of the *mind* of myth. It knows nothing of the drama of the gods so characteristic of the pagan myth, nothing of that sense of the integration of human society with the rhythmic, and essentially historyless, pattern of nature which itself reflects the activity of the gods. Whatever it is that we have in the Bible, it is certainly not myth as we know it elsewhere. And on the other hand, the pagan myths know nothing of the distinctive theology of the Bible but move in a totally different world. A definition of myth that does not protect this distinction cannot be regarded as satisfactory. True, one may, if one cares to do so, say that Israel, in transcending the pagan myth, created "the new myth of the will of God." [13] But one must protest that this is too loose a use of the word to be meaningful: mythology has become to all intents and purposes a synonym for theology.

We must not imagine, of course, that we have disposed of the hermeneutical problem, or rendered it any less difficult, merely by asserting that it is not in any proper sense one of reinterpreting "myth." The problem remains, however we choose to describe it. We still have the task of interpreting a religion that expresses itself in ancient and prescientific

[13] See H. and H. A. Frankfort, in H. Frankfort *et al.*, *The Intellectual Adventure of Ancient Man* (Chicago: University of Chicago Press, 1946), p. 373.

categories to the modern, scientifically oriented mind which no longer thinks—and to a significant degree, cannot think—in those categories. That is anything but an easy task. But the problem that confronts us is not properly with myth, but with a variety of things that can be labeled "myth" only in the attenuated sense that many of them may have had their background or parallels in the thought of the ancient world, which was a world of myth. These include the Bible's pre-Copernican world view, its anthropomorphic way of speaking of God, many of its conceptual patterns, much of its symbolism and imagery—all of which seem strange to the modern mind. This is a whole complex of problems; they are not all of the same kind, nor will they be felt by everyone in the same way. To lump them all under the heading of myth, especially since this involves an inexact use of the word and one that is bound to create misunderstanding, can serve no useful purpose.

(b) This leads to a second point. Since the problem of interpretation has so many ramifications, we are warned not to go at it one-sidedly with a doctrinaire rigidity. Modern man is not necessarily a sophisticated university professor, still less an existentialist. His difficulties with the Bible are by no means in every case the same, nor do they all lie on the same level. Manifestly all cannot be dealt with by any single procedure.[14] There are, indeed, many even today for whom the Bible's language presents no difficulty whatever; they have so long steeped themselves in it that it has become their mother tongue. To proceed to reinterpret it for them, whether in existentialist categories or some other, would simply be to create difficulties where none had existed. On the other hand, there are those—Marxists, for example—whose philosophical presuppositions preclude even belief in God. Such people are not likely to accept the Bible no matter how much we reinterpret it. Here we can do little more than stand our ground and be prepared to counterattack as opportunity offers. With others, the trouble is simply that the Bible is unfamiliar. Never having read it, they find its entire vocabulary strange; a sermon that might edify the faithful will seem to them irrelevant and boring. Here our task is primarily one of education, for these biblical terms make excellent sense—and can make sense to the modern mind, once they have been explained. Still others are deaf to the Bible for reasons by no means as intellectual as we like to think: perhaps a reaction against an overstrict

---

[14] The point is well made, for example, by Austin Farrer in *Kerygma and Myth*, I, 214-15; similarly, G. Brøndsted in *Kerygma and Myth*, II, 300-301.

upbringing, or a manner of life that is not consonant with the biblical teaching, or the atrophy of the spiritual faculties amid the press of daily affairs. Here the appeal is not primarily to reason, but to conscience and duty—if you will (old-fashioned word), an evangelistic appeal. But there are those—and let us never forget it—who want most desperately to believe in the Bible but who for intellectual reasons cannot honestly do so. And their reasons may vary from the most naïve to the most sophisticated and profound. We must seek in each case to discover what these are and strive in every legitimate way to deal with them. And this may involve us in a considerable reinterpretation of the Bible's message in categories more understandable to the individual in question.

But this is to say that there is no single, cut-and-dried technique that the interpreter must always follow. One suspects, indeed, that each situation, each sermon, must remain a problem to itself. Interpretation is *to the congregation*. The direction that it will take will depend upon the text, and the theological literacy, the sophistication, and the prejudices of those addressed. The preacher must make a good exegesis of his congregation. He must ask how they will receive the text—whether with understanding or incomprehension, belief or questioning, enthusiasm or boredom—and attempt to proceed accordingly. If he fails to do this, he will continually be answering questions nobody present has asked, thereby turning the sermon into a theological conversation—with himself.

(c) Finally, however necessary and proper a reinterpretation of the biblical categories may be, there are limits beyond which it cannot legitimately be carried. The substance of the matter must on no account be compromised. Whether Bultmann and others are sufficiently careful in this regard is a question that I do not wish to discuss. But no reinterpretation of the biblical message can be regarded as acceptable that does not hold steadfastly to, and clearly affirm the reality of, those saving events with which the Bible is principally concerned. The gospel must indeed be interpreted existentially, in the sense that it must be so presented that it addresses the hearer in his existential situation and opens up before him the possibility of a new manner of living. It can be so presented because it does in fact offer men a new understanding of existence and because the human situation remains in all ages essentially the same. It must be so presented, else the danger exists that the hearer, feeling no personal involvement, will be content to view the redemptive drama as a more or less interested spectator—or as a critic. Thus the crucifixion and resurrection of our Lord cannot be preached *merely* as events that took place long ago, to the saving efficacy of which the hearer is invited only to give intellectual assent. These are also existential events that happen in the life of every believer: the crucifixion of *his* "old self," *his* baptism into the death of Christ, *his* rising to newness of life. But that is nothing new; Paul had something to say about it long ago (e.g. Rom. 6:3, 6; Gal. 2:20).

But while we must seek to make the gospel existential in the sense just defined, we must not be tempted to interpret it only existentially (i.e., in terms of existentialist philosophy). We must insist upon the objective reality of those saving events of which the New Testament tells, for without these there is no gospel. The gospel does indeed offer us a new understanding of our *Existenz,* but it does this because it has an objective word to speak *to* our *Existenz.* The existential decision to which it summons us is not just a subjective experience. Rather, it is a decision that is based upon trust in the incarnate, crucified, and risen Christ. The gospel declares that events *have taken place,* and on that basis summons to decision. It is acceptance of these events in faith as *eph hapax* and historic, if also suprahistorical, events that makes existential decision possible and meaningful for the Christian. If insistence upon the reality of these events be the offense of the gospel—and I suspect that it is—then so be it. We have no choice save to make it. To try to render the gospel more palatable by interpreting it in purely existential terms is to rob it of its content and fundamentally to compromise it.[15]

III

Up to this point we have been talking of biblical preaching generally. Although we have by no means exhausted the subject, we can tarry with it no longer, but must press on to the matter that principally concerns us: the special problem of preaching from the Old Testament. How ought one to go about doing this? How is one to use the Old Testament in the Christian pulpit? How is one to proclaim its word as a word that is valid for the Christian congregation?

1. That the Old Testament constitutes a special problem cannot be

---

[15] I do not direct this remark at Bultmann or any other person, but simply state my own conviction. Bultmann has more than once been accused of Docetism (e.g. by Karl Barth in *Kerygma and Myth,* II, 111) or of Gnosticism (e.g. by E. Voegelin; *OTCF,* p. 65)—whether with justice or not will not be debated here.

doubted. Nor is the solution to it immediately obvious. But it is evident that, if responsible preaching from the Old Testament is to be done, a further hermeneutical step imposes itself in addition to the three outlined above. After all, one cannot just select an Old Testament text and, having discovered its precise verbal meaning and its theological concern, proceed without further ado to proclaim it to the congregation as a normative word. The more seriously one takes the Old Testament, the clearer this becomes.

To preach from the New Testament is simple. That is certainly *not* to say that the task involved in doing so is an easy one. On the contrary, we have expressly affirmed what every preacher knows, that it is enormously difficult. But the hermeneutical problem is fundamentally simple (I did not say easy). It is simple because the New Testament addresses the church —and we too address the church; the New Testament witnesses to Christ —and we too witness to Christ. The task of the explication, the translation, the application, and the enforcing of its message may be backbreakingly hard; but there is (how shall one say it?) no hermeneutical transfer. One has to translate its word from one century to another, but one does not have to translate it from one aeon to another, out of B.C. into A.D. The New Testament sets forth the faith of the church, preached to and in the name of the church; we too preach to and in the name of the church.

The Old Testament is different in that it was not in the first instance a document of the church at all: it was not written by Christians for Christians. The more seriously we take it in its plain meaning, the more clearly we see that it is the document of a religion genetically related to our own, yet not precisely the same as our own. It is a document of the faith of old Israel, and only secondarily a document of the church. Its message is not *of and by itself* a Christian message. Yet we must preach a Christian message from it (what other kind, pray, are we to preach?), if we are to use it in the pulpit at all. That statement is made quite seriously and with full awareness of its implications. In preaching, say, from Amos or Isaiah, it is simply not enough to grasp the precise meaning of their words within the context of their theology and proclaim that *just so* to the congregation. That would be, indeed, to confront our hearers with the demands and promises of Israel's faith. He who did that might be a Hebrew prophet—and perhaps a better preacher than most of us are. But we do not preach as prophets of Israel, nor do we address old Israel. The basic problem with the Old Testament is that, in all its texts, it occupies a perspective that is not, and cannot be, our own. It stands on the other side of Christ; it looks for a Christ, but it does not *announce* him. And we cannot preach from that perspective, as if Christ had not yet come. So we cannot proclaim the Old Testament's word merely in its own self-understanding. We must proclaim it from an A.D. perspective, in its Christian significance, or the Old Testament will, quite frankly, be of little use to us in the pulpit.

And that is the problem. How can one do this without sacrificing exegetical integrity? It has to be done, if the Old Testament is to be a vehicle of Christian proclamation. Yet it is a first principle that we may not impose Christian meanings on its texts either through exegetical skulduggery or homiletical irresponsibility: honesty and sound method forbid it. Nor can we evade the problem, as so many preachers do, by spiritualizing the text or moralizing from it or by using it as a springboard from which to leap into the proclamation of New Testament doctrine. This can scarcely be called preaching *from the Old Testament*. To preach responsibly from the Old Testament requires that one both adhere rigidly to the plain intention of the text and, at the same time, so bring it to word that it comes to the Christian hearer as an authentic witness to the faith that he claims as his own. Or, to put it otherwise, Christian preaching from the Old Testament must be done in the light of the New Testament revelation and from the A.D. perspective of the New, yet in such a way that neither the New Testament word nor its A.D. perspective is foisted on the Old Testament text. And that is *just* the problem. How is one rightly to do this? How is this B.C. text to be preached as a word to the church without distorting its meaning?

2. That is manifestly a fundamental hermeneutical question—indeed, *the* fundamental question where the Old Testament is concerned. How one will answer it will depend upon the way in which one conceives of the theological relationship of the two Testaments.[16] This has been formulated in such a variety of ways that it is well-nigh impossible to classify them.[17] But two opposing tendencies may be noted: a tendency

---

[16] The point has been clearly recognized by a number of scholars; see esp. Th. C. Vriezen, *Theologie des Alten Testaments in Grundzügen* (Wageningen: Verlag H. Veenman & Zonen, German ed., 1956), pp. 75-76; D. Rössler, "Die Predigt über alttestamentliche Texte," in R. Rendtorff and K. Koch, eds., *Studien zur Theologie der alttestamentlichen Überlieferungen* (Neukirchen: Verlag der Buchhandlung des Erziehungsvereins, 1961), pp. 153-62, esp. p. 153.

[17] A. A. van Ruler, *Die christliche Kirche und das Alte Testament*, pp. 9-12, lists ten

to stress the similarities, or the continuity, between the Testaments on the one hand and, on the other, a tendency to stress the differences. In extreme instances of the former, the messages of the two Testaments may be viewed as virtually identical, in extreme instances of the latter as fundamentally irreconcilable.[18] It is impossible here to review all the ways in which the matter has been stated. But the very want of agreement on the point should be a warning to us not to go at the problem one-sidedly, as if it could be disposed of by appeal to any single catchword or formula. The truth is that the theological relationship of the Testaments can legitimately be conceived of in various ways, most of which have a certain validity, but no one of which is alone entirely adequate to provide the basis for a sound hermeneutic.

(a) Thus, for example, one may understand the relationship of Old Testament to New as one of full parity within the unity of divine revelation. Such a view of the matter is quite commonly held in orthodox Protestantism—especially, perhaps, in the Calvinist tradition. One might state it something like this: Since the Old Testament is the revelation of Israel's God, and since he is also the God who is revealed in Jesus Christ, the Old Testament remains for the Christian a revelation of *his* God and an authentic witness to the faith he claims as his own; as such, it is in all its parts useful for edification and for moral and doctrinal instruction. Sometimes one will hear it said that the Old Testament *is* the Scripture, while the New, in that it brings the glad announcement that Scripture has been fulfilled, supplies the key for the interpretation of Scripture. Here the unity of the Testaments is seen more in terms of an identity of subject: Christ, who is the center of the New Testament revelation, is also the true subject of the Old. A highly christological interpretation is likely to result.[19] On occasion, indeed, the relationship has been stated

---

ways of stating the relationship which he sees as currently advocated, and even he may not have gotten them all (A. Jepsen, *EOTH*, p. 258, n. 16, complains that Luther's position is not represented). I feel that van Ruler's categories do not all stand on the same footing and that one could logically reduce them to five or six—each of them, of course, with variations.

[18] Cf. P. Lestringant, "L'Unité de la Bible" in *Le Problème biblique dans le Protestantisme*, pp. 45-69; see pp. 56-59.

[19] So, for example, with W. Vischer; see *The Witness of the Old Testament to Christ*, esp. pp. 7-34; and see further Ch. II above, pp. 86-88, above. Vischer's theme is again sounded in the title of a recent article, "Everywhere the Scripture Is about Christ Alone" in *OTCF*, pp. 90-101.

in such a way as even to give the Old Testament a certain priority over the New—as, for example, by A. A. van Ruler, who finds the central theme of the Old Testament (which *is* the Scripture) to be the theocracy (the kingdom) which is the goal of God's purpose in history, and who regards Christ as God's last "emergency measure" taken when all else had failed.[20] These ways of stating the matter are indeed different. But all—and others like them—have it in common that the relationship of the Testaments is viewed as one of full parity.

Now there is manifestly a profound truth in this. To say that the God of the New Testament is also the God of the Old and that both Testaments have as their subject his redemptive dealings with men is to make a theologically correct statement, and one insisted upon by the New Testament itself. It is a statement that both safeguards the position of the Old Testament in the canon and demands that it be preached in the church. It does justice to the fact that the Old Testament is not only an irreplaceable source of inspiration and edification for the Christian but also a book that provides him with indispensable instruction in the nature of the faith that he claims as his own. He does indeed receive the Old Testament as a revelation of his God.

Nevertheless, merely to assert the parity of the Testaments within the unity of divine revelation does not, of itself, furnish us with an adequate hermeneutic. It insures that the Old Testament will be preached, yes; but it provides us with no unambiguous procedure to follow in the practical discharge of that task. In particular, it does not give us clear guidance in dealing with the "difficult" parts of the Old Testament. The result is that the problem with which we began remains in full force. Without some further safeguard the practical outcome can be, and in fact is, a selective use of the Old Testament which ignores its troublesome parts,[21] a christological interpretation of it which runs beyond its plain meaning,[22]

[20] See van Ruler's extremely provocative work cited in note 5; for the words in quotes, see p. 65. For a critique of van Ruler's views in English, see the articles of J. J. Stamm and Th. C. Vriezen in *EOTH*, pp. 200-210, 211-223, respectively. Van Ruler's view of the Old Testament is in the Calvinist tradition (and so Vriezen, *EOTH*, p. 214).

[21] On the point, see W. Eichrodt, "Les Rapports du Nouveau et de l'Ancien Testament," in *Le problème biblique dans le Protestantisme*, pp. 105-30, esp. pp. 109-11; also S. Amsler, *L'Ancien Testament dans l'église*, p. 131.

[22] So, for example, in the work of W. Vischer; see note 19, above. But, judging from certain of his published sermons, I do not believe that Vischer's actual handling of the Old Testament in preaching is as consistently christological as this book might lead one to suppose.

or an illegitimate absolutizing of it through according it a validity in its own right, independently of the New.[23]

The problem, let it be repeated, is with the "difficult" texts. Granted that the Old Testament is an integral part of the Christian revelation and is therefore useful for edification and instruction in the faith, what is the preacher to do with those texts that are shocking and morally unedifying? What is he to do with these endless cultic regulations, these ancient customs and institutions, which can in no obvious way serve as a guide for Christian faith and piety? Shall he arbitrarily derive Christian teachings from such passages? Then he has not really *preached* from them but rather has used them for "more worthy" purposes of his own. Shall he ignore such passages? Then he is guilty of that selective use of the Old Testament which is just what he is likely to deplore in the "liberal." Yet if he does neither of these things he runs the risk of urging sub-Christian attitudes and notions in the name of Christ or of imposing a new legalism on the church by proclaiming Old Testament regulations as normative and eternally binding (a thing that has happened at times, not least among devout Calvinists).

It is theologically correct to state the relationship of the Testaments as one of unity within the framework of divine revelation. But such a statement cannot without qualification be turned into a hermeneutical principle, for there is another side to the matter. The two Testaments do indeed have a unity; but there are also differences, and these must be taken into full consideration.

(*b*) Again, one may define the relationship of the Testaments in terms of continuity, in the sense that the Old Testament is viewed as the historical and theological preparation for the gospel. This understanding of the matter has been represented on the theological scene with the widest possible variations. Liberal Protestant scholarship, for example, was at one time quite fond of describing the Old Testament religion in terms of a process of development which, beginning in the most primitive forms, issued eventually in the ethical monotheism and the peculiar institutions of postexilic Judaism which became, in turn, the seedbed of Christianity. Other Protestants—and not a few who would disclaim the epithet "liberal"—laying more stress on the divine element in Scripture, prefer to speak of God's progressive revelation of himself and find in the

[23] Th. C. Vriezen (*EOTH*, p. 222) has, with some justice, seen this danger in van Ruler's position.

Old Testament the steps in his education of his people whereby he prepared the way for the coming of Christ.[24] Roman Catholic theologians, too, in a quite different way frequently speak of the divine pedagogy in the Old Testament and see in it the record of God's providential earthly preparation for the coming of the supernatural redemption in Christ.[25]

That there is truth in this view of the matter, if rightly stated, goes without saying. The Old Testament unquestionably provides both the historical background and the theological preparation for the rise of Christianity, and no one would dream of denying it. Christianity did spring, and in the form it took could only have sprung, from the soil of Israel. The Christ of the New Testament could have come only to this Israel. Moreover, there *is* a progressive element in revelation. Only by insisting upon it can we care for the fact that many features in the Old Testament religion passed into history and were not taken up into the New Testament faith at all. Only by so insisting can we avoid the error of erasing history and safeguard the position of Christ as the crown of revelation. Since this is so, it is quite legitimate to view the Old Testament as the record of the initial steps in God's pedagogy by which he prepared the way for the coming of Christ.

Nevertheless, such a view of the matter cannot by itself provide us with an adequate basis for the interpretation of the Old Testament. To recognize the Old Testament as the historical and theological preparation for the gospel (however one states it) is indeed to underline the necessity of knowing it, and thus to secure its place in the theological curriculum and in the instructional program of the church. But unless something more can be said, the danger exists that the Old Testament will be seen as chiefly of historical interest and will for that reason be tacitly relegated to a subordinate position within the canon of Scripture. To use the term "progressive revelation" as it is commonly understood, or to describe the Old Testament as the preparation for, the educative steps toward, the gospel, inevitably carries with it the implication that the Old Testament

---

[24] This view is so frequently advanced as to require no documentation. For recent examples of it from quite different viewpoints, see L. Hodgson in *On the Authority of the Bible*, pp. 7-8; P. Lestringant in *Le problème biblique dans le Protestantisme*, pp. 64-65.

[25] I am not competent to say if this is the prevailing Roman Catholic view; but one sees it frequently expressed. See, P. Grelot, *Sens chrétien de L'Ancien Testament*, pp. 435-38; P. Heinisch, *History of the Old Testament*, trans. W. Heidt (Collegeville, Minnesota: The Liturgical Press, 1952)—who (p. 3) speaks of "the steps taken by God to prepare mankind for the appearance of the Redeemer."

represents a preliminary phase in the process of revelation, one that was necessary, indeed, but elementary, provisional, and imperfect, and now succeeded by something better. And so viewed, the Old Testament will always remain a problem in the pulpit. After all, if it represents but the steps on the journey to Christ, if it has nothing to offer save foreshadowings of the reality that is given in him, has it anything essential to teach the Christian who lives in the light of the gospel? Does it really say anything that is not said better and more clearly in the New Testament?[26] The preacher who views the Old Testament *merely* as the preparation for the gospel will almost certainly neglect it or use it in a highly selective way. He will confine his preaching to those obviously edifying texts which, ethically and religiously, seem to stand on a level with the New Testament, or which seem most clearly to typify Christ. If he uses the rest at all, he will show his helplessness by spiritualizing it, or by drawing from it those dreary moral "lessons" with which we are all too familiar.

The Old Testament is indeed the preparation for the gospel. But if that is all that we can say about it, we shall never have the full use of it in the pulpit, and with large parts of it we will scarcely know how to proceed at all.

(c) But the Old Testament can also be understood as a propaedeutic to the gospel in another sense. One can see its primary function as that of laying men open to the hearing of the gospel, and thus of providing, if you will, the subjective preparation for the gospel. This understanding of the matter has its roots in the dialectic of law and gospel, which has played such an important role especially in the Lutheran tradition. According to Luther, law and gospel are to be found in all parts of Scripture, in that one reads everywhere *both* of God's righteous demands and judgment (law) *and* his gracious promises and forgiveness (gospel).[27] Law has the function (its "second use") of setting before man God's requirements, making clear to him his inability to meet them and achieve righteousness through his own efforts, and thus of laying him helpless; in that it thus convicts of sin and impels to Christ, it prepares for the reception of the gospel. Now this is certainly a valid understanding of the function of law.

---

[26] The same point is made by J. D. Smart, *The Interpretation of Scripture* (Philadelphia: The Westminster Press, 1961), pp. 79-80.

[27] On Luther's use of law and gospel, see esp. H. Bornkamm, *Luther und das Alte Testament,* pp. 69-74, 103-51; briefer and in English, see R. Prenter in *Biblical Authority for Today,* pp. 98-111.

Moreover, it is one that allows possibilities for practical homiletics which, I feel, have been too largely neglected in my own tradition, in current preaching at least. To be sure, one might argue that in the Bible's own understanding, grace (gospel) is antecedent to law; but there can be no question that law (as Luther used the word) does indeed have the function of preparing men for the hearing of the gospel. Did not Paul speak of the law as a "schoolmaster" (*paidagōgos*, R.S.V. "custodian") to Christ? Indeed, the man who has no understanding of the law is likely to feel little need for the gospel.

In view of this, it is legitimate to ascribe to the Old Testament, with its strong element of "law," the pedagogical function of preparing men for the reception of the gospel. But we are not for that reason to make the mistake of turning "law-gospel" into a formula for describing the theological relationship of the Testaments, as if the Old Testament were synonymous with law, the New with gospel. That is a mistake that Luther himself did not make, although he did not at all times express himself as clearly on the subject as might be wished.[28] The term "law" is simply not adequate to describe the contents of the Old Testament. The Old Testament does indeed contain law; but it also contains gospel (grace, promise). At the same time, the New Testament, though principally concerned with the announcement of the gospel, is not altogether gospel, for it not only contains law in the Lutheran sense of the word, but also large blocks of teachings which occupy a place in its theological structure analogous to that of law in the Old.

Nevertheless, there have been those in recent years—as it happens, in the Lutheran tradition—who, conceiving the relationship of the Testaments in terms of the law-gospel dialectic, have equated the Old Testament with law. One thinks of such scholars as Emanuel Hirsch, Rudolf Bultmann, and —or so it seems to me—Friedrich Baumgärtel, whose views we have mentioned in a previous chapter, as well as certain of their respective followers.[29] These men, albeit in different ways, all accord to the Old Testament a purely pedagogical function and stress its radical discontinuity with the New. In the case of Hirsch, discontinuity reaches the point of

---

[28] Cf. G. von Rad, *Old Testament Theology*, II, 389, and n. 1. Luther did on occasion speak of the Old Testament as "law," the New as "gospel," but only with regard to the fact that law predominates in the one and gospel in the other; cf. Bornkamm, *Luther und das Alte Testament*, pp. 70-71 and the quotation from Luther there.

[29] See Ch. II, pp. 67-73, above, and notes there.

absolute antithesis, with the result that the Old Testament forfeits canonical rank and is found useful only as the great contrast to the New in the light of which the uniqueness of the latter can be appreciated. Bultmann, who finds in the Old Testament a history of complete miscarriage and failure (*Scheitern*), rather than a *Heilsgeschichte* moving to fulfillment in Christ, believes that the Christian hears the Word of God in the Old Testament only indirectly as he gains from it a grasp of his existential situation which prepares him to receive the gospel. As for Baumgärtel, although he finds a continuity between the Testaments in the theme of "promise in Christ" which he sees running through the Old Testament, he too speaks of the Old Testament as a witness of a strange religion which, because it speaks a word outside the gospel, places a mirror before us, shows us ourselves as we too often are, and thus enables us to receive the assurance of the gospel that God has redeemed us.[30]

It would be untrue to say that Bultmann's and Baumgärtel's views regarding the Old Testament are altogether mistaken and without merit, for they include certain valid insights which must on no account be lost from view. If we must insist that the Old Testament does tell of a *Heilsgeschichte*, it is also true that it tells of a very human history of sin and failure, disappointment and judgment. And there is indeed a certain discontinuity between the Old Testament religion and the New Testament revelation, as we shall later affirm explicitly. Moreover, the Old Testament, like all Scripture, does address us in our subjectivity and speak to us of our existential situation, and that not only in those parts properly classifiable as "law." The Old Testament is indeed a pedagogue to the gospel.

Nevertheless, the relationship of Old Testament to New cannot be viewed merely in terms of law that drives to gospel, however this be stated. To do so is to get at but half the truth. It is to subjectivize the Old Testament's word and to forget that it speaks not merely of our human condition, our disappointments and failures, but also of the God whose purpose and grace tower above all human failure, however shattering. It is also vastly to overstress the discontinuity between the Testaments and to leave us with the question if it is really necessary for the church to make use of the Old Testament at all. If it is merely a subjective preparation for the gospel, might not something else serve as well? That is a possibility that Bultmann himself frankly concedes.[31]

[30] See, for example, the article in *EOTH*, esp. pp. 144-56.
[31] See Ch. II, p. 72, above, and n. 41.

To appeal to the Old Testament only as a reflection of our human situation that prepares us for the hearing of the gospel is to straitjacket it, and often enough to do violence to its plain intent. By no means every Old Testament text is amenable to so one-sided an approach. One may find an excellent example of this in one of Baumgärtel's works,[32] where Baumgärtel takes Wilhelm Vischer to task for imposing Christian meaning on the Old Testament text. He cites Vischer's treatment of the incident of Ehud in Judg. 3:12-30,[33] and rebukes Vischer for seeing the sword plunged into the Moabite king's belly as "the word of God—sharper than any two-edged sword" (Heb. 4:12), and for finding in the story biblical support for the right to assassinate tyrants. Now one might indeed agree that Vischer has gone rather far beyond the plain meaning of the text and that his interpretation may be open to criticism. But what does Baumgärtel suggest in its place? He suggests that the story is relevant for us only in that it lets us see ourselves as men just as vengeful and hate-filled as Ehud was, who stand under God's judgment. But is that at all what the text intended to say? One must say that it is not. If Vischer has gone beyond the plain meaning of the text in search of a Christian significance, Baumgärtel has disregarded its plain intention altogether, for it was of all things not written to place a mirror before the reader and convict him of sin. (Sinful man that I am, I have to say that it has no such effect on me.)

The Old Testament does indeed speak to us of our condition and prepare us for the hearing of the gospel. But that is not its only function. To interpret it from this point of view alone is again and again to force it to say what it did not intend to say, while ignoring its true intention.

(d) Finally, it is possible to understand the relationship of the Testaments in terms of their position within the history of God's redemptive purpose (Heilsgeschichte) or, as many prefer to state it, in terms of the schema: promise-fulfillment. This view of the matter has many representatives today, as it has always had. These have it in common that, in one way or another, they see the Old Testament as the history of God's dealings with his people and his gracious promises to them, which points forward to, foreshadows, and finds fulfillment in his decisive redemptive act in Jesus Christ.[34] Little of a positive nature can be said in criticism

---

[32] Verheissung, pp. 94-95.

[33] See Das Christuszeugnis des Alten Testaments (2nd ed.; Zollikon-Zürich: Evangelischer Verlag, 1946), II, 89.

[34] As examples of this general approach (with variations in detail) see: G. von Rad, "Typological Interpretation of the Old Testament," trans. J. Bright, in EOTH, pp. 17-39;

of this view, for it is an eminently correct one. It has the merit of safe-guarding the unity of the Testaments while at the same time allowing for the differences between them. In that it does justice to the fact that there is an element in the Old Testament which is not derived from the New, yet which is essential to the understanding of the New, it prevents the New Testament—understood separately and to itself—from being made the point of departure for a secondary legitimization of the Old.[35] The two Testaments do indeed represent parts of a single redemptive history, and they stand to one another in a relationship of promise and fulfillment: the New Testament itself saw it so.

Nevertheless, even here a word of caution is in order. Correct though this understanding of the matter is, it does not in and of itself provide us with hermeneutical principles that ensure that full justice will be done to the Old Testament in our preaching. We might, to be sure, interpret the Old Testament typologically, as von Rad and others have suggested.[36] For my part, I find this in principle a perfectly legitimate procedure—though it may be doubted that "typology" is a fortunate word for it.[37] These scholars will have nothing to do with exegetical skulduggery, and insist that the plain, historical meaning of the text is to be preserved. But, viewing the Old Testament as the witness to a coherent series of divine acts which are oriented toward, foreshadow, and derive their ultimate significance from God's decisive act in the New Testament, they feel that the fundamental events of the Old Testament, with their attendant demands and promises, may legitimately be interpreted *in their plain sense* as corresponding to, and anticipating in a "typical" or analogical sense, the no less fundamental events of the New. This is certainly not the

---

and von Rad, *Old Testament Theology*, II, 319-429; H. W. Wolff, "The Old Testament in Controversy: Interpretive Principles and Illustration," trans. J. L. Mays in *Interpretation*, XII (1958) 281-91; and Wolff, "The Hermeneutics of the Old Testament," trans. by K. R. Crim in *EOTH*, pp. 160-99; W. Zimmerli, "Promise and Fulfillment," trans. by J. A. Wharton in *EOTH*, pp. 89-122; C. Westermann, "The Way of the Promise through the Old Testament," trans. L. Gaston and B. W. Anderson in *OTCF*, pp. 200-24. Further examples could easily be added.

[35] So D. Rössler (R. Rendtorff and K. Koch, eds., *Studien zur Theologie . . .* , pp. 158-61) in agreement with Zimmerli.

[36] See esp. the works of von Rad and H. W. Wolff cited in note 34.

[37] The question is raised by von Rad himself, *EOTH*, pp. 38-39; cf. also Wolff, *EOTH*, pp. 181-82, n. 74. Other scholars of the same general approach refrain from using the word. I feel that it would be well to avoid it in this connection both because it has too many pejorative connotations, and because what is proposed here is an analogical interpretation rather than typology in the conventional sense.

typology—if typology it is—that we have learned to fear. Since it is based in an essentially correct understanding of the Bible's own theology, and since von Rad and his colleagues are impeccable exegetes, we may be sure that in their hands it will issue in no vagaries and may prove fruitful in the extreme. Indeed, published sermons by certain of these scholars illustrate in a remarkable way their ability to bring the Old Testament to word in its Christian significance without in the least distorting its plain meaning.[38]

Still, it cannot be allowed that this typological-analogical interpretation is by itself sufficient to do justice to the Old Testament. It has limitations and dangers. Perhaps the most obvious danger is that it can so easily be misused. As von Rad himself concedes, the handling of individual texts is not subject to hermeneutical regulation but "takes place in the freedom of the Holy Spirit." [39] Now, of course, this must to a degree inevitably be the case in any attempt to interpret the Scripture: no rule book exists, or can exist, to tell the preacher how to deal with each and every text. But one fears that the average pastor needs more guidance. If he can preach from the Old Testament only as he finds in it analogies to the New Testament events, and if it is left up to him to discover these as best he can, there is the danger that he will be tempted to indulge his fancy to too great a degree.[40] There is also the danger that the true message of the sermon will be a New Testament message but loosely tacked onto the Old Testament text—a procedure that can hardly be called preaching *from the Old Testament*, and one that leaves the hearer wondering why the preacher did not simply base himself on the New Testament in the first place.

But even apart from such dangers—which, after all, result from a misuse of von Rad's principles and are perhaps avoidable—the question remains if a typological-analogical interpretation can in any case do full justice to the Old Testament, or if it will not instead greatly restrict the use that can be

[38] See, for example, H. J. Kraus, ed., *Alttestamentliche Predigten* (Neukirchen: Verlag der Buchhandlung des Erziehungsvereins, 1954); also, various sermons in C. Westermann, ed., *Verkündigung des Kommenden* (Munich: Chr. Kaiser Verlag, 1958).

[39] Cf. von Rad, *EOTH*, p. 38; also Wolff, *EOTH*, pp. 163-64; Wolff, *EvTh* XII (July-August, 1952), 104.

[40] Though I cannot agree with all Fr. Baumgärtel's criticisms of von Rad, he has a point when he expresses the fear (*Verheissung*, p. 124) that "students and pastors who are not named von Rad" will be tempted by this method into uncontrolled subjectivism. I say this because I have recently heard one or two sermons that consciously developed von Rad's principles in which the "typology" was decidedly venturesome—and not a little forced.

made of it.[41] Those who follow this approach believe that the Old Testament speaks a relevant word to the church only through the saving acts of God to which it witnesses, and the attendant demands, promises, and judgments—not through the human figures of its history or the specific historical situations of which it tells.[42] Now it is assuredly true that we want· no allegorizing or spiritualizing of the details of the Old Testament narrative, no moralizing from its various characters. But is this net spread broad enough? Will it serve to catch the whole of the Old Testament, or will important parts slip past and be lost from use? To put it otherwise, if the Old Testament can speak relevantly to us only as it offers analogies to the saving events of the New, what of those places where no such analogies can, without forcing, be found? Are they to be regarded as irrelevant, and silenced? [43] And if the Old Testament offers but analogies to the New, foreshadowings of what the New gives plainly, if it does not have a word for the church which *is* its own, yet more than analogy—is it really needed in preaching? Is it any more than a book of illustrations? I raise these points as questions only.[44] But they reflect the fear that a typological interpretation, legitimate as it may be within limits, cannot do full justice to the Old Testament's word.

But, even if one leaves typology quite aside, there is still the question if the place of the Old Testament in present-day preaching can be assured *solely* on the basis of the concept of *Heilsgeschichte* or the schema: promise-fulfillment. If the Old Testament is presented *merely* as the history of God's redemptive acts leading on to Christ, as the record of his promises now long ago fulfilled, the danger exists that preaching will become a rehearsal of past events to which the present-day hearer may stand as a spectator, and from which he may at best derive information.[45] And if this is all that the Old Testament seems to offer—a promise that has been fulfilled, a history that has been completed—its relevance in preaching will inevitably be thrown into question. A satisfactory hermeneutic must avoid this danger. The Old Testament must be so presented that it

---

[41] On the place and the limitations of typological interpretation, see especially W. Eichrodt, "Is Typological Exegesis an Appropriate Method?" trans. J. Barr in *EOTH*, pp. 224-45.

[42] For a specific statement of this, see M. Noth, "The 'Re-presentation' of the Old Testament in Proclamation," trans. J. L. Mays in *EOTH*, pp. 76-88, esp. pp. 86-88.

[43] Similarly, H. Wildberger, *EvTh* XIX (January-February, 1959), 89-90.

[44] For similar questions, see W. Pannenberg, *EOTH*, pp. 326-29; A. Jepsen, *EOTH*, pp. 258-62; also J. D. Smart, *The Interpretation of Scripture*, pp. 116-20.

[45] M. Honecker, *EvTh*, XXIII (March, 1963), 167-68, makes a similar point.

involves the hearer—in such a way that he sees its history as *his* history, its promise in some way as promise *to him*. That may be to say—and I think it is—that place must be allowed for the truth (for there is a truth) in the use of the Old Testament as a "tutor" to the gospel, and its word to old Israel so presented that the modern hearer receives it as a word to his own condition.

The truth of the matter is that, however legitimate it may be—and is— to understand the relationship of the Testaments in terms of *Heilsgeschichte* or promise-fulfillment, neither formulation, unless defined very broadly indeed, is alone quite adequate to cover the case. Certainly the whole of the Old Testament cannot neatly be classified as promise, the whole of the New as fulfillment. If there is promise in the Old Testament, there is also an element of fulfillment; and if there is fulfillment in the New Testament, there is also the promise of things yet to come. More than that, there is much in the Old Testament that only by stretching terms beyond recognition can be labeled promise, and much more that is indeed promise but that finds no fulfillment in the New Testament or elsewhere—and indeed not a little that is abrogated in the New Testament.[46] Equally, the entire Old Testament cannot readily be subsumed under the rubric of *Heilsgeschichte*: there is much in it that fits in that category loosely, or not at all. The Old Testament both is, and is not, a *Heilsgeschichte*. It is, in that it focuses upon that saving purpose which God worked in and through Israel's history, and which the New Testament announces as accomplished in Jesus Christ. But the history of Israel, of which the Old Testament also tells, was not in itself a *Heilsgeschichte* but a very human history, and like all human history marked by nobility and greatness, yes, but also by sin and stupidity, questioning and rebellion, tragedy and the frustration of hope. It was a history that led on to Christ— and equally to the rejection of Christ.

We conclude, then, that the theological relationship of the Testaments cannot be dealt with summarily merely by catchword appeal to the concept of *Heilsgeschichte* or to the schema: promise-fulfillment. These formulations of the relationship are eminently correct and contain truth that must on no account be sacrificed. But they do not contain the whole truth.

---

[46] W. Zimmerli, who works with the formula of promise-fulfillment, is fully aware of this (see "Promise and Fulfillment" in *EOTH*, pp. 89-122); see also H. Wildberger, *EvTh* XIX, 88; K. Frör, *Biblische Hermeneutik*, pp. 139-42; A. A. van Ruler, *Die christliche Kirche und das Alte Testament*, pp. 35-36.

IV

But have we, then, reached an impasse? We have argued that one's interpretation of the Old Testament will depend upon one's understanding of its theological relationship to the New. But, having reviewed various of the more commonly proposed formulations of that relationship, we have concluded that, although each of them contains some element of truth, no one of them is by itself adequate to serve as the basis for a satisfying hermeneutic. Does this mean that we stand "before the door of the Old Testament without a key," [47] and that we must either give up the attempt to preach from it or resign ourselves to proceeding as best we can on the basis of intuition and good judgment? I make bold to submit that it does not. I submit that there is a key that will open the whole of the Old Testament for us as a word to the church, while at the same time providing us with a measure of hermeneutical control. I should further submit that this key is to be found in the theological structure of the two Testaments observed in the preceding chapter.

1. This does not mean that we are going to propose another precise formulation of the relationship of the Testaments to replace those described above. The point is precisely that no single formulation can be forged into a master key that will unlock all doors. The theological relationship of the Testaments is a complex one, and our understanding of it must be flexible enough to do justice to the truth that lies in all the above formulations if our use of the Old Testament is not to be sharply restricted. [48]

No hermeneutic can be regarded as satisfactory that does not allow the preacher to work with all parts of the Old Testament and to bring his text to word in its Christian significance, yet without exegetical distortion. True, some texts are both easier and more important than others. But the preacher should be able to preach from *any* text and make it heard for what it has to say, be it much or little. A hermeneutic that enables him to preach only from obviously edifying passages and leaves him helpless before the rest will not do. And, obviously, the text must be proclaimed in its Christian significance (we can preach no sermons save Christian sermons). That is to say, the text must be interpreted in full recognition of Christ as

[47] I paraphrase the title of one of Fr. Baumgärtel's articles, "Ohne Schlüssel vor der Tür des Wortes Gottes?" *EvTh* XIII (December, 1953), 413-21.

[48] Cf. L. E. Toombs, *The Old Testament in Christian Preaching*, pp. 22-34, who reviews various ways of stating the relationship of the Testaments, and himself refuses to state it in any single formula.

the crown and norm of revelation. Yet, at the same time, care must be taken that whatever interpretation is given derives from the plain sense of the text and remains true to it. These are heavy demands. Hermeneutical principles based upon too narrow a formulation of the relationship of the Testaments will inevitably fail to meet them all.

The Old Testament is a most variegated book, and it will be heard by the Christian in a variety of ways. It contains every conceivable type of literature; it exhibits diversity of theological concern and many levels of spiritual insight—some of which last are fully consonant with Christian teaching, some of which are not. It tells of the events of an ancient history, some of which affect us even yet, some of which were of no great significance at all. It records words spoken in the course of that history— prophetic words, words of piety and wisdom—some of which address the Christian with full immediacy, some of which seem strange if not repellent. It describes the conduct of men caught up in that history—good men, bad men, morally pale-gray men—who respond to the claims of their God in faith and unfaith, obedience and gross disobedience, praise and most bitter complaint. Some of them are outstanding examples, some most emphatically are not. The Old Testament is, in a word, the deposit of the life of an ancient people, their customs and institutions, their beliefs and practices; some of these have carried over into Christianity, some have not. It is, on the surface of it, impossible to suppose that such a variegated book will at every place relate to the New Testament and address the Christian in the same way.

That there is a theological connection between the Testaments is not to be denied: the New Testament both affirms that there is and defines its nature. As has already been indicated, the Old Testament's theology understands the whole course of Israel's history in terms of God's dealings with his people and his redemptive purpose for them and through them. It is a history that moves between promise and fulfillment. The story of Israel's origins from the call of Abraham, through the Exodus deliverance, to the entry into the land of Canaan, is cast in a framework of promise and fulfillment. Israel's history in the Promised Land—her exile from it and her ultimate return to it—is understood as a history guided by God's sovereign will, subject to the stipulations of his covenant, and interpreted through his prophetic word of summons and warning, judgment and promise. And through all the pages of that history, through tragedy and beyond it, we see—expressed in manifold forms—a continued reaching out, a continued straining toward history's ordained conclusion: the triumph of God's rule in the earth. The Old Testament—let it be affirmed explicitly—does indeed tell of a *Heilsgeschichte* that moves toward promised fulfillment.

But—again as already indicated—there is something lacking in that *Heilsgeschichte*. It is an unfinished *Heilsgeschichte*, a *Heilsgeschichte* that does not arrive at *Heil*. Down to the end of the Old Testament, hope lay still over the horizon; one turns its last page to find Israel still in a posture of waiting—for God's future. And it is just at this point that the New Testament lays hold of the Old and claims it. Claims it, in that it announces that this long history of promise, of hope and disappointment, has come at last to fulfillment in Jesus of Nazareth, who is the promised Christ, sent "in the fulness of time" to bring God's kingdom to men. Claims it, in that it knew of no God save him whom Jesus called "Father," and had no doubt that this was the very God who had been active in Israel's history. Claims it, in that it saw the Old Testament as "the Scriptures" which Christ had fulfilled and the Word of that same God. Claims it, in that it saw Israel's history continued in the church, which is the new Israel, the people to whom God had, through Christ, given the promised new covenant.

This serves to define one of the ways—and perhaps the most important one—in which the Christian must view the relationship of the Testaments. By the claim of the gospel itself the Testaments are inseparably bound to each other within the unity of a single redemptive history that moves between promise and fulfillment. The fact of this unity must be kept steadily in mind in any attempt to interpret the Old Testament. The two Testaments have to do with one and the same God, one history, one heritage of faith, one people. Since this is so, the Christian must claim the Old Testament, as the New Testament did, for it belongs to him no less than it did—and does—to Israel. Indeed, the Christian has through Christ in the truest sense been made an Israelite, grafted onto Israel like a wild branch onto a tree (Rom. 11:17-24). He must therefore see the Old Testament's history as *his* history,[49] the history of his own heritage of faith, its God as *his* God, its saints and sinners as men who had to do with

---

[49] Cf. A. A. van Ruler, *Die christliche Kirche* . . . , pp. 31-32; also P. R. Ackroyd, *ET*, LXXIV (March, 1963), 166-67, who uses the amusing illustration (credited to Professor N. W. Porteous) of the Frenchman who, having taken out British citizenship, discovered that his country had now won the battle of Waterloo.

that God. The Christian who refuses to see it so flies in the face of the New Testament's witness and does no less than reject his own past. The unity of the Testaments within a single redemptive history must at all times be affirmed.

But it is not so simple as that. As Christians, we do indeed read in the Old Testament of the ancient past of our heritage of faith and hear there the Word of our God. Yet the more seriously we take the Old Testament in its own self-understanding, the more forcibly it is brought home to us that it does not speak to us exactly of our own religion. Its religion is one that is genetically akin to our own, yet not the same. It is bound up with the fortunes of a people who, if theologically our people, are nevertheless another people. Its institutions are for the most part strange to us; its beliefs are not precisely those found in the confessional documents of our churches. In a word, it is not the Christian religion. It hoped for a Christ (Messiah), but it could announce no fulfillment of that hope; indeed, so different was the Messiah of its expectation and the Christ of the New Testament that many could see in the latter no fulfillment at all. It was a religion that strained forward through tragedy and disappointment toward a destination; but from the pages of the Old Testament it is not at all clear what that destination would be. It turned out to be both Christ *and* the rejection of Christ. The Old Testament religion is genetically related to Christianity, yes—*and* genetically related to normative Judaism.

All this means that the Christian both can and must read his Old Testament, as it were, in two directions: forward with history in its plain, historical meaning, and backward in the light of the New Testament's affirmations about it.[50] Nor is he to do now the one, now the other, as the impulse strikes him, but both simultaneously. Because the New Testament has claimed the Old, and because Christ is for us the crown and norm of revelation and thus the key to its true significance, we have to read and understand the Old—i.e., interpret it—in the light of what the New affirms. We have to hear the Old Testament through Christ, for it is at his hands that we—who are not Jews—have received it. That is to say, we have to refer each of the Old Testament's texts to the New for verdict, whether it be ratification, modification, or judgment. At the same time, because the Old Testament has a word that concerns us which is not the same as the New Testament's, and because we are exegetically honest,

[50] See P. S. Watson, *ET*, LXXIII (April, 1962), 198, for a similar understanding.

we have to read the Old Testament in its plain meaning—i.e., exegetically —facing forward with history toward a future that is not yet clear. We have to hear its word before Jesus Christ, which was when it was spoken, and we have to follow that word ahead to Christ—who fulfills and judges. In short, we have to hear and accept the Old Testament as the *Old* that it is, inseparably related to the New, yet not the same as the New.

Clearly, then, the theological relationship between the Testaments is no simple one. How shall it be stated? Certainly no catchword, no neat formula, will do. Indeed, one suspects that any formulation will leave something to be desired. For my part, I can at the moment think of no better way of putting it than in the form of what may seem a commonplace: The Old Testament is the history of our own heritage of faith—but before Christ; it is the record of the dealings of our God and a revelation of our God—but before Christ.

But this is to say that the relationship of the Testaments is inevitably a dual one: it is a relationship of continuity *and* of discontinuity.[51] The continuity lies in the obvious fact that Christianity is historically a development out of Judaism; the discontinuity in the equally obvious fact that Christianity is not a continuation, or even a radical reform, of Judaism, but an entirely separate religion. The continuity lies in the fact that the theological structure of the two Testaments is fundamentally the same, with the major themes of the theology of the Old carried over and resumed in the New; the discontinuity lies in the fact that these themes receive radical reinterpretation in the New in the light of what Christ has done. Above all, continuity lies in the New Testament's affirmation that Jesus is the Christ (Messiah), who has fulfilled the law and the prophets; the discontinuity lies in the fact that this fulfillment, though foreshadowed in the Old Testament, is not necessarily deducible from the plain sense of the Old and was in fact so surprising that the majority of Israelites could not see it as fulfillment. The New Testament, while unbreakably linked with the Old, announces the intrusion of something New and, therewith, the end of the Old. It affirms the fulfillment of Israel's hope—and pronounces radical judgment on that hope as generally held. It announces the fulfillment of the law—and the abrogation of the way of the law. In a word, the two Testaments are continuous within the unity of God's redemptive purpose; but their discontinuity is the discontinuity of two aeons. The

[51] This point has often been made; for an exceptionally clear statement, see Th. C. Vriezen, *Theologie des Alten Testaments* . . . , pp. 74-93.

Old Testament is a book of the old aeon, B.C., the New of the new aeon, A.D.

2. Neither aspect of this twofold relationship is for a moment to be lost from view in attempting to interpret the Old Testament. To do so is ruinous. To ignore the continuity is to forget that the New Testament has claimed the Old, to rip the gospel from its anchorage in history and, thereby, to mutilate it. To ignore the discontinuity is to forget the claim of the New Testament to be "New"; it is also to level the Testaments, stop history dead in its tracks, and ignore the fact that we do not and cannot practice the religion of old Israel. Both aspects are to be held in view in dealing with all parts of the Old Testament. It is not as if some of its texts were continuous with the New Testament, others discontinuous— though it is true that now one feature predominates, now the other. In each of its texts the Old Testament stands with the New in a relationship *both* of continuity *and* of discontinuity. At no place may we forget either of these aspects, for under both the Old Testament is a book that points to Christ and, at the same time, speaks its indispensable word to men in Christ. Let us suggest how this is so.

(*a*) First as regards continuity. Viewed from the side of the New Testament, the Old Testament is an integral part of that history of redemption which is brought to completion in Jesus Christ. As such, it has become a document of our faith, and speaks to us an objective word regarding the nature of our faith and the God whom we worship. Though a document of B.C., it speaks through Christ in and to A.D., for it both takes on a new significance in the light of the gospel and rounds out and completes our understanding of the gospel.

Within the continuity of redemptive history the two Testaments stand as the two acts of a single play—albeit a play with a surprising denouement. The relationship between them is one of beginning and completion, promise and fulfillment, or however one wishes to express it. Now in any two-act play, Act I is as important as Act II for the understanding of the whole. Without Act II, Act I is incomplete and unsatisfying; but without Act I, Act II is incomprehensible and impossible. By the same token, events in Act I point to, and take on significance in the light of, Act II; and events in Act II point back to, and are clarified by, events in Act I. But the whole play is finally to be understood in the light of its conclusion, for it is only from this point that the true significance of all that has gone before can be grasped. This means that one can find a Christian significance in the Old Testament and preach a Christian message from it, because its whole history, from the Christian's point of view, leads on to Christ and finds its proper conclusion in him.

This in no way grants the preacher permission to read Christian meaning back into the Old Testament text. That is just what he may not do; such a procedure amounts to a flat refusal to hear the Old Testament. But one can very well see retrospectively in past events a deeper significance than was apparent at the time, and that without in the least attributing to the actors in those events insights that they did not have. Thus we who live today are in a far better position to grasp the full significance of the American Civil War than were the participants in it, who could at best have had only a partial understanding of what the results of their actions would be. Just so, anyone who comes to the last page of a detective novel, and learns at last "whodunit," sees in retrospect that many a seemingly casual word or unimportant incident in earlier chapters had a significance that he had entirely overlooked at the time. Or, a man may look back upon his earlier years and recall some action, some decision, that seemed at the time of no great importance, and realize that it had affected the entire course of his life; but, if he is honest, he does not attribute to himself as he was then a foreknowledge that he knows he did not have.

Just so, the Christian finds that the whole story of the Old Testament takes on a new and deeper significance in the light of what he affirms to be its conclusion. How could it be otherwise? As he hears the kerygmatic recitation of the mighty acts of God toward Israel, upon which her faith was based, he must inevitably think of that other kerygma proclaiming God's supreme and decisive act, upon which *his* faith is based, and which for him lends to the whole story of Israel an eternal significance which it otherwise would not have. As he reads of the covenant that made Israel a people, of Israel's chronic failure to abide by its stipulations, of the disaster that overtook her, and of her hope for a new covenant (Jer. 31:31-34), can he avoid a thought of that other covenant which he celebrates about the Lord's table, and through which he, who is of himself nothing, has membership in the people of God (I Pet. 2:9-10)? In like manner, Israel's messianic hope, her law, her ritual of atonement, her celebration of the kingship of Yahweh—and much more—take on new depths of significance for him in the light of the New Testament's affirmations. In short, in a thousand Old Testament passages he sees—and without reading a single thing *into* those passages—depths of significance not apparent to old Israel, because he knows where the story came out! Since this is so, the preacher may legitimately and without distortion read the Old Testament in the light of the New, find a deeper significance in it, and use it as a vehicle of Christian preaching.

But that is not the whole of it, nor is it enough. To say that Christ is the key to the understanding of the Old Testament is indeed to *permit* the use of the Old Testament in the pulpit, but scarcely to require it.[52] And the Old Testament not only *may* be used in the Christian pulpit, it *must* be. The Christian gospel cannot be preached only from Act II of the drama of redemption without misunderstanding and distortion. If the New Testament is the key to the significance of the Old, the Old is no less the key to the understanding of the New. As Act I of the drama of redemption, the Old Testament not only points to Christ and takes on a new significance in the light of Christ; it also speaks to the Christian its own distinctive and indispensable word regarding the nature of his God and his faith, and thus fills out and completes his understanding of the gospel.

Precisely because the New Testament claims the Old, it presupposes the faith of the Old. For this reason, many essential features of the Christian faith are not explicitly developed in the New Testament because adequately presented in the Old and taken for granted.[53] This is true, for example, of the whole social dimension of the gospel, its relation to the corporate problems of society, which, no doubt in good part because of the humble position of the earliest Christians, receives relatively little stress in the New Testament. How poor we would be if we could not appeal to Israel's prophets at this point! And how impoverished our piety and devotion would be if we could not sing praises to our God with psalms, as the church has always done! One thinks, too, of the eschatological hope of Israel, of which Christ is said to be the fulfillment. The New Testament hails him as Messiah and Son of man, and describes him as the suffering servant; yet it nowhere explains what these terms mean. Why should it? Does one not know this from the Old Testament? Apart from the Old Testament, indeed, it is impossible to understand the significance of our Lord's work as the New Testament writers saw it. Likewise, the New Testament tells of the making of the new covenant and understands the relationship of the believer to his Lord and to his fellow believers as a

---

[52] See J. L. McKenzie, OTCF, p. 112, for a clear statement of the point.

[53] S. Mowinckel makes the point splendidly; see *The Old Testament as Word of God*, trans. R. B. Bjornard (Nashville: Abingdon Press, 1959), pp. 30-31.

covenantal one; yet it nowhere troubles to explain what a covenant is. But, again, why should it? Is it not sufficiently clear from the Old Testament? And we might go on.

The Old Testament must be used in the Christian pulpit because, in more ways than can be suggested here, it guards the gospel from misunderstanding and perversion.[54] By anchoring it to the specific history of a specific people, it saves the gospel from vaporizing into a set of abstract ideas, or hardening into a philosophy or a system of doctrine. By stressing the corporate dimension of God's dealings with his people, it guards Christian belief from slipping into a private piety, a subjective sentiment, a disintegrating individualism, as it so often threatens to do. By its very realism, its frank earthiness, it holds the gospel to life as it is lived in this world and blocks it from a flight into an otherworldly piety which, with its eyes fixed on heaven alone, is content to let this world go its merry way to perdition. It is, indeed, only by holding the Testaments together that the "new" of the New Testament is secured and is seen to be not a code of ethics, or an idea of God, or a "better religion," but an eschatological announcement. Because it so complements and secures the gospel, the Old Testament is indispensable in preaching. Wherever it has been neglected, there the gospel has suffered distortion.

(b) The Old Testament, then, in its continuity with the New, both takes on a new significance in the light of the New and speaks to the Christian an objective word regarding the nature of his God and his faith. But that is only the half of it. There is also discontinuity between the Testaments, and it must never be forgotten, for under this aspect too the Old Testament has an indispensable word to speak. This time it is more a subjective word, a word to man regarding himself and his condition. And it, too, is a word that both points to Christ and continues to address men in Christ.

That a discontinuity exists between the Testaments is evident to every thoughtful reader and can be illustrated in a variety of ways. But it does not lie exclusively—or even primarily—in the fact that the Old Testament religion is an ancient one, expressive of a culture quite other than our own, or in the fact that many of its institutions, beliefs, and practices have not carried over into Christianity. Nor does it lie in the fact that the Old

---

[54] For fuller discussion, see Emil Brunner, "The Significance of the Old Testament for Our Faith," trans. B. W. Anderson in *OTCF*, pp. 243-63; Mowinckel, *The Old Testament as Word of God, passim*; also, H. Wildberger, *EvTh*, XIX, 83-89.

Testament's understanding of God is not always on a level with that of the New, or that words and deeds recorded in its pages may on occasion strike the Christian as shocking. It is rather that the entire perspective of the Old Testament is B.C. Every word of it was spoken before Christ, by and to men living before Christ and caught up in a history that was moving toward a destination the nature of which was not yet clear. They were men addressed and claimed by the very God we acknowledge as our own; yet the fullness of the purpose of that God lay for them over the horizon and out of sight. The Old Testament therefore poses questions, raises problems, expresses hopes, to which it can give no final answer, solution, or fulfillment. It points beyond itself, beyond its own possibilities, toward a consummation it could neither see nor produce. Every text of the Old Testament comes from a history that moves toward an unseen future. In the light of the New Testament we affirm that it found its true conclusion in Christ. But from the Old Testament itself it is impossible to tell where that history would lead; it led in fact both to Christ, and away from Christ, to normative Judaism.

Precisely because it has this B.C. perspective, the Old Testament can address us with an unusual immediacy, for we live—all of us—to some degree in B.C. It is true that the new age has come—and come fully—in Jesus Christ; it has come whether men are aware of that fact or not. At the same time, B.C. is not—theologically speaking—simply an epoch in history that ended with the birth of Christ: it is a condition of living. It is the condition of standing, whether through ignorance or by decision, outside, or not fully subject to, the messianic kingdom of Christ.[55] It is the condition of those who have never heard the gospel or who, having heard it, have refused it in favor of some "salvation" more congenial to their way of thinking. As far as such men know, or can believe, no Messiah (Christ) has ever come. Thus we see that our world, two thousand years after Christ, is still for the most part living in B.C. So, too, this country of ours, in spite of its long Christian heritage and its many churches, is deeply mired in B.C., for it can scarcely be called a Christian country. What is more, neither the church nor the best of its people is clear of B.C. Though we are told that we who are Christians have been made "a new creation" in Christ (II Cor. 5:17), who is as it were a second Adam (Rom. 5:14; I Cor. 15:22, 45), we know that this is so most imperfectly. The power of

[55] Fr. Hesse, *EOTH*, pp. 285-313, esp. pp. 304-307, though generally stressing the discontinuity of the Testaments more sharply than I should, makes this point splendidly.

this age continues, and there is a warring within us (Rom. 7:23); in each attitude and each action whereby we defy Christ's rule we discern the old Adam, B.C. Each of us ever remains *simul iustus simul peccator.*

The Old Testament, then, stands in discontinuity with the New because it speaks a B.C. word, not an A.D. word. But this very fact gives it an amazing continuity *with* B.C. *man:* it can speak to his condition. Not through its institutions, laws, religious practices, and ancient thought patterns—which are doubtless as strange to him as to anyone else, if not a great deal stranger, but in its humanity—in its hopes and aspirations, its piety and sin, in the way in which its people understand and respond to the claims of their God. If there is a "typical" element in the Old Testament, and one that enables it to address modern man with immediacy, it lies just here. The Old Testament's history is a thing of the past; the events that happened then will never be repeated and will parallel events of today only by coincidence, and then only in broadest outline. Its institutions and ritual practices are of another world altogether, and they cannot be brought over into our world. Its characters may appear as more or less Christlike, but few of them are really typical of Christ, and then not in themselves, but only by virtue of their function in the divine purpose; most of them are not even safe moral examples. But the human situation is typical. It is typical because human nature remains essentially unchanged, and because men do find themselves in typical situations and react to circumstances, their fellowmen, and their God in typical ways. And these Old Testament men, just because they have to do with *our* God, and because they are good, bad, ambiguous, spiritually discerning and obtuse, are typical of men today who have to do with the same God, and who are likewise good, bad, ambiguous, spiritually discerning and obtuse. For my part—and I confess it freely—I feel an affinity with these "saints" of the Old Testament that is not always easy to feel with those of the New, who so often seem far beyond me. In their hopes and aspirations, their piety and their questionings, their shortcomings and disappointments, I recognize myself—in my own B.C.-ness.

This B.C. perspective of the Old Testament is the essential complement to the A.D. perspective of the New. Because of its very humanity, and because it drives ahead toward a future it never attains, the Old Testament raises questions, poses problems, which every sensitive reader sees are his own problems, the problems of the world and of all mankind. And just because it involves B.C. man in the problems, yet can give to them no

207

final solution, it impels him toward some better solution—beyond the limits of B.C. Even the Christian hears the Old Testament in this way. He cannot, just because he has the New Testament, read the Old merely as a long history of hope and disappointment which has at last been brought to fulfillment in Christ, and which he may—because he has Christ—receive as information. He cannot stand as a spectator to this B.C. history, for it is also his own history: he himself, theologically speaking, stands yet with one foot in B.C. The Old Testament's word therefore mirrors even before him the predicament that, but for Christ, besets him, and impels him anew to the gospel.

The Old Testament does indeed have the function of preparing men for the hearing of the gospel. This does not mean that we are to think of the Old Testament as law, the New as gospel, and assign to the Old only a pedagogical function, as some have done. The Old Testament, as we have already said, is both law *and* gospel (in Luther's sense); and in the Old Testament no less than in the New, gospel is antecedent to law (in the exegetical sense). To assign to the Old Testament *only* a pedagogical function is at best to use it halfway, and ultimately to misuse it. But it does have a pedagogical function, and that not only in its law, but as a whole. The Old Testament as a whole is theologically antecedent to the gospel, finds solution in the gospel, and thus in all its parts—its gospel as well as its law, its promises as well as its stipulations and judgments—opens men to the hearing of the gospel.

The Old Testament as a whole impels to solutions beyond the bounds of B.C. The more seriously I take the *theology* of its law (covenant stipulations), the more clearly I see in it the demand for a righteousness quite beyond me, as it was beyond old Israel—a righteousness which neither my busy religiosity nor my sincerest efforts can produce. The more seriously I take the prophetic denunciation of Israel's sins, the more clearly I see that these are precisely the sins of my society, my church—and me; and in their word of judgment I hear also God's word of judgment on my society, my church—and me. The more seriously I contemplate Israel's dream of messianic peace —of swords beaten into plowshares and triumphant security as the appointed destination of the national history—the more clearly I see that this is just the hope of the B.C. man within me. And the frustration of that hope through the length of Israel's history teaches me that it is something I shall never have on my little B.C. terms. The Old Testament's word, rightly heard, places me in my B.C. dilemma, shows me the wreckage of my B.C. hopes, and thereby creates in me the readiness to hear of some better hope—beyond all B.C. The Old Testament, as it were, addresses me through old Israel, draws me along the line of Israel's history—which so parallels my own B.C. history—to the proper conclusion of that history, which is Christ.

So viewed, the Old Testament cannot be dispensed with in preaching the gospel. Without the Old, the New is not new. One can enter A.D. only out of B.C. One must be claimed of God in one's B.C.-ness before one can be claimed by God's Messiah, who comes in A.D. Just because the Old Testament speaks the word of *our* God in and to B.C., it is the indispensable prolegomenon to the preaching of the gospel. Though the sermon may not be from an Old Testament text and may not even allude directly to the Old Testament, it must nevertheless put the hearer in an Old Testament position—of waiting. It must address this religious but imperfectly Christian man, this man seeking peace on his own B.C. terms, and place him in his B.C. predicament, drive him into the *cul-de-sac* of his B.C. expectations, to the limits of his B.C. capabilities, so that his ears may be opened to the hearing of the gospel. If this is not somehow done, we run the risk of doing what we so often in fact do: offering men a salvation for which they really feel no need. Or we will address our hearers as Christian men, because they are such in name and in fact, forgetting that the whole baggage of B.C.—its legalism, its sin and false hope—has been dragged behind them, bumping and clanking, into the church. The Old Testament speaks to us an objective word of the nature of our God and our faith—let that be repeated. It also speaks to us an indispensable word of our own condition, before Christ; it will continue to do so as long as the last relic of B.C. remains.

3. In view of its great variety and the twosided nature of its relationship to the New Testament, it is evident that the Old Testament will not everywhere address the Christian in the same way. And this requires that the principles by which we attempt to interpret it be left flexible if full justice is to be done to it in our preaching.

Let it be repeated: No hermeneutic can be accounted satisfactory that does not allow the preacher to operate with any and all Old Testament texts and to bring them to word in their Christian significance, yet without in any way twisting or departing from their plain sense. A hermeneutic that silences parts of the Old Testament, or enables us to hear only the "easy" parts, or arbitrarily imposes meaning upon the text, or uses it as the vehicle for a sermon the content of which is really drawn from the New Testament, will not do. Equally, an uncritical procedure that betrays the preacher into imposing Old Testament institutions, directives, and attitudes directly on the Christian will not do. This means that we cannot frame set questions which we may then put to each and every Old Testament text.[56] We cannot always and monotonously ask: In what way does this text witness to Christ? Or: How, as law, does it clarify the gospel, or convict of sin and impel to Christ? Or: What does it have to say of our *Existenz*? Or: How does it offer "promise in Christ"? Or: What element in it is typical of the New Testament revelation? Or (and so our tedious moralistic preaching): What lessons can we learn from it to guide our conduct? No single set question can possibly do justice to every text. We have to be prepared to ask all the above questions, and more. Or, rather, we must let each text pose its own questions, whatever these may be. We must be prepared to hear each text in its plain intention, yet in its Christian significance.

Manifestly, then, our hermeneutical principles must be flexible and broadly based. But this is not at all to say that we are to go at the Old Testament charismatically, dealing with each text as the impulse strikes us. Rather, our interpretation is to be controlled by the theology expressed in the text with which we are dealing, in its relationship to the theology of the Old Testament as a whole, and as that in turn relates to the theology of the New. Let us attempt to explain.

As was observed in the preceding chapter, the Old Testament as a whole is expressive of a peculiar and distinctive faith which, though never worked out systematically, was from earliest times onward articulated about certain overarching and unifying themes. Essentially, this was an understanding of history, and of life within history, in terms of God's dealings with his people, his demands upon them, and his promises to them; it centers upon his supreme overlordship, his kingly rule over his people and in the world. Not a text of the Old Testament but expresses some facet of this structure of believing or shows us men in dialogue with it. We also observed that the New Testament takes up the faith of the Old and announces its fulfillment in Christ. The theology of the New Testament is something new, to be sure; but it is one that presupposes and reinterprets the theology of the Old. The New Testament, no less than the Old, has its focus upon the rule (kingdom) of God in earth, save that in the New this kingdom, though its final victory lies yet in the future, is announced as present

[56] H. W. Wolff, *EOTH*, pp. 160-62, makes this point splendidly—though one may ask if to seek the "typical" in the Old Testament may not itself be to pose a set question.

fact in Christ.[57] The theological structure of the two Testaments is essentially the same; each of the major themes of the Old has its correspondent in the New, and is in some way resumed and answered there. By virtue of this fact a hermeneutical bridge is thrown between the Testaments which gives us access to each of the Old Testament's texts and defines for us the procedure that we must follow in attempting to interpret them in their Christian significance.

It is impossible to do more than indicate that procedure in its broad outlines; we shall attempt to illustrate it more specifically in the next chapter.[58] Interpretation of the Old Testament must begin, as all interpretation must, with a grammatico-historical exegesis of the text (with all that that entails) aimed at arriving at its precise verbal meaning. That goes without saying. An interpretation that will not begin there cannot be called an interpretation *of the text*. But, again as elsewhere, exegesis must proceed in theological depth. That is to say, it must seek to discern behind the words of the text those theological concerns, those facets of the Old Testament's structure of faith, that express themselves in it. Thus, for example, if one is dealing with a historical narrative, one must ask for what theological purpose this story was related. If with a prophetic word, one must inquire after those theological convictions that prompted it and gave it its shape. If with a psalm, one must ask what aspect of Israel's understanding of her God is expressed in it and what function it had in the life of the community or the individual. And so on. Thus far, interpretation of the Old Testament follows a path in no essential different from that of the New.

But, in the case of the Old Testament, a further step imposes itself. Having determined the theology that informs his text, the preacher must—because he is a Christian and has received the Old Testament from the hands of Christ, who is its fulfillment—bring his text to the New Testament, as it were, for verdict. He must ask what the New Testament has done with this aspect of the Old Testament faith in the light of Christ. Does it announce its fulfillment? Does it ratify it and take it over intact? Does it modify it or give it a new significance? Or pass judgment upon it

---

[57] W. Eichrodt has repeatedly pointed out that this is the binding element between the Testaments: cf. *Theology of the Old Testament,* I, 26; see Eichrodt, *EOTH,* p. 239, and in *Le problème biblique* . . . , p. 121.

[58] I believe that the remarks of J. L. McKenzie, *OTCF,* pp. 112-14, point in the same general direction as that taken here; cf. also D. Rössler, "Die Predigt Über Alttestamentliche Texte," pp. 161-62.

and abrogate it? Or what? Moreover, he must concern himself for the "existential placement" of his text, if he is rightly to apply it to his people. Its original situation is an ancient one, in the life of old Israel, not at all the situation of the people he must address. The preacher therefore has the task of "re-aiming" his text. And, since the human situation remains essentially unchanged, and since Israel is continued in the church, he can do this. He must ask who was the speaker of this word then, and who its addressee, in order that he may determine how it is rightly to be heard, and to whom it speaks today. But, although he must interpret the Old Testament's word in the light of the New, he does not for that reason leave his text behind and rush hastily on to preach a New Testament message. That would not be to preach from the Old Testament. Rather, he preaches from the Old Testament text itself—this very word in its plain meaning—but in the light of what its theology has become in Christ.

The foregoing is but a statement of principles, and a summary one at that. It is not suggested that their application will always be easy, or that they will automatically serve to solve all the problems. But I believe that they define a hermeneutical procedure that is both subject to some exegetical control and flexible enough to enable the preacher to attack all varieties of texts and to bring from them what they have to say, be it much or little. It is my further conviction that every Old Testament text, if rightly heard, has its word for us today, a word of the God who claims us, or a word of ourselves as we stand before that God.

V

PREACHING FROM THE OLD TESTAMENT:

THE PRINCIPLES ILLUSTRATED

In the preceding chapter we endeavored to outline those hermeneutical principles that ought—so it was argued—to guide the preacher in his use of the Old Testament in the pulpit. It now remains to give them concrete illustration in the hope that their implications may be made clearer thereby. There are dangers in attempting to do this. A good point can easily be damaged, rather than established, by poorly chosen or badly presented illustrations, and I am keenly aware of that fact. If the illustrations that follow should have such an effect where the reader is concerned, I shall have reason to regret having offered them. Yet principles are abstract things. However fine they may sound, they mean little if they are given no tangible expression, and if they cannot withstand testing, in the specific situation. This is emphatically the case with hermeneutical principles. In no area is the adage more true that the proof of the pudding is in the eating. Hermeneutical principles exist to serve practical interpretation. It is only as they are applied to specific texts, and tested there, that one can be sure whether they are valid and workable or not. Our discussion, therefore, cannot be regarded as complete if it is left in the realm of theory; the risk of illustrating it—even of illustrating it badly—must be taken.

Ideally, adequate illustration would require the writing of sermons on all types of texts, each of them accompanied by detailed exegesis and theological exposition—a thing that neither space nor the reader's patience would permit. The examples offered below are in no sense intended as sermons, or as outlines of sermons, and I should be greatly embarrassed if any reader should suppose that they are. Rather, they are hermeneutical exercises aimed solely at illustrating the principles set forth in the preceding chapter. They represent the sort of thinking that the preacher should do with regard to his text *before* he begins the actual preparation of the sermon. The exegetical and theological analysis of the text that must precede any attempt to interpret it is in each case presupposed; it is hinted at but, for reasons of space, not carried out in detail. Texts have been selected virtually at random, but with emphasis on some of the more "difficult" ones—the thought being that if principles can be applied successfully in such cases, then even more readily so elsewhere. I trust that the interested reader will test the approach here followed in the case of still other texts, and if he finds it inadequate or unworkable, will seek for a better one of his own.

I

But first, let us review the task that confronts the interpreter, as outlined in the preceding chapter, using as examples a pair of very familiar passages, one from the Old Testament's law, one from its gospel: the Ten Commandments and the new covenant passage in Jer. 31:31-34. These texts have been chosen because they are "easy" (in the sense that they are obviously of great importance, are relevant, and create no theological problems for the Christian), and because they allow for an unusually clear illustration of principles. We shall proceed summarily here, suggesting the steps that are to be taken, but no more.

1. Supposing, then, that I wish to preach on the Ten Commandments (and I certainly should), how ought I to go about it? Obviously, the first step is a careful exegesis of the text. Until I have discovered what the various commandments mean, I can say nothing of value about them and cannot consider preaching on them. I have therefore to grapple with such questions as these: What is the precise force of the words "before me" in the first commandment? Does the commandment not to take the name of God in vain refer to profanity, or to something even more serious? Does "you shall not kill" prohibit the taking of life generally, or only arbitrary, unauthorized killing, specifically murder? And so on. To answer such questions is the task of exegesis. It is not always an easy task. Still, by

diligent study of the text with the aid of the best helps available, I can discharge it tolerably well. And I find a wealth of preaching material, for here are (or here are what seem to be) basic rules of religion and morality which every age and generation has found relevant and valid.

But this does not mean that I am ready to preach. To expound the various commandments in their verbal meaning merely as commandments would be unsatisfactory. The result would be moralistic preaching—very good moralistic preaching, no doubt, but still moralistic preaching and not gospel. It would, moreover, be shallow preaching (all moralistic preaching is shallow), for it would be to abstract the Commandments from their theological context and leave them entirely without motivation. So, obviously, I have to view the Commandments in theological perspective.

To do that plunges me at once to the very heart of the Old Testament faith, for the Ten Commandments are no less than the classic statement of the stipulations of the covenant that made Israel a people. Law is anchored in gospel (grace). Behind the Commandments, informing them and giving them motivation, there sound the kerygmatic words, "I am Yahweh your God, who brought you out of the land of Egypt, out of the house of bondage." The Sinaitic covenant took the form of a suzerainty treaty, in which the Great King would remind his vassals of his beneficent acts toward them which obligate them to perpetual gratitude, and then would lay upon them the stipulations which they must meet if they expect to continue in his favor. Here Yahweh, the divine Overlord, reminds his people of his prevenient grace to them in rescuing them from slavery and calling them to himself, and then—in the Commandments—lays down the terms to which the people must conform if the covenant bond is to be maintained. Specifically, they are to acknowledge no other divine overlord (god) save him, and they are to live in community with one another and with him in obedience to his covenant law. Viewed in this light, the Ten Commandments are seen not as abstract religious or moral principles at all, but as a description of the conduct required of God's people in response to his unmerited favor. And it is only in this light that the Commandments can legitimately be proclaimed.

But still I am not ready to preach on the Commandments. I am not, because neither I nor my people occupy their theological perspective. I am not a member of that people that was led forth in the Exodus deliverance and formed in covenant with Yahweh at Mt. Sinai under the law of Moses. I know of a new and greater Moses; and I am a member of that new Israel to which, on the night in which he was betrayed, he gave the new covenant in his blood. The saving act of God to which I must in gratitude respond is not one of deliverance from slavery in Egypt, but from bondage to sin and death. Moreover, I know that Christ in no way abrogated the law, but announced its fulfillment and, in so doing, radically reinterpreted it and gave it new depths of meaning (classically, in the Sermon on the Mount). The Commandments of God therefore remain valid for me; but they have been ripped from their setting in the Sinaitic covenant and placed in an entirely new theological setting. And it is only in that setting that I can hear them and proclaim them. I have, in a word, to interpret the theology of the Commandments in the light of the New Testament revelation.

This does not mean that I am to impose New Testament meaning upon the ancient Decalogue. Far from it! But I have to proclaim it against the background of God's gracious act in Christ, and in the light of Christ's reinterpretation of the law. The commandment is still, "You shall not kill"—and I have never done that. But I cannot forget Christ's word that to be angry with the brother and to insult him is itself to violate the commandment—and that I have done repeatedly. The commandment is still, "You shall not commit adultery"—and surely I can avoid that. But Christ has declared that to lust is already to commit adultery—and that I have frequently done. The commandment is still to worship no god but God—and I have never participated in nameless pagan cults. But I have seen the revelation of this God in Jesus Christ and have heard Christ's claim to absolute lordship—and that lordship I have denied again and again. I read nothing into the Old Testament text; but I have to read it in the light of the New Testament's affirmations about it. And, as I do so, the law begins to discharge its function as a "tutor" (*paidagōgos*) to Christ. The point is no longer merely that we ought to keep the Commandments (as indeed we should), but precisely that we have not done so and cannot—neither we nor old Israel. And it is as we are driven to realize this, to realize our inability to achieve righteousness through the law, that we are driven anew to the justification that comes from God through faith. Anchored in gospel, the law impels to gospel. At the same time, because it has not been abrogated but fulfilled, the stipulations of covenant continue to remind us that the response demanded to the grace of Christ is the recognition of his supreme and sole lordship and obedience to his commands in every encounter with the brother.

2. Let us now turn to that other passage mentioned above: the promise of the new covenant in Jer. 31:31-34. What procedure should be followed here? Again, as always, the first step must be an exegesis of the text that lays bare its precise verbal meaning (in this case, a task that is relatively easy, for the text is straightforward enough). And, again, it is necessary to view the text in the light of the prophet's total message and to grasp those facets of his theology that find expression in it. This last is a large assignment. Rightly to fulfill it, I must wrestle with the place of covenant in the Old Testament's theology, and specifically in Jeremiah's own theology, and must understand how in his mind it had been irrevocably broken and voided by the sins of his people. I must take seriously his attack upon the conceit of his contemporaries that God was unconditionally committed to the nation's defense through the covenant with David, his announcement of the judgment that was coming, and the crash that vindicated his words and swept away all hope, for it is against this background of despair that his word of hope is to be read. I must then seek to understand what Jeremiah intended to convey by this promise of a new covenant, what he meant by the writing of God's law on every heart, by the knowledge of God which all would share—and much more. A large assignment indeed! But when it is completed, I have before me a message that is exceedingly profound—and profoundly moving.

Still, I cannot proceed, straightaway and without further ado, to proclaim that message. I cannot, because Jeremiah speaks from a perspective that is not my own, from which I cannot preach. Jeremiah lived centuries B.C.; he could only *hope*—and promise that hope would one day be fulfilled. But I live in A.D., and have heard the gospel's affirmation that this hope has been made fact in Jesus Christ, who has given to his church the promised new covenant. I know that Jeremiah's words point to Christ and find fulfillment in him, and I must preach upon them in the light of that fact: I cannot do otherwise. And that sets before me a problem. If I base myself on a strict exegesis of the text, as I have been taught to do, and faithfully expound its plain intention, then I will be guilty of preaching from a B.C. perspective, without gospel, as if Christ had not yet come. Yet if I preach from a New Testament perspective (as I must), I run the risk that Jeremiah's word will seem to my hearers of purely historical interest—a hope long ago fulfilled, a promise long ago made good—and of no existential concern to them.

How is one to avoid such a dilemma? Clearly, we have to hear Jeremiah's words in the light of the New Testament's affirmation about them: that goes without saying. But we have to contrive to hear them *as Jeremiah's words*. That is to say, we must hear them as the B.C. words they are, and with B.C. ears. And these last we have, for, as observed in the preceding chapter, we stand all of us with a foot in B.C., since we are most imperfectly Christian men. We must know those false hopes that Jeremiah attacked —this conceit of unconditional divine protection, this identification of God's purposes with our own best interests—as *our own* false hopes, for such they are. We must see in the crash that demolished those hopes the divine *No* to all *our* B.C. hopes, and be impelled by it to seek a better hope—in God's new covenant of grace. We must follow that better hope, that promise of a redeemed and righteous society, ahead till we are driven beyond the limits of *our* B.C. possibilities and come at last to understand that no effort of ours, whether political or religious, can bring it to pass. Then and only then, when we know at last our hopelessness will our ears be really open to the gospel's affirmation that hope has been proffered *us* and the new covenant given *to us* through Jesus Christ. We cannot, in short, merely affirm that Jeremiah's word points to fulfillment in Christ; we must allow it to point *us* out of *our* B.C.-ness to Christ. As it does this, it *addresses* us and begins to serve its proper function—as a preparation for the gospel.

But that is not all. Jeremiah's word not only points to Christ; it continues to address us who have accepted Christ and who seek to live in covenant with him. Because Christ has announced the fulfillment of this word, we may see in it a suggestion of what he intended his church to be: the community of those who have accepted his grace and acknowledged him as Lord, who are inwardly committed to obey his commandments and to exhibit his grace before the world. And precisely because we are so often no such thing, precisely because Jeremiah's picture of the redeemed society of new covenant is no snapshot of us, his words come as words of warning and judgment to the church. They remind us of what our relationship to Christ ideally is, bring home to us our grievous short-comings, and warn us that the sins that fractured the old covenant ever threaten to damage the new. So Jeremiah's words, rightly heard, address the committed Christian too, strip him of complacency and self-righteous-ness, and impel him anew to cast himself in penitence upon the grace of God in Jesus Christ.

II

In the case of the two examples just given, the hermeneutical issues are, I believe, relatively clear. They are passages that are obviously of tremendous theological importance and relevance. Let us now turn to another prophetic text, likewise of great theological importance, but whose contemporary relevance and "preachability" may seem far less obvious, perhaps because the principles that ought to guide the preacher in interpreting it are less obvious: Isa. 7:1-9. The passage reads:

In the days of Ahaz the son of Jotham, son of Uzziah, king of Judah, Rezin the king of Syria and Pekah the son of Remaliah the king of Israel came up to Jerusalem to wage war against it, but they could not conquer it. When the house of David was told, "Syria is in league with Ephraim," his heart and the heart of his people shook as the trees of the forest shake before the wind.

And the Lord said to Isaiah, "Go forth to meet Ahaz, you and Shear-jashub your son, at the end of the conduit of the upper pool on the highway to the Fuller's Field, and say to him, 'Take heed, be quiet, do not fear, and do not let your heart be faint because of these two smoldering stumps of firebrands, at the fierce anger of Rezin and Syria and the son of Remaliah. Because Syria, with Ephraim and the son of Remaliah, has devised evil against you, saying, "Let us go up against Judah and terrify it, and let us conquer it for ourselves, and set up the son of Tabeel as king in the midst of it," thus says the Lord God:

> It shall not stand,
>> and it shall not come to pass.
> For the head of Syria is Damascus,
>> and the head of Damascus is Rezin. . . .
> And the head of Ephraim is Samaria,
>> and the head of Samaria is the son of Remaliah.
> If you will not believe,
>> surely you shall not be established.' "

In this passage we have a word spoken by Isaiah the prophet at the command of his God, and addressed to Ahaz, King of Judah. It was spoken in the year 735 or 734 B.C., in a time of dire national emergency. It is a word thoroughly characteristic of Isaiah, and one that strikes a note that recurs again and again through his book; manifestly it was a word of desperate relevance to the situation that it addressed. But what has it got to say to men today? That is our question, and it is a legitimate one. This is a most ancient word, addressed to a long-ago situation that will never in history be repeated, and one to which the modern situation is similar only broadly and by coincidence. And we are inclined to be impatient with the details of this ancient history, this poking in dusty closets, and are tempted to bypass it and to ask only what moral or what teaching we may extract from the passage for the edification of our hearers. And thereby we lose the word. The prophetic word was always a specific word, addressed to the "then and there" of a specific situation; it is only as we take that "then and there" seriously that it can begin to speak to the "here and now."

1. So our first question must be: What was it that Isaiah was saying to Ahaz in *that* situation *then?* That is to say, we have to begin with a grammatico-historical exegesis of the text. We cannot carry out that task in detail here. But, although there are textual and exegetical difficulties to be dealt with, it becomes at once abundantly plain *what* Isaiah wanted the king to do.

The situation is familiar, or should be. The shadow of the monster—Assyria—loomed on the horizon. Tiglath-pileser III had taken the path of Empire. As he sent his armies lancing into the West, a coalition was formed to oppose him, the ringleaders of which were Rezin, king of the Aramean state of Damascus, and Pekah ben Remaliah, who had seized the throne of northern Israel. Judah had apparently been invited to join this coalition, for in a business like this there must be no laggards—at least, not to one's rear. But Ahaz, aware of the dangers of such a venture, would have no part of it. So the allies marched against him; they would give him a proper hazing, remove him, and put one ben Tabeel (apparently a prince of Aramean blood who was amenable to their wishes) on the throne in his place. And now they were coming, and Ahaz was scared. He was in a trap and could see no way of escape. "His heart and the heart of his people shook as the trees of the forest shake before the wind." What ought he to do? He could see but one course: He would strip his treasury, send tribute to the Assyrian king, make himself his vassal, and implore his aid (II Kings 16:5-9). This would cost his country its independence, but it would save his skin.

Isaiah seems to have known of this plan, and he disapproved of it completely. So, taking his son Shear-jashub, he went out to meet the king as the latter was inspecting his water supply in preparation for the siege. The boy's name ("a remnant will return") was symbolical and could carry either a threatening or a promising connotation. We cannot dwell on the point here; but presumably the boy was taken along because the king would know his name and derive a message from it. In any event, Isaiah's word to the king is clear. He said, in effect: Don't take this course, your majesty. Pull yourself together. Be calm. Don't be afraid of these little kings that attack you. God is in control, and he has not ordained what they propose. It won't happen! Believe, your majesty—for

> If you will not believe,
> surely you shall not be established.

Or, better to catch the Hebrew wordplay: "If you do not stand firm—i.e., in trust—you will not be stood firm—i.e., in your position."

But here we are likely to go astray. The scene is a dramatic one, and we find ourselves fascinated by it. We see before us two men—and what a contrast in character! There is the prophet—a veritable lion of a man who, from all that we know of him, did not understand the meaning of the word "fear." And there is the king—if not a physical coward, then a moral coward, an irresolute man who took counsel of his fears (or so he is depicted here). And we are tempted to stop at that and derive a moral from it. One ought to be bold like Isaiah, having faith, trusting God. One ought not to be like Ahaz, an unbeliever and a coward. But what a shallow handling of the text! A whole theological dimension has been missed. The passage was, of all things, not written to provide either Israel or ourselves with moral lessons for our edification. Isaiah's quarrel with Ahaz was not just that he lacked courage or was politically unwise; it was a *theological* quarrel. "If you will not believe"—believe what? "If you will not stand firm"—stand firm on what? On the basis of what Isaiah had just said? Yes, but much more than that: Isaiah's word of assurance was itself based in theology.

2. So we have next to ask what that theology was. That is to say, we have to go behind *what* Isaiah said to the king and inquire concerning the theological convictions that moved him to speak in this way.

As is generally recognized, Isaiah's words on this occasion, as well as on many another, sprang from his unswerving belief in Yahweh's faithfulness to his covenant with David. The theology of the Davidic covenant receives its clearest expression in the oracle of Nathan (II Sam. 7:4-16) and in certain of the Royal Psalms (see especially, Pss. 2; 72; 89; 132). It was a very time-conditioned theology, but it was officially affirmed in the Jerusalem temple and was the theology that gave the Davidic dynasty its legitimacy. Its gist was that Yahweh had chosen Zion forever as the place of his earthly abode and promised to David a dynasty that would never end. True, the king could by his sins bring chastisement upon himself and his people; but God has promised never to take his gracious favor from David—the dynasty will endure. More than that, God has promised it victory over its foes and a far-flung domain, with the kings of the nations fawning at its feet. This theology, reaffirmed in the cult, was no less than the ideological basis of the existing order in Judah. Isaiah himself was deeply rooted in it. And now, when the nation was in danger and the promises themselves seemed threatened, he begged his king to have faith *in the promises.*

Just there lay the seat of Isaiah's quarrel with Ahaz, and the difference between them. Isaiah *did* believe; and faith was to him a lifelong source of courage (see such passages as 14:32; 28:16; 30:15; 37:33-35). And Ahaz did *not* believe. Oh, no doubt he did believe, in a formal way. On his coronation day he had heard the proclamation, "You are my son, today I have begotten you" (Ps. 2:7). He was familiar with the promises to David, had heard them reaffirmed in the temple, and no doubt gave them credence: after all, his own position was given legitimacy by them. But, in a pinch, he was not one to place his trust in so airy a thing as theology. He would trust in Assyrian steel, the sort of help a man can see.

So Isaiah's word: Believe, O king! Trust the gospel that has been given you! Stand firm in faith! This nation was founded in God's sure promises to David, and they are its help in time of danger. Take the theology you have been affirming "in church" seriously! Back your pious words with deeds! If you cannot, the promise will not be promise to you, but judgment. Yes, the dynastic promises are sure. (In the next passage, vss. 10-17, into which we cannot go here, Isaiah gives the sign of Immanuel to that effect.) But this is also sure: that an unbelieving king and an unbelieving people will be judged in history by the very theology they so piously affirm.

Thus Isaiah's word to the "then and there" of 735/34 B.C. It was a most relevant word; and in its relevance to the ancient situation we find the clue to its relevance in the "here and now." Still it says: "If you will not believe the promises. . . ."

3. But it is not so simple as that. The question still remains: What can I legitimately do with that word? How can I rightly proclaim it in the church? Can I proclaim it as God's word to my people, just as it is? That is exactly what I *cannot* do. Obviously, I cannot invite my people in

dangerous times to repose their trust in the promise made to David of a dynasty that would never end and in the inviolability of Jerusalem and its temple. That would be laughable: the Davidic line and the temple have been gone with the wind these thousands of years. If I attempted to preach such a theology, I would not be taken seriously.

But what then? Shall I transfer the promises from that political order to this and urge my people to trust God always to protect this Christian nation? That is something we B.C. men like to hear, even when we don't quite believe it: that the present order is secure, for God has established it and tabernacles in its midst; let it trust him and make no entangling alliances, for he will defend it from all its foes and make its future yet more glorious. Is that, then, the Word of the passage for us? No! That is, to use Jeremiah's word (Jer. 7:4, 8), precisely a lie. It is a lie that was buried under the rubble of Jerusalem, yet has had many reincarnations. To revive it again would make it no less a lie. What eternal promises, pray, has God made to the American nation—or any other nation, for that matter?

The more seriously I take the theology of the Davidic covenant, the more clearly I see that it is a theology that points beyond itself and its own possibilities. The promises are such that they could never find fulfillment on their own terms. The kingly ideal (e.g. Ps. 72) lay beyond the capabilities of the Davidic dynasty, or any of its representatives: it was never remotely reality. In time there developed (and first with Isaiah himself: 9:1-7; 11:1-9) the expectation of an ideal king of David's line (perhaps it would be the next one, who knows?) under whose just and beneficent rule all the promises would be fulfilled. But that hope, too, was disappointed: no such ideal Davidide appeared; the dynasty ended, and the temple lay in ruins. Yet hope was not abandoned. Ever it looked ahead, beyond tragedy, frustration, and despair, for the coming of a King, the Anointed One, the Messiah, who, endowed with God's power, would bring victory and peace to his people and establish God's kingdom on earth. Repeatedly disappointed, this hope was driven ahead through the years of Israel's history, down the corridors of B.C. time, till, at the turning point of the years and the end of all B.C., the midnight darkness was brightened and there came the announcement: "Good news . . . to you is born this day in the city of David a Savior, who is Christ [Messiah] the Lord" (Luke 2:10-11). Here, so the gospel affirms, and so all Christians must affirm, the promises made to David find at last their fulfillment.

What is more, this Christ, who is the fulfillment of the Davidic promises, has himself given eternal and unconditional promises, far greater than those made to David. Not to a nation, a political order, but to his disciples, to his church. Not promises of security, protection from physical harm, triumph by physical force, but sure promises nevertheless. He has promised that his church will endure and that "the gates of hell shall not prevail against it"; he has promised his presence in it "even to the end of the age"; he has promised to those who receive him life both now and forever. And more. These are unconditional promises; and we are invited to trust in them unconditionally. The structure of the covenant with David thus remains valid for us; but its content has been radically transformed in the light of the gospel.

4. So it is that Isaiah's words have for us been caught up into a new theological context, and in that context they continue to speak: they speak through Christ to the church. But it is Isaiah's own words that speak. We read nothing into them; they address us in their plain meaning. They were spoken in the first instance to Ahaz, who was a king of Judah, a ruler of God's people, responsible for the conduct of his country's affairs, both political and religious. But they also address those of us, whether ministers or laymen, who have positions of leadership in the church and are responsible for guiding its corporate policies and overseeing its spiritual well-being. Nor is it the church's designated leadership alone that is addressed, for, if we believe in the priesthood of all believers, every mature Christian shares in this responsibility—and can exercise it, too, at least where the local congregation is concerned. We are all of us to some degree in Ahaz' position: we have all (and not just the church's leaders) received promises, and we are all invited to trust them.

So Isaiah's word speaks through Christ to the church. And it is still a word of summons—to trust in the gospel and its promises. We need to hear that word, for it is no easier to do so in this year of grace than it was in Ahaz' day. The political situation of 735/34 B.C. will never be repeated and, of itself, scarcely concerns us. But the existential situation concerns us, for it is very much our own. It is a time when the church is threatened, and when the promises of Christ seem unreal and not to be depended upon. Where now the glorious days of the past? They seem to us like the golden age of David must have seemed to Ahaz and his contemporaries. Where now the promised triumph? It seems far away, and getting no nearer. Indeed, we see the church yielding ground almost everywhere, deserted and attacked even by its former friends. Can it be that the future is not the promised victory, but a post-Christian age? Can it be, as certain theologians would have it (strange theologians, who would practice theology without *theos*), that the God of the promises is "dead"? There is unease among us, and the feeling that we dare not meet this emergency merely with trust in the gospel and its promises. We are not willing to surrender the church, no. But we feel that it is up to us to find some course of action by which we may reestablish its position and save it. But that is to say that its future depends upon us; and the end of that is cowardly fear.

And to us there comes Isaiah's word: Stand firm in the promises of Christ and his gospel, and do not fear. Let the church cast herself on the promises and live from them. Let her be elevated by them above disaster and the threat of disaster. Do not fear these yapping dogs of men, these burned-out fagots of men, who would destroy the church. God did not ordain them: they cannot win! Let the church trust her future to the gospel that has been given her and place ultimate trust in nothing else, whether power, or cleverness, or zealous activity, or good works. Believe —and be established as the church!

But Isaiah's word, now as then, is a two-sided word. It is also a word of stern warning and judgment. And it is aimed at the Ahaz in us, for we are very like him. This cowardly little man of unfaith is a veritable paradigm of our want of faith: piously affirming the promises on Sunday, lifting songs of praise to God, halfway believing in fair weather, mechanically parroting "credo, credo," yet when the chips are down believing not at all; preferring to trust in institutional power, money, physical growth, programs of good works and political action, alliances with the existing order—anything that may serve to establish our position before the world; feeling that to trust in the gospel and its promises would be just a little naïve.

And to this Ahaz that is in us Isaiah's word comes: *No* to your unfaith! If you will not stand firm, trusting in the gospel that is given you, there is no future for you, O church, for you will not stand as the church; and the promises will not be promise to you, but your judgment—in history. This Ahaz to whom I spoke was wise: he saved his country by his cleverness and very nearly cost it its soul; and he made his name a hissing and an execration in his people's memory. It was in the faith—the messianic faith—that I proclaimed that my country *lived,* even beyond its death.

Now you who are the church must hear my word through Jesus Christ, who is the fulfillment of the promises to David, and the Messiah: save your life through human means, and you may succeed; but you will lose it while saving it. If you would save your life, O church, you must risk it in faith.

Somewhat in this way, I believe, Isaiah's word from the eighth century B.C. speaks through Christ to the church. And it places us squarely before the most important question: Do you dare to live by faith in the gospel? Do you dare to believe the promises?

> If you will not believe,
> surely you shall not be established.

III

As our next example, let us turn to a narrative text—a passage already alluded to briefly in Chapter III: the story of David's sin with Bathsheba found in II Sam. 11:1-12:25. (The text is much too long to reproduce here; let the reader consult his Bible.) This story, as is well known, is a part of the so-called History of the Throne Succession or Court History of David, which comprises the whole of II Sam. 9–20 plus I Kings 1–2, but which also builds upon, and presupposes knowledge of, the account of Nathan's oracle to David in II Sam. 7, the stories of the Ark in I Sam. 1–6 and II Sam. 6, as well as certain of the stories of the rise of David to power and his struggle with Saul in I and II Samuel. As is generally agreed, the History of the Throne Succession is a document virtually contemporary with the events of which it tells (it was reduced to writing in the reign of Solomon) and is an invaluable source of historical knowledge.

1. Although it is presupposed that one will begin by making an exegetical study of it, the story of David and Bathsheba is not one that requires a great deal of explanation. It is a familiar story, most lucidly told, a master-piece of Hebrew narrative prose. The details of the incident are abundantly plain. David's sin is clear and plain—if not to David, at least to the narrator and to us; and Nathan's rebuke is plain—as plain as a slap in the face. It is not necessary to spend words explaining a story so lucidly clear.

But, when all is said, it is not a pretty story. Like so many in the Old Testament, it leaves the preacher vaguely embarrassed; it brings home to him the helplessness that he frequently feels before the Old Testament text. It is not that he is necessarily prudish. It is not that he doubts that such things happened or is so naïve as to suppose that they do not still happen. Nor is it that he does not recognize in Nathan's rebuke the authentic word of Israel's God, for he knows that this was ever his word against crimes that make light of his law and do violence to the covenant brother. He is also aware that this is still the word of God against egregious crimes such as lust, adultery, and cowardly murder. God by no means condones such crimes: he knows that. It is just that he does not quite know what to do with such a text in the pulpit. Probably none of his hearers have ever been guilty of such a crime. He would prefer not to discuss so sordid a story before them, and he can see no profit in doing so. Indeed, he questions the wisdom of children—and children in the faith —being taught such stories: heroes of the faith ought not to behave in this way, and it might be disillusioning to some to learn that they did. He almost wishes that this had not been recorded of David. Granting that he did it, would it not be better to forget it, to pass it by in charitable silence (as the parallel account of the Chronicler in fact did), and remember only the good?

The truth is that he feels that the sermon ought to edify, to bring forth some positive teaching, some moral, some example of right conduct for the upbuilding of the flock. And, try as he may, he can find nothing of the sort here. The story offers no example save a horrible example: an example of what one ought under no circumstances to do. Perhaps one can, by dint of some straining, find an example in David, in that when Nathan's rebuke finally penetrated his skull, he openly confessed his fault—and so ought we to do. Or perhaps an example can be wrested from Nathan, who was courageous enough to denounce sin, to call a dirty spade what it was, even to the face of the king—and so, God knows, ought we to be. But if *that* is all the preacher can get from the story, he is playing with it, and he knows it—or ought to know it. The story simply was not written to present either David or Nathan as an example. Nor was it written to bring home to Israelites the wickedness of adultery covered up by cowardly murder (though it may incidentally have had that effect, as it does with us). Let the preacher seek of the story edifying examples, and he may get them; but he will get nowhere. He will get only what the story did *not* aim to say, while ignoring completely what it sought to convey.

2. But, then, what *did* the story aim to say? What is its theological

227

concern? At first glance it may seem to have none, or as little as any part of the Bible. It is, as we have said, a part of the History of the Throne Succession, which may have been an eyewitness account, or seems at least to have been based upon one. This account tells of the later years of David's reign, and how Solomon succeeded him on the throne. And it does this with an objectivity that is almost "modern," so much so that its author has with some justice been called the first true historian in all history. His aim seems to be (though this is not actually the case) merely to tell what happened. Specifically, he tells how David, having succeeded Saul and reached the climax of his victorious reign, was promised a dynasty: his son would succeed him. He then tells how the throne actually passed not to Absalom, not to Adonijah, not to some other—but to Solomon. And he seems content to depict David as he actually was. In telling of the affair with Bathsheba he seems to have no aim save to inform his readers that it happened and that it reflected no credit on David. How, then, can one find in so sordid a tale a handhold for a sermon, when its author did not, apparently, have any desire whatever to preach one?

Yet it is just here that the word of the passage begins to speak. It speaks first in the clarity—the pitiless clarity—with which David is presented. Here is no attempt to idealize David. Here is honest reporting. We see before us no plaster saint viewed through rose-colored spectacles, no shining, immaculate hero. Rather we see a very human man, a man both good and bad, brave and cowardly, a man neither black nor white, a morally pale-gray man. He was a great and exceedingly able man, brave, loyal, magnanimous, devout in his own way, a man held in honor by his people; and as such the narrator depicts him. He was also a willful man, a slave to his own passions who, disregarding the law of his God and the rights of his fellowman, committed an unforgivable sin; and that, too, the narrator records, neither glossing over it nor excusing it. Indeed, he depicts David as a man whose conscience was so dull that, even when his sin was rebuked, he did not see the light until the lamp was flung in his face: surely this prophet is talking about someone else! And when he did see the point? "I have sinned . . ." (vs. 13). Yet, as the narrator tells the story, one senses no profound contrition. David does not cry: My God, what have I done? O God, that I could make amends, could retract this thing, for it will haunt me till the day I die! Have mercy upon me, O God, who am unworthy of all mercy! No, he wrestles in prayer with his God, hoping to escape the consequences of his sin: perhaps the child will live.

And when that proved impossible, we see an almost fatalistic acceptance of what can't be cured. And then life goes on: he will have an heir—and by the very woman he had stolen; and that heir will be Solomon.

Shall we, then, give the story an edifying ending? Shall we say that in the end David emerged a chastened man, a changed man? Not as the narrator tells the story. Still trying to make an edifying example of David, preacher? Don't try. Down to the end he remained the same old David. Through his last years as the narrator portrays them we see still a man who was loyal to his God in his own way, brave, able to endure the worst without whining, who loved his sons to a fault and was on occasion magnanimous to those who had been disloyal to him. Yet we also see a man who, on his very deathbed, ordered unforgiving vengeance on those who had crossed him—as both his old retainer Joab and his enemy Shimei might have testified (I Kings 2:5-9). For all his greatness, David remained to the end of his life an ambiguous man, an unchastened man—and no saint.

A pitiless description of David indeed. But is that all? If it were, we could do little with the story. But it is not all. The History of the Throne Succession also presents this David as God's designated king to whom sure promises have been given, and through whom God's purposes for his people are to be set forward. The author sees God's hand at work in this very human history. The whole story is set in a context of assurance and hope, a hope that points toward the future. The story of Bathsheba ends—with Solomon born. An heir will sit on the throne. The future of the dynasty is secure, as God has promised. David may sin and be punished, may be hero and villain all at once, but God's promises are sure. Through David and his line there is a future for Israel. To David the promises have been given—because God so willed it.

So the word. But it is a well-nigh unbelievable word. It leaves us asking if such a thing is really possible. Is it possible that God's purpose in history can be set forward by such an ambiguous man, a man so unlike Christ and so like ourselves? And the text intends to say: Yes, it is possible—for God so willed it.

3. But it is a well-nigh unbelievable word. We wonder if we can really take it seriously. It offends our moral sensibilities. Surely God's kingdom on earth is to be set forward by good people, people without notorious vices, not by men like this. And so we are tempted to argue with the word, and we find ourselves arguing with history.

That David became in a peculiar way the foundation of the future hope of his people, a hope that sustained them and held them together, is not debatable: it is a simple historical fact. David's great achievement was never to be forgotten. It was, after all, under his rule that Israel became for the first and last time a strong nation among the nations of the earth; for the first and last time all the land thought of as having been promised was hers. In the minds of many, it must have seemed that the promises of God to the patriarchs—of land, great posterity, and blessing—had been amply fulfilled in David. His was a golden age that could not be forgotten. The very memory of it, transfigured, was projected upon the future, and gave form to the hope that sustained Israel through the years. As pointed out in the preceding section, a theology grew up about David. It is the theology that we see classically expressed in Nathan's oracle (II Sam. 7:4-16) and in certain of the Royal Psalms. Reaffirmed in the temple cult, clutched to the nation's heart, it became an article of faith that Yahweh, who dwells among his people on Mt. Zion, has promised to David a dynasty that would never end. True, kings might sin and be punished; but nothing that the worst of them could do could cancel the "sure mercies" promised to David. It was the nation's confidence that what God had begun in David would *never end,* but would lead on to his promised future.

That hope reached out continually for its fulfillment. Always—and as it had in fact been in the case of David himself—there was a tension between the king of the dynastic ideal and the kings of reality. Here is the ideal:

> Give to the king thy justice, O God,
> Thy righteousness to the royal son!
> May he judge thy people with righteousness,
> Thy poor with justice! . . .
> May he live while the sun endures,
> and the moon, through all generations! . . .
> May he rule from sea to sea,
> From the River to the ends of the earth!
> May his foes bow down before him,
> His enemies lick the dust!
> (Ps. 72:1-2, 5, 8-9, translation mine.)

And the reality? It could hardly have been more different. For the most

230

part the reality was powerlessness, defeat, shameful subservience to foreign powers, and kings who were a travesty of the ideal.

Yet the ideal was not surrendered. It gave rise to the expectation of a king of David's line, "a shoot from the stump of Jesse," who, endowed with all the charismatic graces, would fulfill the dynastic ideal and make all the promises actual. The harder the times, the more eyes were strained toward this coming One. Alongside the entire Davidic dynasty, B.C. to the very last man, there lived the hope of a king beyond all B.C., such as B.C. never saw. And Israel lived toward that hope. To be sure, it was a hope that knew, and could know, no fulfillment on its own terms. No such ideal Davidide appeared; the eternal dynasty turned out not to be eternal. Nor did any messianic revolution, any intervention from heaven, take place to restore it. Hope, ever disappointed yet never surrendered, was hurled out ahead toward a solution that nothing in B.C. could give. Yet in that hope Israel *lived*: that is a simple historical fact.

The gospel announces the end of B.C. and the fulfillment of hope in the Christmas proclamation: "To you is born this day in the city of David a Savior, who is Christ the Lord" (Luke 2:11). Here, we affirm, is the answer to the desire of the nations and the solution to man's B.C. dilemma; here is the fulfillment both of the covenant law by which David was condemned and of the prophetic promises attached to his dynasty. And this messianic hope which, we affirm, finds its fulfillment in Christ did begin with ambiguous David: that is historical fact. David, judged and condemned by covenant law, was nevertheless a link in the chain of redemptive history, because—so it would seem—God so willed it.

And so it is throughout the Old Testament. Its heroes are not always heroes and very seldom are saints. Call the roll of the heroes of faith as given in Heb. 11: not one is depicted as perfect, and many are not even admirable. Even Abraham, that paragon of faith, passed off his wife as his sister in the interests of his own safety. Jacob, to put it bluntly, was a cheat and a crook, whose duplicity became proverbial. Moses took life in anger. Rahab was a harlot. Jephthah was so dark-minded as to offer his own daughter as a sacrifice. Samson was a bullyboy and a lecher with not a saintly trait to his name. Samuel and the prophets—even these great men were in no case without their faults. Of all these heroes of faith here listed, not one is depicted as a saint. And it is time that we took this fact of biblical history seriously. It is time that we stopped combing the Bible for these dreary moral lessons of ours and tut-tutting whatever in its story displeases us. It is time that we stopped evaluating its characters from the pinnacle of some lofty Christian idealism and patronizing them for their spiritual and moral shortcomings. If we are going to take the biblical witness at all seriously, we must set ourselves down before the fact that it was in *this* history, and through these very human and often clay-footed men, that God worked his redemptive history; and it was to *this* history, and no other, that he sent his Christ. And in this history ambiguous David played an essential part.

4. But is that all? Does the story do no more than inform us that David was a sinner in the sight of God, yet that God nevertheless chose to use him as an instrument of his redemptive purpose? If that be all, the story may indeed cause us to reflect on the grace of God, who deigns to use even sinful men in his service; but it would seem otherwise to be only of historical interest, the record of an incident that happened long ago, and of no direct concern to us.

But that is not all. It is not all because the theology of the story has been caught up in Christ and through Christ addresses the church. It is caught up in Christ because the God who spoke through Nathan is also the God revealed in Christ; because the promises given to David find their fulfillment in Christ; and because this chain of redemptive history, begun in David and fufilled in Christ, continues in Christ and his church. This Christ, who is the fulfillment of the promises to David, has also given promises. And they are eternal and unconditional promises. As David was promised a dynasty and triumph over his foes, so Christ has assured his church of his presence in it forevermore. As Israel awaited fulfillment in the messianic reign of peace that would come, so the church awaits the triumph "when every knee shall bow . . . and every tongue confess that Jesus Christ is Lord" (cf. Phil. 2:10-11). At the same time, as David was subject to covenant law, so we of the church are subject to the stipulations of the new covenant—hard, impossible stipulations: "You . . . must be perfect, as your heavenly Father is perfect" (Matt. 5:48); and again: "If you love me, you will keep my commandments" (John 14:15).

So, through Christ, the theology of the story involves us. It involves us because it places us in David's theological position. The story is ancient; it happened long ago, and will never happen just so to any of us. We do not stand in David's physical position. But we are nevertheless in David's theological position. We are, because we are members of Christ's church, his elect to whom his promises have been given, recipients of his covenant, bound to live under his law, yet sinners deserving of his wrath. We can, therefore, no longer be mere spectators to the story. It is no longer to us a story *about* David, of purely historical interest. It is no longer even a word *to* David, from which we can perhaps draw some lessons. It has become, through Christ, a word addressed *to us*.

Through Christ, Nathan shouts at each of us, "You are the man!" and will not let us evade. If we did not receive this word through Christ, we might well try to evade. I am the man? Surely not. I have never been guilty of such a crime; I never did my neighbor to death in order to have his wife. This is a word for notorious sinners—not for respectable church-men like myself. But Christ answers: Not for you? Have you not heard how I have fulfilled and reinterpreted covenant law? Never murdered? How fine! But I say to you that whoever is angry with his brother and shows contempt of him is guilty before the law. Never committed adultery? How righteous you are! But I say to you that to feel the tug of lust is already to commit adultery. You are indeed the man! And as Nathan's words speak through Christ, we know that we have committed David's sin again and again—and, like David, were too dull of conscience to know it. Yes, we are all of us the man: God's elect, recipients of his promises, called to exhibit his grace and set forward his kingly rule on earth, yet rebels who defy his law and harm the brother, who bring shame on his church, and are without merit and without deserving.

So the story, taken with theological seriousness, puts us in our proper position and teaches us what it is to be *simul iustus simul peccator*. Through Nathan's rebuke it condemns us. It reminds us that every sin against the brother is a sin against Christ. It teaches us that nothing we can do—no sloughing off of bad habits, no little works of piety and merit—can erase the wrong that we have done. It constrains us to cry out in the words of the psalm placed by tradition in this setting:

> Against thee, thee only, have I sinned, . . .
> Create in me a clean heart, O God,
>   and put a new and right spirit within me (Ps. 51:4, 10.)

Having done that, we are prepared to hear the word of grace which we really could not hear before: To you, who are no better than David, are the promises given—because God so wills it.

IV

As our next example, let us select a psalm. And, to illustrate our belief that even the most difficult of Old Testament texts have, if rightly approached, some word to speak to the church, let us turn not to one of those greatly beloved psalms that have through the centuries nurtured the faith and the piety of Christians, but to one that sensitive spirits have always found shocking and offensive: Ps. 137. Following is the text of that psalm as printed in the *Hymnbook* of my church, for use as a unison reading by the congregation:

> By the waters of Babylon,
> There we sat down and wept,
> When we remembered Zion.
> On the willows there
> We hung up our lyres.
> For there our captors
> Required of us songs,
> And our tormentors, mirth, saying,
> "Sing us one of the songs of Zion!"
> How shall we sing the Lord's song
> In a foreign land?
> If I forget you, O Jerusalem,
> Let my right hand wither!
> Let my tongue cleave to the roof of my mouth,
> If I do not remember you,
> If I do not set Jerusalem
> Above my highest joy! (Ps. 137:1-6.)

1. A careful exegetical study of the text is, of course, presupposed; we shall not delay upon it here. Our task is, rather, to ponder the theological problem posed by Ps. 137, and to come to grips with it as a word of God to the church. To be sure, if the reader has before him only the above-mentioned *Hymnbook,* he might be inclined to say: What problem? Where is any problem here? I see no problem. And, indeed, in the text as it is printed there is none; it is a very easy text, from which the pastor can readily draw edifying lessons. The pathos of it touches our hearts over a gap of two millennia and a half. This devotion to Zion—it is exemplary! Would that we all had such devotion! "If I do not set Jerusalem above my highest joy"—would that all our people felt so toward the church! Surely

234

these are the words of a saint—of a man devoted to God, and the things of God, to the depths of his being. He endures tragic suffering; yet in it he is sustained by a loyalty and a faith that will not let him go. Is he not an example for the flock?

But wait. The text, as the reader well knows, has been expurgated. Of course, I for one have no difficulty in understanding why, and in a way I am glad: it is a shocking text, not at all the sort of thing one expects to hear in church. Let us read the psalm to the end—just three verses more (vss. 7-9):

> Remember, O Lord, against the Edomites
>   the day of Jerusalem,
> how they said, "Rase it, rase it!
>   Down to its foundations!"
> O daughter of Babylon, you devastator!
>   Happy shall he be who requites you
>   with what you have done to us!
> Happy shall he be who takes your little ones
>   And dashes them against the rock!

And so the psalm ends. One can readily see why *that* was omitted from the hymnal: it would be embarrassing to read such a thing in church on Sunday.

I say, one understands. But is this a theologically legitimate procedure? To omit part of a text for reasons of space is one thing, and perfectly proper; to do so on moral and theological grounds, as was assuredly the case here, is another. It points to an understanding of the use of Scripture that is at least questionable. It tacitly implies that Scripture ought at all times to be morally edifying and that it is proper to skip over such parts as do not meet that standard. It advertises that there are parts of Scripture that we wish were not there, that we prefer not to hear, and will not hear or trust our people to hear. Granting that the conclusion of Ps. 137 is not very suitable for use in the service of worship, would it not have been better to have omitted the psalm altogether? By expurgating it we come close to saying that we do not recognize its conclusion as having any useful word for the congregation, and that there are parts of Scripture, of which this is one, that ought to be withdrawn from public use.

So there is indeed a problem, and we must face it. What place does Ps. 137 legitimately occupy in the church's rule of faith and practice? In

235

what sense does it speak any word of God to the congregation? Of course, one might reply that the psalm is not a word from God at all and does not pretend to be. On the contrary, it is the word of a man—an all-too-human man. It does not articulate any cardinal theme of the Old Testament's theology, save in a negative way; it is the outburst of an individual who cries out at the misery that has befallen his nation—so his theology has declared—as the judgment of God. His words are no more a directive from God than is, say, the story of Lot's incest or of David's sin with Bathsheba; they are in no sense presented as an example for us to follow. True. But that does not relieve us of the problem. We declare the Scriptures to be our supreme rule of faith and practice, and we do this not least because we believe that we hear the Word of our God there. But in what sense can that be so of this text, half so exemplary, half so utterly unacceptable? In what way can it, if we dare to hear it all, serve to nurture our faith and guide our conduct? Can it be that the hymnal has, after all, pointed the way: take the psalmist's devotion as an example to follow, and pass his bitter hate in charitable silence? Is that, perhaps, the way in which we must approach the Old Testament as a whole?

I submit that it is not. I submit that we shall never hear the Old Testament's word rightly unless we are willing to hear it all. That is to say, we must hear it in its full humanity. There is a drive toward incarnation in the biblical revelation. According to the Bible's own affirmation, it pleased God to reveal himself not through timeless teachings, or some heavenly *gnosis,* but through the events of a particular history, and to and through men who were caught up in that history, and who were in every case men of like passions with ourselves and subject to all the limitations of our flesh. And God's final revelation of himself was given—so the New Testament declares—when "the Word became flesh and dwelt among us," in the form of a man who had a body like our own and feelings like our own, and whose mortal life, like ours, ended in death. It is incumbent upon us to take this aspect of the biblical revelation seriously. We cannot attempt to abstract it from its human form without being guilty of a tacit sort of Docetism. We cannot demand that God's Word be always spoken from heaven with the tongues of archangels. We cannot demand that the Bible give us nothing but correct teachings and safe moral instruction, and be offended at it when it does not. We must receive the biblical word in its humanity, and as a whole, or we cannot rightly hear it at all.

And just so with Ps. 137. We cannot expurgate it according to taste, extracting from it its edifying sentiments and thereby turning its author into a saint. If we do that, we will not *hear* the psalm. This man who put Jerusalem above his highest joy was not a saint. He who loved Zion so devotedly and hated his foes so passionately was *the same man.* Indeed, it would not be too much to say that he hated so because he loved so. We cannot have half this man. We cannot hear his exemplary words of devotion rightly unless we are willing to hear of the tragedy and bitterness from which they sprang.

2. So we must begin with this text—as with all others—by asking the right questions. And the first question in this case is not, What lessons may we learn, what example may we derive, from this text? It is not even, What positive theological teachings are expressed here? For here is a man who responds in anguish to what his theology has affirmed was the judgment of God, but is to him sheer, stark tragedy. The first question is: Who is this man?

In one sense, that is an easy question to answer. He is a Jew exiled in Babylon. He has seen the destruction of his country, of his home, of the temple where he worshiped, and of all that he held dear. He has been hauled away to a strange land, and he is homesick, heartsick, filled with longing. And he hates! With reason, too, when one thinks of the Babylonian rape of Jerusalem, the butchery, the wanton destruction, and the humiliation. And Edom. The dirty traitors, with their last-minute stab in the back! He is a lost, homeless man, a bitter, hate-filled man. He is a snarling, beaten animal of a man, but for the thought of Zion. And if this increases his hate, it also sustains him: the memory of things past has become the substance of his hope for the future, if hope there is at all.

And what is this Jerusalem that he mourns? His country's capital city, of course, his own home and his father's home before him; in it stood the temple, the earthly habitation of his God; in it stood David's eternal throne. Jerusalem is to him no less than the seat of the visible rule of God on earth, his visible church, supporting the visible earthly order. And he yearns for this visible church and mourns its destruction. And who are these whom he hates? The enemies of Zion, of course, of this visible church, who have defiled it and laid it in ruins. And he hates them with a hatred that defies description. Yet it must be said that whatever one thinks of his spirit, his love and his hate, it is at least rightly directed: he loves the right things—God and his church, and the things of God—and, if hate he must, he hates the right things—the enemies of God's church.

237

But, again, who is this man? A Jew in exile 2,500 years ago? Yes—but more. He is a type; he is typical of that man in every age who is godly and devoted to the things of God, yet who—theologically speaking—lives in B.C. His name is Legion. He is claimed by God with a claim that will not let him go, yet he understands and responds to that claim from a pre-Christian perspective and in a not-yet-Christian spirit. God-fearing, he loves God's visible church. He loves it for itself, yes, but also as the bulwark and ground of the good life he has known, the giver of blessings both material and spiritual. He is sincerely devoted to the church and counts it his highest joy to serve it. He is heartbroken over its reverses; he yearns for its restoration and victory, and for the triumph of God's kingdom in the world. And he hates those enemies of religion who would destroy the church. Yes, hates! No, he is not so crude about it as to wish to dash their babies' brains out against a rock. But they are his enemies, and he does not love them. He would like to see them wiped from the face of the earth, at the cost of what innocent suffering he neither considers nor cares, so that the church that he loves might thrive again. He is God's wholly committed man, yet a man who is estranged from God's spirit. He is man whose longing only God can fill, man whom God must surely judge. He is man yearning for some gospel, some good news of God's intervention, yet man to whom the gospel must come as a strange thing. We know this man well: there is more than a little of him in most of us.

3. Manifestly, then, we cannot read this text to itself or receive it as God's Word for us in and of itself. Like every other Old Testament text, this psalm must be read in the light of the gospel, which is the terminus toward which, theologically speaking, the Old Testament history tends. As we have said, the Old Testament tells of a history of redemption, a *Heilsgeschichte*. It describes God's dealings with Israel, his purpose for Israel and, through Israel, for the world. It tells how he called a people to himself in the Exodus deliverance, gave them his covenant and law, spoke his word to them, acted in their history in judgment and mercy, and gave to them the promise of his ultimate triumph and the consummation of his purpose. But that promised consummation did not materialize in the pages of the Old Testament; its history of redemption remains incomplete. And because the New Testament announces that completion in Jesus Christ, the Christian is obliged to read the Old in the light of what he affirms to be its true conclusion.

But the Old Testament is not merely a redemptive history. The history of Israel is not itself a *Heilsgeschichte,* but a very human history, the history of an ancient people quite different from ourselves. The actors in that history were all human beings, some of them good, some of them bad, most a mixture of both, none of them perfect. They responded to the claims of their God in faith and unfaith, obedience and disobedience, submission and violent protest. The history of which they were a part led on in fact to Christ, and also to the rejection of Christ. The two Testaments, therefore, stand in a dual relationship to each other. They are bound together in the continuity of God's redemptive purpose; they stand in the discontinuity of B.C. to A.D. Christ, we affirm, fulfills the hope and the piety of the Old Testament; he is also the judge of that hope and that piety. It is through Christ that we have a part in Israel's history, and it is through him that we receive the Old Testament; it is through Christ that we must read it, and every text in it.

Now Ps. 137 stands midway of that history and looks for its ending. This exiled Jew is an actor in that history. He lives far in B.C.; he is claimed by God, and he longs for God's intervention. And we know that that longing, and the history of which this man is a part, will in the end lead to Christ: to accept or to reject. We see in this man no less than a paradigm of man on the way to Christ, man whose history must in the end come to Christ. As we read his words in the light of the gospel, we know that his longing for Zion, his spiritual homesickness, has no answer save in Christ; we also know that Christ will judge this man, who is anything but an example for the godly. Nor can we stand as disinterested spectators to this man's outburst and evaluate it from some position of detachment. We see a bit of ourselves in this man. We know that we too are on our way to Christ, not yet free of B.C.; we know that we too must confront Christ, who is both the fulfillment of our longing and our judge.

4. So it is that the psalm, read in the light of the gospel, speaks a word to our condition. But that raises a question. If we read the psalm in this way, are we not forced to reject its concluding verses as unworthy and sub-Christian? Is it not just this man's hatred, so utterly contrary to Christ's spirit, that Christ will judge? Ought we not, therefore, to evaluate the psalm similarly?

Yes, but it is not so simple as that. It is not simply that Christ judges this man's hate and fulfills his devoted longing. If that were the case, the *Hymnbook* would indeed be correct: expurgate his hate, forget it, and

239

use his piety for purposes of edification. But that is not the case. No, Christ judges *both* his piety *and* his hate and fulfills *both* his longing *and* the passionate involvement that created his hate. *This whole man* is on the way to Christ and must confront Christ. And *this whole man*, like the Old Testament itself, will be found to stand to Christ—if we may put it so—in a relationship simultaneously of continuity and of discontinuity. And this man is a paradigm of ourselves.

In Christ is the fulfillment of his longing and hope *and* the judgment of his B.C. hope. His hope will never be fulfilled as he wants it; he will never have it on his own terms (and no more will we). He would like to go back to *status quo ante*: he never will. Oh, he will return, or his son will, to Jerusalem; and the temple will be rebuilt there. But what a poor fulfillment! No mighty overturn of pagan power here, no reestablishment of the lost glory of David, with Jerusalem the center of a far-flung domain. Just a tiny law community, privileged by the Persian king. And would some messianic deliverer come to smash the foes of Zion? Some apocalyptic intervention to establish God's rule in triumph? No. His longing will know nothing but frustration until he hears at the issue of the years—and heeds—the voice of One announcing, "The kingdom of God is at hand."

In Christ this man's B.C. longing is fulfilled and judged: judged while fulfilled. In Christ he learns that God's purpose is not to glorify Israel and smash its foes, nor yet to glorify his church and secure the best interests of Christian people. Rather, it is his own glory, which it is man's chief end to serve. It is his purpose to *use* his church, his new Israel, in the service of a yet greater Zion and its King, to whom every knee shall one day bow. It is *that* Zion, *that* Jerusalem that calls this man to fulfillment. Here is your home, your only home, and the answer to your homesickness. Here is your home and your destination; all other homes are but lodging places for a night. Baptize your piety and devotion into the service of that Zion. Place it above your highest joy. Seek its welfare— and find peace and rest.

And his hate? That too must confront Christ. And Christ judges it, of course. Christ cannot condone such hate; his command is, rather, "Love your enemies and pray for those who persecute you," turn the other cheek, go the second mile (cf. Matt. 5:44, 39, 41). The Christian cannot wish his enemies dashed against a rock or blown to bits; he cannot repeat such words. That is the truth of their expurgation: they are not Christian words. Yes, Christ judges this man's hate. But he does not expurgate the passionate involvement that created it. Christ does not call expurgated men, plaster saints, into his kingdom, but sinners. We cannot divide this man and take only the half that we like. He hated greatly not least *because* he loved greatly. Just to judge his passion and eliminate it would be to destroy the ardent devotion that made him God's committed man. *This whole man* must be baptized into Christ. His hatred must be judged and surrendered that the passionate involvement that created it might be transmuted into zeal for the kingdom. Here is a man the kingdom can use. Here is no pale man, tolerant of the kingdom's foes because the kingdom does not greatly claim him. Here is no sentimental fool who thinks that to love the enemy means that the kingdom *has* no enemies. Here is the man who, by God's grace, will love the enemy; but he will know the enemy very well. Here is the man of zeal against the forces of sin, indifference, secularism, and pagan ideology that would destroy the church and send it into exile. Here is the man who labors mightily and prays earnestly for the defeat of the foes of Christ's kingdom. He is a man out of B.C., godly, homeless, hating, who must confront Christ. But he is also the passionately involved man who, redeemed in Christ, can truly pray, "Thy kingdom come, thy will be done. . . ." He is man to whom the gospel must be preached.

V

For our final illustration, let us turn to the book of Joshua and ponder the problem that confronts us in attempting to preach from it. As the reader is well aware, Joshua tells the story of the conquest of the Promised Land and takes its name from the one who was Israel's leader in that enterprise. We shall take as our text two passages, Josh. 11:16-23 and Ch. 23. The first of these passages forms the conclusion of the conquest narrative itself. The second, which takes the form of a valedictory address by Joshua, delivered in his old age, is the grand conclusion of the book as a whole. Here the unknown author of the book, presupposing that the reader has read and pondered all that has gone before, sums up, reiterates, and hammers home the point that he has been trying to make throughout the entire account as he has presented it. Although this double text is a rather long one, it might be well to reproduce essential portions of it here, since it is probably not familiar to all. The first passage reads:

241

So Joshua took all that land, the hill country and all the Negeb and all the land of Goshen and the lowland and the Arabah and the hill country of Israel and its lowland [the extent of the land conquered is further specified]. . . . And he took all their kings, and smote them, and put them to death. Joshua made war a long time with all those kings. There was not a city that made peace with the people of Israel, except the Hivites, the inhabitants of Gibeon; they took all in battle. For it was the Lord's doing to harden their hearts that they should come against Israel in battle, in order that they should be utterly destroyed, and should receive no mercy but be exterminated, as the Lord commanded Moses [vss. 21 and 22 tell of further conquests]. . . . So Joshua took the whole land, according to all that the Lord had spoken to Moses; and Joshua gave it for an inheritance to Israel according to their tribal allotments. And the land had rest from war.

The second part of the double text reads:

A long time afterward, when the Lord had given rest to Israel from all their enemies round about, and Joshua was old and well advanced in years, Joshua summoned all Israel, their elders and heads, their judges and officers, and said to them, "I am old and well advanced in years; and you have seen all that the Lord your God has done to all these nations for your sake, for it is the Lord your God who has fought for you. Behold, I have allotted to you as an inheritance for your tribes those nations that remain, along with all the nations that I have already cut off, from the Jordan to the Great Sea in the west. The Lord your God will push them back before you, and drive them out of your sight; and you shall possess their land, as the Lord your God promised you. Therefore be very steadfast to keep and do all that is written in the book of the law of Moses, turning aside from it neither to the right hand nor to the left, that you may not be mixed with these nations left here among you, or make mention of the names of their gods, or swear by them, or serve them, or bow down yourselves to them, but cleave to the Lord your God as you have done to this day. For the Lord has driven out before you great and strong nations; and as for you, no man has been able to withstand you to this day. One man of you puts to flight a thousand, since it is the Lord your God who fights for you, as he promised you. Take good heed to yourselves, therefore, to love the Lord your God. For if you turn back, and join the remnant of these nations left here among you, and make marriages with them, so that you marry their women and they yours, know assuredly that the Lord your God will not continue to drive out these nations before you; but they shall be a snare and a trap for you, a scourge on your sides, and thorns in your eyes, till you perish from off this good land which the Lord your God has given you." [The text continues in the same vein to the end of the chapter; but this will suffice.]

1. Now it is safe to say that, as far as its message is concerned, we could hardly have chosen a more difficult text. Some would say it is an impossible text, from which a Christian sermon simply cannot be preached. The book of Joshua is anything but the best-loved book in the Bible. It is a book with which many preachers feel that they cannot honestly operate; now and then one hears the wish expressed that it was not in the Bible at all. It tells a bloody tale of battle, violence, and wholesale slaughter, a slaughter in which God assists with his mighty acts; the smoke of burning towns and the stench of rotting flesh hangs over its pages. What is worse, not only did God assist in this slaughter; it is more than once stated that he expressly commanded it. It is a story of fanaticism, of holy war and wholesale sacrificial destruction (the *herem*). And the author of the book tells of this slaughter with approval, and with a more than gentle hint that he regrets that it was not carried out more completely. And sensitive folk cry out, as they always have: What is such a story doing in the Bible? How can such conduct, and such a notion of God, be reconciled with the teachings of Jesus? Did God really give such orders? What edification and guidance for faith and living can such a story possibly have? You simply cannot preach from this book, and you ought not to teach it to children. Shield our gentle ears from violence such as this!

How can one preach upon such a text? Well, certainly *not* as an example for Christian living. This is the sort of text upon which our moralistic preaching simply breaks down. We cannot urge Christians to take up holy war against the church's foes, to carry fire and sword against them or drop bombs on them, and assure them that in doing so they would be committing an act of faith. That would be both monstrous and contrary to the express command of Christ, who enjoined us to love our enemies and warned us that to take the sword is to perish by it. To use the stories of Joshua as examples to follow would be nothing short of hermeneutical blasphemy, and I know of no preacher who would dream of doing such a thing. But then, who told us that the Bible was there to provide us with inspiring examples? He who searches his Bible for points upon which to moralize will find himself helpless before large parts of it. And if that is what we think the present text ought to provide, then we cannot use it. The institution of holy war and its use in the conquest of Canaan is a bit of ancient history—leave it there. It is not—and, in Christian theology, is not intended to be—a model for the church to copy. Even the author of Joshua used the stories of conquest for a theological purpose and scarcely expected his people to take up holy war against the surrounding nations.

2. So we have to look more narrowly at the theology expressed in our text and in the book of Joshua as a whole, of which our text is the summation. We have to ask what theological intention the author had in telling these stories of holy war and conquest. It must be confessed that he does idealize holy war and glorify it. He seems to look back with some nostalgia to the time when all Israel fought shoulder to shoulder as Yahweh's military levy, every man of them a soldier. Yet there is a certain unreality about it. After all, when he wrote, the institution of holy war—and the tribal order that supported it—was a dead letter, and had been for centuries. And even if he had wished to revive the institution, against whom did he propose to use it? Where now the Canaanites, the Hittites, the Hivites, the Girgashites, and the Perizzites who had been the objects of its fury? Gone into the limbo of history these hundreds of years. Did he, then, seek to arouse his countrymen to battle against neighboring nations? There is no hint of such a thing. No, the enemy now is internal; it is those pagan gods and pagan practices that have infiltrated Israel itself and, in his view, threaten the life of the nation.

One understands that this is a word from the late seventh century B.C. The book of Joshua—together with the books of Judges, I and II Samuel, I and II Kings, and probably the narrative portions of Deuteronomy—is a part of a great historical corpus, perhaps the work of one hand, perhaps of several, composed (so I should argue, with many others) in the last days of the kingdom of Judah (though later supplemented during the Exile). This was a dark and dangerous time, when shadows were growing long. What now of the glorious promises by which Israel lived: of secure possession of her land, of a far-flung domain, a population as numerous as the stars, and protection from all her foes? What now of the eternal promises to David? One could not be sure. Indeed, it looked as if all the promised blessings might at any moment be taken away. And even as our historian wrote, Jeremiah was striding the streets of Jerusalem saying that that was exactly what was going to happen.

Our historian (we shall use the singular number) is concerned for his nation's life. He does not merely relate history; he preaches from it. He tells of past events in order that he may project them into the present as lessons and as warnings. That he was strongly influenced by the theology of the Deuteronomic law, which had been the basis of Josiah's great reform in 622 B.C., is obvious and universally recognized. One recalls how Deuteronomy in positively classical fashion addresses Israel of the seventh century as if she were still standing *before* the promises—as if the promise of land, long ago fulfilled, were not yet fully fulfilled and still subject to conditions. Again and again the exhortation sounds: Hold fast to your God, obey his commandments as they are written in the law of Moses, and it will go well with you; disobey his commandments, go chasing after other gods, and you will face disaster and the revocation of the promises. This note is taken up by our historian. He tells the history of his people from Moses to his own day and seeks to show that at every step of the way the Deuteronomic theology has been vindicated by the events. And he begs his people to heed this lesson before it is too late. The book of Joshua is a part of this history. Here the historian reminds his people how their ancestors, because devotedly loyal to their God and obedient to his orders, were enabled to overcome insuperable odds and were given the Promised Land. And in our text he concludes that part of the story with a warning for all the future: The Promised Land is yours; but you will not be allowed to keep it forever unless you stand clear of foreign people, foreign gods, and foreign ways, and cleave to Yahweh your God as soldiers totally obedient to his orders.

3. Now we can understand that theology a little, and we sense that it conveyed a most relevant message to the people of Judah at the end of the seventh century B.C. and the beginning of the sixth. Yet manifestly we cannot preach that word just so to the church. We cannot because our situation is entirely different. We are not citizens of the kingdom of Judah, living in and around Jerusalem, facing the possibility that our land will be taken from us. What is more, we cannot preach it because it is not yet a Christian word; it is very much a pre-Christian word and, in some of its sentiments, sub-Christian. Yet even in our text it is a word that, while telling of events of the distant past, is concerned principally with the present and the future: it is a word that looks ahead. The historian tells of the conquest of the land, and he sees the promises as fulfilled; yet he also sees them as subject to condition and facing an uncertain future, a future that would depend upon the reception of the word. Who could tell what

that future would bring? As a matter of fact, this was a word sounded at one minute before midnight; hardly was the ink dry upon it when Nebuchadnezzar's army came and did its work—and the Promised Land was taken away.

So the promises were hurled out ahead to seek some greater fulfillment than they were given under Joshua. The reader knows how, in the literature of the sixth century, the Exile was viewed as a new Egyptian bondage out of which God would lead his people in a glorious new Exodus through the wilderness, back to the Promised Land (so *passim* in Isa. 40–55; cf. also Jer. 31:7-14; Ezek. 20). The reader also knows how this hope, disappointed and yet again disappointed, was pushed into the still farther future, till it assumed truly eschatological dimensions and took the form of the expectation of a definitive divine intervention, the great Day of Yahweh, when, with portents and wonders, God would step in to rescue his people and fulfill his promises. And, projected into the future along with this expectation, there went also the imagery and the theology of holy war, itself progressively assuming cosmic proportions. All through the later literature of the Old Testament (e.g. Isa. 24–27; 34; Ezek. 38–39; Joel 3 [Heb. 4]; Zech. 14) we see it—this expectation of the great eschatological combat. Even to the eve of our Lord's coming, we know that Qumran sectarians were awaiting "the war of the sons of light against the sons of darkness," in which they expected to participate. Unsheath your swords, O Israel! Soon the eschatological battle begins. Be ready to fight for your God, for beyond the struggle lies the fulfillment of all God's promises, the age of his triumphant rule.

We see, then, that this bit of the Old Testament's theology pointed out beyond itself toward a greater fulfillment. It was a fulfillment greater than mere possession of the land, an eschatological fulfillment that it would never get on its own terms, never in all B.C. In its own way (dare we say it?) it pointed to Christ, who is the fulfillment of all promise and the bringer of God's kingdom to men.

The New Testament, then, announces that fulfillment, that new age, in Jesus Christ. But what, one might ask, has it got to do with the bloody institution of holy war? At first glance one is tempted to say, nothing at all; rather, it abrogated it completely and threw it from the canon. In the New Testament there is no talk of slaughtering the foes of Christ, no slightest suggestion of ushering in his kingdom through a military campaign (as if the church could). On the contrary, we hear of a spiritual kingdom that does not use the weapons of this earth: "My kingship is not of this world; if my kingship were of this world, my servants would fight" (John 18:36). No conquest by the sword, no holy war, here. Plenty of people wanted Jesus to lead such a war against Rome; but that was just the sort of Messiah he was not and would not be. The New Testament completely repudiates holy war as an institution. Or, better, it did not attempt the historical madness of trying to revive an institution already in fact obsolete for hundreds of years when the stories about it were written. In the New Testament's theology victory by the sword is a great heresy; wherever the church has attempted such a victory, she has achieved shattering inner defeat.

But what of the *theology* of holy war? The New Testament by no means repudiates it. Rather, it consistently eschatologizes it and imparts to it a spiritual (though none the less real) quality. The Old Testament looked forward to the eschatological struggle; the New Testament throws everything into the context of eschatology. The eschatological struggle was begun in Jesus Christ and *won* on Good Friday and Easter. Here the back of Satan's resistance was broken, and the "last enemy" death sent in rout. But the struggle goes on, and will go on to final victory at the Last Day. And when the New Testament seeks to describe that Last Day, it borrows much of the symbolism of the Day of Yahweh, and not a little of that of holy war. And in this (already begun) eschatological struggle the Christian participates as a soldier of Christ (see, e.g., classically, Eph. 6:10-20; II Tim. 2:1-4; 4:6-8). This war is not fought with conventional weapons against visible foes. The foes are spiritual—though terribly real, and often enough real men—and the battle and weapons are spiritual. But it *is* a war, a no-quarter fight to the death. And to the soldier of Christ who engages in it faithfully there is given the sure promise of victory, and a crown.

The church has always known this. Not only is it in the New Testament, as we have said; it is enshrined in the church's symbolism and liturgy, not least in her hymnody. How many hymns sound this note! "Stand up, stand up for Jesus, ye soldiers of the cross"; "Onward, Christian soldiers, marching as to war"; "Am I a soldier of the cross, a follower of the Lamb"; "The Son of God goes forth to war, a kingly crown to gain"; "Fight the good fight with all thy might"; "Soldiers of Christ, arise, and put your armor on." And more. Indeed, it is probable that on no other theme, save Christmas, Passion Week and Easter, is it easier to find hymns. This martial note is a proper and well-recognized part of the church's heritage.

4. So it is that the theology of Joshua—the promise, the battle, and the victory—has been caught up in the New Testament and given a new and profounder meaning in Christ. But does that not mean that we may now safely dispense with Joshua and its tale of holy war, which so profoundly shocks us, and concentrate solely upon the New Testament's witness? I think not. We still need the Old Testament's witness in these matters. And, as we see what this bit of ancient theology has become in Christ, *these very texts* speak to us through Christ in their own right and give us a word of their own that we very much need to hear. It is, as it was in the first instance, a word of exhortation and warning.

We are, in truth, theologically speaking in a position similar to that of the people the author of Joshua addressed. The New Testament and history itself have conspired to put us there. Like Israel of the late seventh century, we stand between promises long ago fulfilled and an uncertain future which seems to throw the validity of the promises into question; we stand between victory won in Christ and a final victory of which we can see no sign. Though the Word and the Spirit assure us of the promises, we need to be confronted with the gravity of the emergency that is upon us, and of the total claims of the gospel on us.

We have, I think, to find this martial note again, for we have all but lost it. We sing our martial songs, and the sanctuary rings with brave words. But we are not a very soldierly people. We are parade-ground troops reluctant to dirty our uniforms; we are soldiers who refuse orders, sleep on duty, serve when convenient, and often enough traitors to the cause. God's military levy? We are a ragtag, bobtailed militia, of no use in the eschatological battle—save that God, in his grace, has deigned to use us anyhow. Indeed, this talk of the life of faith as a combat embarrasses us. It seems scarcely in good taste. We do not like to think of the church as militant at all, but rather as caught up in a stream of steady fraternal progress. We are men of tolerance and good will who find it hard to believe that the God of the Bible (though infinitely more loving) is not necessarily as tolerant as we. Feeling no animus toward the enemies of God, we fraternize with them till we no longer recognize them as enemies and are ready to make almost any compromise with them in the interests of peace. When the Bible talks of their total destruction, we vaguely feel this to be

248

unworthy. Yet we expect the promise of Christ's victory on earth to be made good to us and through us, his most unmilitant church.

It is not hard to imagine old Joshua shouting at us over the centuries: I have something to say to you! It is not the heart of the gospel, perhaps, but it is a word you need desperately to hear. Since you will receive it through Jesus Christ, you will know it is no summons to fight holy war as I did (though you might do well to remember that your heritage of faith is genetically linked to just these events; and that might warn you not too smugly to limit the ways in which God may choose to advance his purpose in history, either then or now). But you need engage in no such holy war, indeed are forbidden to do so. You have received greater promises than I ever dreamed of, and a far greater fulfillment in Christ, who is the end of the history of which I was a part. He is your covenant Lord, he is your commander who gives you your orders, and it is to him that you owe your allegiance. All is new. But this one essential thing has not been altered: As in the past, so now and in all the future, victory is given and the promises made good to God's obedient soldiers who follow his orders without question, who trust his leading implicitly, and who make no compromise with his foes. Only such know anything of promises.

So be reminded—Joshua continues—of the history that lies behind you, of the promises already made good to you in Jesus Christ, and of the victories already won in his name. This was no battle to conquer a tiny corner of this earth's territory. Rather, it is the eschatological combat unleashed in Jesus Christ "against the principalities, against the powers, against the world rulers of this present darkness, against the spiritual hosts of wickedness in the heavenly places" (Eph. 6:12); it is also a continuing combat, for Christ and under Christ, for the spirits of men on this earth. And the victories have been amazing. How far you have come since the church's beginnings! What numbers you have won! What territories gained! And not physical conquest only, but victories over the human spirit beyond counting! Time would not suffice to tell of those unnumbered thousands, obedient to Christ's commission, through whom Christ's kingdom has been advanced on earth. To be sure, the story of your past is not altogether a pretty one (any more than is that of ours), and you ought never to idealize it. But it is nevertheless a story of great victory, great conquest, which has brought men of all nations into submission to the kingly rule of Christ. And this I would have you to understand, now that the age of your great conquests lies long in the past and the future seems uncertain: These were victories you did not win and could never have won in your own strength. It was God himself who fought for you. You won in the strength of Christ and his gospel, as soldiers obedient to his commands. This was something I understood very well, and you must understand it too. I know that you were revolted by our practise of the *ḥerem,* and I would not wish you to revive the institution, now that I too have come to Christ. But try to understand us a little. That *ḥerem* was our attempt (think of it what you will) to give recognition to the fact that the battle had been God's, and the victory God's; we dedicated the spoils entirely to him, keeping nothing for ourselves. You must never indulge in such a practice, of course. But you might well take it as a much-needed reminder that the spoils of your victories too (converts won, good works done, advances made) belong wholly to God and his glory, and are not for your own aggrandizement.

Then Joshua addresses us, as long ago his voice addressed Judah of the seventh century B.C.: Understand the gravity of the emergency that confronts you, and be reminded of the conduct that is required of you if you would win through. The eschatological holy war unleashed in Jesus Christ, and already won in him, still continues, and will continue while time endures. The promises will not be continued to you if you refuse to take it seriously. The foe is a dangerous foe, and fiendishly clever. He not only confronts you at gunpoint; he will infiltrate your very ranks if for a moment you relax your vigilance. I shocked your sensibilities, perhaps, when I exhorted my people to stay clear of foreigners and foreign ways. No doubt you thought it intolerant of me. But the fact remains that if you temporize with the foe he will destroy you from within and leave you no longer a church. Be reminded, then, of the seriousness of the struggle. This is no mock battle you are engaged in, but a no-quarter combat. It does not end in negotiation and compromise, but in the total victory of God and the total defeat of his foes. Christ will not be content to rule part of his kingdom; he intends to rule it all. You may think what you will of my long-ago actions, but the total nature of the struggle you may never for an instant forget: your very survival is at stake.

So Joshua might speak to us, were he here to do so. The word he gives us is not the heart of the gospel, perhaps; but it is a word we need very much to hear, and do hear through Christ. It is a word of stern warning with very little optimism in it. It does not promise anything. But it leaves the future open. It places us, as it did its hearers long ago, before the needful decision, and points us to the way of survival—and perhaps victory—as Christ's church.

Many further examples could be given, and perhaps better ones than the foregoing, without beginning to exhaust the subject, for the variety of the Old Testament's texts is almost limitless. But there is space for no more. I trust, however, that these few will have served to illustrate the sort of thinking that one must do about an Old Testament text before attempting to preach from it, and to suggest some of the ways in which the Old Testament may legitimately address us today. I hope that the reader will be stimulated to further thinking and experimentation of his own.

Whatever is to be said of the above illustrations, it is my firm conviction that the Old Testament, rightly used, has an indispensable place in the preaching and teaching of the church. Because it is bound to the New in the continuity of redemptive history, it not only finds fulfillment and a new significance in the light of the New, but also supplements, fills out, and clarifies the message of the gospel in an essential way; it speaks to us in its own right a word of our God and our faith which it is necessary for us to hear. At the same time, because it is the cry to which the New Testament is the answer, the road of which the New Testament is the destination, it is the essential preparation for the hearing of the gospel; it speaks to us a word of our own condition before Christ and points to Christ. The two Testaments, therefore, belong together in our preaching and must be held together. Together they are the church's canon of Scripture, its supreme rule of faith and life, and they must be the authoritative source of its proclamation. It is as both Testaments are proclaimed and taught in the church that "the whole counsel of God" is heard, and men are built up in knowledge of the faith and empowered to fuller obedience.

SELECTED BIBLIOGRAPHY

(Note: The following list makes no pretense to completeness. It includes a selection of works which I have myself read or consulted in the preparation of this book and which have, negatively or positively, influenced my thinking. It is offered in the hope that it will be of assistance to readers who wish to pursue the subject further. Preference has been given, where possible, to works in English.)

Ackroyd, P. R. "The Place of the Old Testament in the Church's Teaching and Worship," *ET*, LXXIV (March, 1963), 164-67.

Aland, Kurt. "Luther as Exegete," *ET*, LXIX (November, 1957), 45-48; LXIX (December, 1957), 68-70.

Alexander, J. N. S. "The Interpretation of Scripture in the Ante-Nicene Period: A Brief Conspectus," *Interpretation*, XII (1958), 272-80.

Amsler, S. *L'Ancien Testament dans l'église*. Neuchâtel: Delachaux et Niestlé, 1960.

————. "Texte et événement," *Hommage à Wilhelm Vischer*, ed. D. Lys. Montpellier: Causse, Graille, Castelnau, 1960, pp. 12-19.

Anderson, B. W., ed. *The Old Testament and Christian Faith (OTCF)*. New York: Harper & Row, 1963. (Note: Various articles in this volume are also listed separately.)

————. "The New Covenant and the Old," *OTCF*, pp. 225-42.

Barr, James. *The Semantics of Biblical Language*. London: Oxford University Press, 1961.

————. "The Meaning of 'Mythology' in Relation to the Old Testament," *VT*, IX (1959), 1-10.

————. "Revelation Through History in the Old Testament and in Modern Theology," *Interpretation*, XVII (1963), 193-205; reprinted in *New Theology No. 1*, M. E. Marty and D. G. Peerman, eds. New York: The Macmillan Company, 1964, pp. 60-74.

Barrett, C. K. "Myth and the New Testament," *ET*, LXVIII (September, 1957), 359-62.

Bartsch, H. W., ed. *Kerygma and Myth*. Trans. R. H. Fuller. London: S.P.C.K., Vol. I, 1953; Vol. II, 1962.

Baumgärtel, Fr. *Verheissung.* Gütersloh: C. Bertelsmann, 1952.

————. "Das alttestamentliche Geschehen als 'heilsgeschichtliches' Geschehen," *Geschichte und Altes Testament (Festschrift A. Alt),* ed. G. Ebeling. Tübingen: J. C. B. Mohr, 1953, pp. 13-28.

————. "Ohne Schlüssel vor der Tür des Wortes Gottes?" *EvTh,* XIII (December, 1953), 413-21.

————. "Der Dissensus im Verständnis des Alten Testaments," *EvTh,* XIV (July/August, 1954), 298-313.

————. "The Hermeneutical Problem of the Old Testament," trans. Murray Newman, *EOTH,* pp. 134-59.

Baumgartner, W. "Die Auslegung des Alten Testaments im Streit der Gegenwart," *Zum Alten Testament und seiner Umwelt.* Leiden: E. J. Brill, 1959, pp. 179-207.

Bernhardt, K. H. *Die gattungsgeschichtliche Forschung am Alten Testament als exegetische Methode.* Berlin: Evangelische Verlagsanstalt, 1956.

Blackman, E. C. *Biblical Interpretation.* Philadelphia: The Westminster Press, 1957.

————. *Marcion and His Influence.* London: S.P.C.K., 1948.

Boisset, J., ed. *Le problème biblique dans le Protestantisme.* Paris: Presses Universitaires de France, 1955. (Note: Some of the articles in this volume are also listed separately.)

Bornkamm, H. *Luther und das Alte Testament.* Tübingen: J. C. B. Mohr, 1948.

Brown, R. E. "The *Sensus Plenior* in the Last Ten Years," *CBQ,* XXV (1963), 262-85.

Brunner, Emil. "The Significance of the Old Testament for Our Faith," trans. B. W. Anderson, *OTCF,* pp. 243-64.

Buess, E. *Die Geschichte des mythischen Erkennens.* Munich: Chr. Kaiser Verlag, 1953.

Bultmann, Rudolf. "Prophecy and Fulfillment," trans. J. C. G. Greig, *EOTH,* pp. 50-75.

————. "The Significance of the Old Testament for the Christian Faith," trans. B. W. Anderson, *OTCF,* pp. 8-35.

Buttrick, G. A. *et al.,* eds. *The Interpreter's Dictionary of the Bible (IDB).* 4 vols. Nashville: Abingdon Press, 1962.

Childs, B. S. *Myth and Reality in the Old Testament.* (*SBT,* 27). London: SCM Press, 1960.

————. "Prophecy and Fulfillment: A Study in Contemporary Hermeneutics," *Interpretation,* XII (1958), 259-71.

Coppens, J. *Les harmonies des deux Testaments.* Tournai and Paris: Casterman, 1949.

Cullmann, Oscar. *Christ and Time.* Trans. F. V. Filson. Philadelphia: The Westminster Press, 1950.

————. "La necessité et la fonction de l'exégèse philologique et historique de la Bible," *Le problème biblique dans le Protestantisme,* pp. 131-47.

Cunliffe-Jones, Hubert. *The Authority of the Biblical Revelation.* London: James Clarke & Company, 1945.

Daniélou, Jean. *From Shadows to Reality.* Trans. Dom Wulstan Hibberd. Westminster, Maryland: The Newman Press, 1960.

Delitzsch, Fr. *Die grosse Täuschung.* Stuttgart and Berlin: Deutsche Verlags-Anstalt, Vol. I, 1920; Vol. II, 1921.

Dentan, R. C. *Preface to Old Testament Theology.* Rev. ed. New York: The Seabury Press, 1963.

Dodd, C. H. *The Authority of the Bible.* London: Nisbet & Co., 1938 [New York: Harper Torchbooks].

————. *According to the Scriptures.* London: James Nisbet & Company, 1952.

Eichrodt, Walther. *Theologie des Alten Testaments.* Stuttgart: Ehrenfried Klotz, Vol. I, 6th ed. 1959; Vols. II and III, 4th ed. 1961. *Theology of the Old Testament* (Vol. I), trans. J. A. Baker. Philadelphia: The Westminster Press, 1961 (see esp. pp. 512-20).

————. "Les rapports du Nouveau et de l'Ancien Testament," *Le problème biblique dans le Protestantisme,* 105-30.

————. "Is Typological Exegesis an Appropriate Method?" trans. James Barr, *EOTH,* pp. 224-45.

Eissfeldt, Otto. "Israelitisch-jüdische Religionsgeschichte und alttestamentliche Theologie," *Kleine Schriften,* I, ed. R. Sellheim and F. Maass. Tübingen: J. C. B. Mohr, 1962, pp. 105-14 (originally published, *ZAW,* XLIV [1926], 1-12).

Fairbairn, Patrick. *The Typology of Scripture.* Reprinted Grand Rapids, Michigan: Zondervan Publishing House, n.d.

Farrar, F. W. *History of Interpretation* (Bampton Lectures, 1885); reprinted Grand Rapids, Michigan: Baker Book House, 1961.

Farrer, Austin. "Important Hypotheses Reconsidered: VIII Typology," *ET,* LXVII (May, 1956), 228-31.

Ferré, N. F. S. "Notes by a Theologian on Biblical Hermeneutics," *JBL,* LXXVIII (1959), 105-14.

Filson, F. V. *Which Books Belong in the Bible?* Philadelphia: The Westminster Press, 1957.

Fohrer, G. *Messiasfrage und Bibelverständnis.* Tübingen: J. C. B. Mohr, 1957.

Forstman, H. J. *Word and Spirit: Calvin's Doctrine of Biblical Authority.* Stanford, California: Stanford University Press, 1962.

Frör, K. *Biblische Hermeneutik.* Munich: Chr. Kaiser Verlag, 1961.

Fullerton, Kemper. *Prophecy and Authority.* New York: The Macmillan Company, 1919.

Geyer, H. G. "Zur Frage der Notwendigkeit des Alten Testaments," *EvTh,* XXV (April/May, 1965), 207-37.

Goppelt, L. *Typos: Die typologische Deutung des Alten Testaments im Neuen.* Gütersloh: C. Bertelsmann, 1939.

Grant, R. M. *The Bible in the Church: A Short History of Interpretation.* Rev. ed. New York: The Macmillan Company, 1948.

Grelot, P. *Sens chrétien de l'Ancien Testament.* Tournai: Desclée et Cie., 1962.

Haller, E. "Ad virtutes exegendi," *EvTh,* XXV (July, 1965), 388-95.

Hanson, R. P. C. *Allegory and Event.* London: SCM Press, 1959.

von Harnack, A. *Marcion, Das Evangelium vom fremden Gott.* 2nd ed. Leipzig: J. C. Hinrichs Verlag, 1924; reprinted, Darmstadt: Wissenschaftliche Buchgesellschaft, 1960.

Hartlich, C., and Sachs, W. *Der Ursprung des Mythosbegriffes in der modernen Bibelwissenschaft.* Tübingen: J. C. B. Mohr, 1952.

Hebert, A. G. *The Throne of David.* London: Faber & Faber, 1941.

―――――. *The Authority of the Old Testament.* London: Faber & Faber, 1947.

Henderson, Ian. *Myth in the New Testament.* (*SBT,* 7.) London: SCM Press, 1952.

Hendry, G. S. "The Exposition of Holy Scripture," *SJT,* I (1948), 29-47.

Hermann, R. "Offenbarung, Wort und Texte," *EvTh,* XIX (March, 1959), 99-116.

Hertzberg, H. W. "Ist Exegese theologisch möglich?" *Beiträge zur Traditionsgeschichte und Theologie des Alten Testaments.* Göttingen: Vandenhoeck & Ruprecht, 1962, pp. 101-17.

―――――. "Das Christusproblem im Alten Testament," *ibid.,* pp. 148-61.

Hesse, Fr. "The Evaluation and the Authority of Old Testament Texts," trans. J. A. Wharton. *EOTH,* pp. 285-313.

―――――. "Haggai," *Verbannung und Heimkehr* (*Festschrift W. Rudolph*). Ed. A. Kuschke. Tübingen: J. C. B. Mohr, 1961, pp. 109-34.

Higgins, A. J. B. *The Christian Significance of the Old Testament.* London: The Independent Press, 1949.

Hirsch, E. *Das Alte Testament und die Predigt des Evangeliums.* Tübingen: J. C. B. Mohr, 1936.

Hodgson, Leonard *et al. On the Authority of the Bible.* London: S.P.C.K., 1960. (Contributions by L. Hodgson, C. F. Evans, J. Burnaby, G. Ebeling, and D. E. Nineham.)

von Hofmann, J. C. K. *Interpreting the Bible*. Trans. Christian Preus. Minneapolis: Augsburg Publishing House, 1959 (original publication in German, 1880).

Honecker, M. "Zum Verständnis der Geschichte in Gerhard von Rads Theologie des Alten Testaments," *EvTh*, XXIII (March, 1963), 143-68.

Jacob, Edmond. *Theology of the Old Testament*. Trans. A. W. Heathcote and P. J. Allcock. London: Hodder & Stoughton, 1958.

————. "Considérations sur l'autorité canonique de l'Ancien Testament," *Le problème biblique dans le Protestantisme*, pp. 71-85.

Jenssen, H. H. *Der historische Jesus: Das Problem der Entmythologisierung der Evangelien für Glaube und Verkündigung*. Halle: M. Niemeyer, 1957.

Jepsen, A. "The Scientific Study of the Old Testament," trans. J. Bright, *EOTH*, pp. 246-84.

Jeremias, Joachim. "The Present Position in the Controversy concerning the Problem of the Historical Jesus," *ET*, LXIX (August, 1958), 333-39.

Johnson, R. C. *Authority in Protestant Theology*. Philadelphia: The Westminster Press, 1959.

Jones, G. V. *Christology and Myth in the New Testament*. New York: Harper & Bros., 1956.

————. "Bultmann and the Liberal Theology," *ET*, LXVII (June, 1956), 268-71; LXVII (July, 1956), 313-17.

Knight, G. A. F. *A Christian Theology of the Old Testament*. Rev. ed. London: SCM Press, 1964.

————. *Law and Grace*. London: SCM Press, 1962.

Knox, John. *Marcion and the New Testament*. Chicago: University of Chicago Press, 1942.

Kraeling, E. G. *The Old Testament Since the Reformation*. London: Lutterworth, 1955.

Kraus, H. J. *Geschichte der historisch-kritischen Erforschung des Alten Testaments*. Neukirchen: Verlag der Buchhandlung des Erziehungsvereins, 1956.

Kümmel, W. G. *Das Neue Testament: Geschichte der Erforschung seiner Probleme*. Freiburg/München: Verlag Karl Alber, 1958.

————. *Promise and Fulfillment*. (SBT, 23.) Trans. Dorothea M. Barton. London: SCM Press, 1957.

Lampe, G. W. H., and Woollcombe, K. J. *Essays on Typology*. (SBT, 22.) London: SCM Press, 1957.

Lestringant, P. "L'unité de la Bible," *Le problème biblique dans le Protestantisme*, pp. 45-69.

de Lubac, Henri. *Exégèse médiévale: Les quatre sens de l'Écriture*. Paris: Aubier, Vol. I, 1959; Vol. II:1, 1961; Vol. II:2, 1964.

Lys, D., "L'Appropriation de l'Ancien Testament," *Etudes Théologiques et Réligieuses*, XLI (1966), 1-12.

Macquarrie, John, *The Scope of Demythologizing*. London: SCM Press, 1960.

Malevez, Leopold. *The Christian Message and Myth*. Trans. Olive Wyon. London: SCM Press, 1958.

McKenzie, J. L. "Problems of Hermeneutics in Roman Catholic Exegesis," *JBL*, LXXVII (1958), 197-204.

————. "Myth and the Old Testament," *CBQ*, XXI (1959), 265-82; reprinted in *Myths and Realities*, Milwaukee: The Bruce Publishing Co., 1963, pp. 182-200.

————. "The Significance of the Old Testament for Christian Faith in Roman Catholicism," *OTCF*, 102-14.

Michalson, Carl, ed. *Christianity and the Existentialists*. New York: Charles Scribner's Sons, 1956.

————. "Bultmann against Marcion," *OTCF*, pp. 49-63.

Miegge, Giovanni. *Gospel and Myth in the Thought of Rudolf Bultmann*. Trans. Stephen Neill. Richmond: John Knox Press, 1960.

Miskotte, K. H. *Wenn die Götter Schweigen: Vom Sinn des Alten Testaments*. Trans. from the Dutch by H. Stoevesandt. Munich: Chr. Kaiser Verlag, 1963.

Mowinckel, Sigmund. *The Old Testament as Word of God*. Trans. R. B. Bjornard. Nashville: Abingdon Press, 1959.

Muilenburg, James. "Preface to Hermeneutics," *JBL*, LXXVII (1958), 18-26.

Nineham, D. E., ed. *The Church's Use of the Bible, Past and Present*. London: S.P.C.K., 1963. (Contributions by C. K. Barrett, H. Chadwick, J. N. D. Kelly, Beryl Smalley, E. G. Rupp, E. Carpenter, G. W. H. Lampe, and the editor).

Noth, Martin. "The 'Re-presentation' of the Old Testament in Proclamation," trans. J. L. Mays, *EOTH*, pp. 76-88.

Pannenberg, W. et al. *Offenbarung als Geschichte*. 2nd ed. Göttingen: Vandenhoeck & Ruprecht, 1963. (Contributions by Pannenberg, R. Rendtorff, T. Rendtorff, and U. Wilckens.)

————. "Kerygma und Geschichte," *Studien zur Theologie der alttestamentlichen Überlieferungen (Festschrift G. von Rad)*, ed. R. Rendtorff and K. Koch. Neukirchen: Verlag der Buchhandlung des Erziehungsvereins, 1961, pp. 129-40.

————. "Redemptive Event and History," trans. S. Guthrie, *EOTH*, pp. 314-35.

Phillips, G. E. *The Old Testament in the World Church, with Special Reference to the Younger Churches*. London: Lutterworth, 1942.

Phythian-Adams, W. J. *The Fulness of Israel*. London: Oxford University Press, 1938.

————. *The People and the Presence*. London: Oxford University Press, 1942.

Porteous, N. W. "Second Thoughts II. The Present State of Old Testament Theology," *ET*, LXXV (December, 1963), 70-74.

von Rad, Gerhard. *Old Testament Theology*. Trans. D. M. G. Stalker. New York: Harper & Row, Vol. I, 1962; Vol. II, 1965 (see esp. Vol. II, Part III).

————. "Verheissung," *EvTh*, XIII (December, 1953), 406-13.

————. "Typological Interpretation of the Old Testament," trans. J. Bright, *EOTH*, pp. 17-39.

Reid, J. K. S. *The Authority of Scripture*. London: Methuen & Co., Ltd., 1957.

Rendtorff, R. "Geschichte und Überlieferung," *Studien zur Theologie der alttestamentlichen Überlieferungen* (*Festschrift G. von Rad*). Ed. R. Rendtorff and K. Koch. Neukirchen: Verlag der Buchhandlung des Erziehungsvereins, 1961, pp. 81-94.

Richardson, A., and Schweitzer, W., eds. *Biblical Authority for Today*. A World Council of Churches Symposium. London: SCM Press, 1951.

Richardson, A. "Is the Old Testament the Propaedeutic to Christian Faith?" *OTCF*, pp. 36-48.

Robinson, J. M., and Cobb, J. B., eds. *The New Hermenuetic*. New York: Harper & Row, 1964.

Rössler, D. "Die Predigt über alttestamentliche Texte," *Studien zur Theologie der alttestamentlichen Überlieferungen* (see under R. Rendtorff, above), pp. 153-62.

Rowley, H. H. *The Unity of the Bible*. London: Carey Kingsgate Press, 1953.

————. "The Authority of the Bible." *Joseph Smith Memorial Lecture*. Overdale College, Selly Oak, Birmingham, England, 1949.

van Ruler, A. A. *Die christliche Kirche und das Alte Testament*. Trans. from the Dutch by H. Keller. Munich: Chr. Kaiser Verlag, 1955.

Rust, E. C. *Salvation History*. Richmond: John Knox Press, 1962.

Rylaarsdam, J. C. "The Problem of Faith and History in Biblical Interpretation," *JBL*, LXXVII (1958), 26-32.

Schulte, H. "In de Tatsachen selbst ist Gott: Die Bedeutung des Alten Testaments für die christliche Verkündigung nach D. Bonhoeffers letzten Briefen," *EvTh*, XXII (August, 1962), 441-48.

Schneemelcher, W., ed. *Das Problem der Sprache in Theologie und Kirche*. Berlin: A. Töpelmann, 1959.

Smalley, Beryl. *The Study of the Bible in the Middle Ages*. Oxford: Basil Blackwell, 1952.

Smart, J. D. *The Interpretation of Scripture*. Philadelphia: The Westminster Press, 1961.

Snaith, N. H. *The Inspiration and Authority of the Bible*. London: The Epworth Press, 1956.

Stendahl, Krister. "Implications of Form-Criticism and Tradition-Criticism for Biblical Interpretation," *JBL*, LXXVII (1958), 33-38.

Stone, Darwell. "The Mystical Interpretation of the Old Testament," *A New Commentary on Holy Scripture*, C. Gore, H. L. Goudge, and A. Gillaume eds. New York: The Macmillan Company, 1929; Part I, pp. 688-96.

Tasker, R. V. G. *The Old Testament in the New Testament.* Philadelphia: The Westminster Press, 1947.

Thornton, L. S. *The Form of the Servant.* London: Dacre Press, Vol. I, 1950; Vol. II, 1952; Vol. III, 1956.

Throckmorton, B. H. *The New Testament and Mythology.* Philadelphia: The Westminster Press, 1959.

Toombs, L. E. *The Old Testament in Christian Preaching.* Philadelphia: The Westminster Press, 1961.

Van Dusen, Henry P. "Liberal Theology Reassessed," *USQR*, XVIII (1963), 343-55.

Vawter, B. "The Fuller Sense: Some Considerations," *CBQ*, XXVI (1964), 85-96.

Vischer, W. *Das Christuszengnis des Alten Testaments.* Zollikon-Zürich: Evangelischer Verlag, Vol. I, 7th ed., Vol. II:1, 2nd ed., 1946. *The Witness of the Old Testament to Christ*, I (from 3rd ed., 1936), trans. A. B. Crabtree. London: Lutterworth, 1949.

————. *Das Kerygma des Alten Testaments* (*Kirkliche Zeitfragen*, Heft 8). Zürich: Zwingli-Verlag, 1955.

————. "La méthode de l'exégèse biblique," *RThPh*, X (1960), 109-23.

————. "Everywhere the Scripture Is about Christ Alone," trans. T. Wieser, *OTCF*, pp. 90-101.

Voegelin, Eric. "History and Gnosis," *OTCF*, pp. 64-89.

Vriezen, Th. C. *Theologie des Alten Testaments in Grundzügen.* Wageningen: Verlag H. Veenman & Zonen, German ed; 1956. *An Outline of Old Testament Theology*, trans. S. Neuijen. Oxford: Basil Blackwell, 1958.

Watson, P. S. "The Nature and Function of Biblical Theology," *ET*, LXXIII (April, 1962), 195-200.

Weiser, A. *Glaube und Geschichte im Alten Testament*, *BWANT*, 4 Folge, Heft 4, 1931; reprinted in book with same title, Göttingen: Vandenhoeck & Ruprecht, 1961, pp. 99-182.

————. "Vom Verstehen des Alten Testaments," *ZAW*, LXI (1945/48), 17-30; reprinted in same volume as above, pp. 290-302.

Westermann, Claus, ed. *Verkündigung des Kommenden.* Munich: Chr. Kaiser Verlag, 1958.

————, ed. *Probleme alttestamentlicher Hermeneutik.* Munich: Chr. Kaiser Verlag, 1960. Eng. trans ed. by J. L. Mays, *Essays on Old Testament Her-*

meneutics (EOTH). Richmond: John Knox Press, 1963. (Note: Various articles in this volume are also listed separately.)

————. "The Interpretation of the Old Testament," trans. D. Ritschl, *EOTH*, pp. 40-49.

————. "Remarks on the Theses of Bultmann and Baumgärtel," trans. D. Ritschl, *EOTH*, pp. 123-33.

————. "The Way of the Promise through the Old Testament," trans. L. Gaston and B. W. Anderson, *OTCF*, pp. 200-224.

Wildberger, H. "Auf dem Wege zu einer biblischen Theologie," *EvTh*, XIX (January/February, 1959), 70-90.

Wolf, H. H. *Die Einheit des Bundes: Das Verhältnis von Altem und Neuem Testament bei Calvin*. Neukirchen: Verlag der Buchhandlung des Erziehungsvereins, 1958.

Wolff, H. W. "The Old Testament in Controversy: Interpretive Principles and Illustrations," trans. J. L. Mays, *Interpretation*, XII (1958), 281-91.

————. "The Hermeneutics of the Old Testament," trans. by Keith R. Crim, *EOTH*, pp. 160-99.

————. "Das Alte Testament und das Problem der existentialen Interpretation," *EvTh*, XXIII (January/February, 1963), 1-17.

Wood, J. D. *The Interpretation of the Bible*. London: Gerald Duckworth & Co., 1958.

Wright, G. E. *God Who Acts*. (*SBT*, 8.) London: SCM Press, 1952.

————. "History and Reality: The Importance of Israel's 'Historical' Symbols for the Christian Faith," *OTCF*, pp. 176-99.

Zimmerli, W. *Das Alte Testament als Anrede*. Munich: Chr. Kaiser Verlag, 1956.

————. "Promise and Fulfillment," trans. J. A. Wharton, *EOTH*, pp. 89-122.

INDEX TO BIBLE REFERENCES

(Numbers in italic indicate references in footnotes.)

OLD TESTAMENT

APOCRYPHA

NEW TESTAMENT

INDEX OF PERSONS AND SUBJECTS

(Numbers in italic indicate references in footnotes.)